GERMAN IDEALISM
AND THE JEW

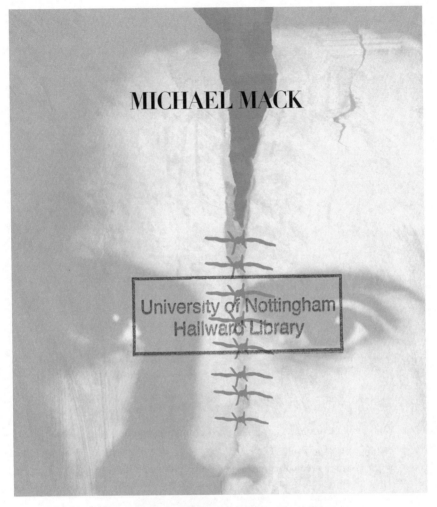

MICHAEL MACK

GERMAN
IDEALISM
AND THE JEW

The Inner Anti-Semitism of Philosophy and German Jewish Responses

THE UNIVERSITY OF CHICAGO PRESS • CHICAGO AND LONDON

Michael Mack is a Minerva–Amos de Shalit fellow at the Franz Rosenzweig Research Center for German Jewish Literature and Cultural History, Hebrew University of Jerusalem. He is the author of *Anthropology as Memory: Elias Canetti's and Franz Baermann Steiner's Responses to the Shoah* (2001).

The University of Chicago Press, Chicago 60637
The University of Chicago Press, Ltd., London
© 2003 by The University of Chicago
All rights reserved. Published 2003
Printed in the United States of America

12 11 10 09 08 07 06 05 04 03   1 2 3 4 5

ISBN: 0-226-50094-2 (cloth)

Library of Congress Cataloging-in-Publication Data

Mack, Michael.
    German idealism and the Jew : the inner anti-semitism of philosophy and German Jewish responses / Michael Mack.
        p.   cm.
    Includes bibliographical references and index.
    ISBN 0-226-50094-2 (alk. paper)
    1. Idealism, German. 2. Antisemitism—Germany—History.
I. Title.

B2745 .M33 2003
305.892′4043—dc21

                                                2002152500

            10 05760124
♾ The paper used in this publication meets the minimum requirements of the American National Standard for Information Sciences—Permanence of Paper for Printed Library Materials, ANSI Z39.48-1992

Contents

ACKNOWLEDGMENTS

Several institutions and individuals supported the conception and the completion of this study and substantially influenced its content and form. Sander L. Gilman invited me to work with him at the University of Chicago. I am most grateful to him for his generous encouragement, help, and advice. His pioneering work on anti-Semitism has been invaluable. In the same way, his groundbreaking work on the interrelations between perceptions of the body and conceptions of the mind helped sensitize me to issues that dwell at the interface between the biological and the spiritual.

At the University of Chicago, where much of this book was written, Paul Mendes-Flohr provided the sincere support, invaluable advice, and untiring encouragement that enabled its completion. His work on German Jewish writing and thought shaped the conception of counternarrativity as developed in *German Idealism and the Jew*. Moreover, his work on dual identities substantially influenced my approach to German Jewish writing and thought.

Paul Mendes-Flohr introduced me to T. David Brent of the University of Chicago Press. I am most grateful to David for all his invaluable help, brilliant advice, and strong encouragement. I cannot imagine a better editor and interlocutor than he. Many thanks, too, to Jane Zanichkowsky for her meticulous copyediting.

I am most grateful to the anonymous readers for the University of Chicago Press. Each has helped improve the structure and the content of this book. I am particularly grateful to Dominic Boyer (one of the anonymous readers who dropped his anonymity) for his detailed and invaluable report. At the University of Chicago, Eric L. Santner encouraged me to discuss Franz Rosenzweig's work as part of the argumentative structure of *German Idealism and the Jew*. He gave me a copy of his manuscript for *On the Psychology of Everyday Life: Reflections on Freud and Rosenzweig.* I am most grateful to him for his brilliant advice and for very stimulating and helpful conversations about Sigmund Freud, Franz Rosenzweig, Giorgio Agamben, and Slavoj Zizek. Moishe Postone offered helpful advice as regards my analysis of Marx's notion of value. He also contributed to a critical reading of Kant and Hegel. Michael Fishbane invited me to teach the university's Judaic civilization course. I am most grateful for his help. Teaching this course was a very enriching and stimulating experience and furthered the completion of this book. Françoise Meltzer and Rick Rosengarten encouraged and supported work on the manuscript. Donald Levine helped me focus on sociological issues related to the topics discussed. Conversations with Oded Schechter about Kant, Hegel, and counternarratives proved to be very creative and very helpful. I thank the following friends and interlocutors at the University of Chicago: Leo Kass, Joel L. Kraemer, Robert Pippin, Jonathan Lear, Homi K. Bhabha, Franklin J. Gamwell, David Levin, Samuel Jaffee, Cass Fisher, Jenny and Ben Sachs, Sivan and Daniel B. Monterescu, Todd Herzog, and Katie Trumpener.

Work on this project has benefited from conversations with several scholars in different disciplines. I am most grateful to the encouragement and comments of Aleida and Jan Assman, Gillian and John Beer, Berel Lang, Nonica Datta, Andrei Markovits, William Collins Donahue, Jakob Johannes Köllhofer, David Roberts, Seyla Benhabib, Hans Otto Horch, Michael Brenner, Andreas Gotzmann, Hans Joas, Jonathan M. Hess, Martin Jay, Anson Rabinbach, Wolf-Daniel Hartwich, Bettine Menke, and Friedrich P. Vollhardt.

This book also has benefited from much institutional support. I thank the German Academic Exchange Service (DAAD), which awarded me a generous postdoctoral fellowship at the University of Chicago. I also thank the Calgary Institute for the Humanities for awarding me its postdoctoral fellowship for 2001–2002. At Calgary, I completed the revisions to the manuscript. I am most grateful to Joel Robert Schulz for all his help and encouragement.

A much earlier and shorter version of chapter 2 appeared as "The Metaphysics of Eating: Jewish Dietary Law and Hegel's Social Theory" in *Philosophy and Social Criticism* 27, no. 5 (2001): 59–88. I am grateful to Sage Publications for permission to reprint a revised version of this article. Another version of chapter 3 appeared as "Richard Wagner and the Trajectory of German Transcendental Philosophy" in *Telos* no. 123 (spring 2002): 81–105; reprinted by permission of Telos Press, Ltd. A different version of chapter 9 appeared as "Freud's Other Enlightenment" in *New German Critique* 85 (winter 2002): 3–32; reprinted by permission of *New German Critique*. I thank the editors for their input and patience.

Introduction: The Political, Philosophical, Theological, Sociological, and Literary Critical Ramifications of Anti-Semitism

There is not just one Enlightenment, but a number of Enlightenments.
— Rosenzweig, *The Star of Redemption*

History and Philosophy

This book challenges a common paradigm underlying standard accounts of the history of ideas. Historians, philosophers, theologians, psychologists, sociologists, and literary critics tend to see anti-Semitism in general and Nazi anti-Semitism in particular as a reaction against the Enlightenment. To be sure, some studies have drawn attention to the presence of anti-Semitic musings in German idealist philosophy. Paul Lawrence Rose's *The German-Jewish Question: Revolutionary Antisemitism in Germany from Kant to Wagner,* for example, does precisely this but no more. There has been a lack of attempts to critically reflect on the relation between anti-Semitism, on one hand, and philosophy, aesthetics, and social theory, on the other.

Scholars of anti-Semitism could not make sense of the presence of irrationality in the self-declared "rational" philosophies of Kant, Hegel, and Feuerbach. Can one ignore anti-Semitism in philosophical writings? An affirmative answer would imply that anti-Semitism is an autonomous entity that has nothing to do with other social and cultural issues. This, however, is clearly not the case. One simply cannot appraise a body of work, disregarding its prejudicial content. Moreover, "the phenomenon of anti-Semitism is never discrete; it exists always and only as part of some larger complex."[1] This implies that the anti-Semitic aspect of a larger entity has implications for the understanding of this larger entity. Following Theodor W. Adorno's hermeneutic strategy, this study reads philosophical, literary, and documentary historical texts with "X-ray eyes."[2] It examines them in such a way as to make their "hidden content" and their "hidden puzzles as transparent as the Cabbalists of old tried to make the Torah."[3] This kind of reading attends to the force field within specific texts. The reader encounters such fields in the minutiae of the book he or she is reading. Contradictions generate the force of such fields. It is these contradictions within the work of Kant and Hegel that link their anti-Semitic fantasies to specific historical realities.

How can we explain the contradictory presence of a Christian paradigm in Kant's secular philosophy? In his ground breaking study *The History of Anti-Semitism* Léon Poliakov argued that Kant's anti-Semitic "outlook was . . . Christian rather than 'racist.'"[4] This is not to say that Poliakov trivialized the issue. On the contrary, he delineated the public impact of this kind of metaphysical anti-Semitism.[5] This impact was especially great on a culture as susceptible to metaphysics as the German one clearly was (and perhaps still is). This metaphysical kind of anti-Semitism has remained a "dark riddle." Scholars sometimes belittled its significance. Sometimes they denied its existence. Sometimes they attributed importance to it (as Poliakov did) but shied away from reflecting on it.

Previous studies pitted religious against secular anti-Semitism. One form (the religious) was considered to be somewhat less harmful than the other (the secular). In perhaps the most systematic attempt to define anti-Semitism, the historian of medieval culture Gavin I. Langmuir tries to avoid such a dichotomy between the religious and the secular by defining anti-Semitism in terms of fantasy. This notion plays a significant role in the present study, and it is therefore worthwhile discussing differences between my approach and that of Langmuir. In his clear and convincing analysis, Langmuir characterizes fantasy by the absence of empirical observation. In this way anti-Semitism emerged in the twelfth century. This century witnessed the rise of "irrational beliefs that attribute to all those symbolized as 'Jews' menacing characteristics or conduct that no Jews have been observed to possess or engage in."[6] Most important, Langmuir analyzes the causes of such fantasies. According to this analysis, chimerical beliefs arise when a given community finds itself in a state of crisis and can no longer take its religion, or, as Langmuir puts it, its nonrational beliefs as self-evident. In such a situation, the irrational beliefs of anti-Semitism come into being: "Irrational beliefs appear when individuals confuse nonrational beliefs central to their sense of identity with knowledge, attempt to defend those beliefs against rational doubts by suppressing their own capacity to think rationally and empirically about the characteristics of certain objects, events, and people, and attribute empirical characteristics to them that have never been observed."[7] By describing the rational as oriented toward accurate observation of the empirical, Langmuir gives a contemporary definition of reason. He thus characterizes anti-Semitism by both "abstraction" and, concomitantly, by the absence of a realistic examination of the external world.[8]

What does this mean for a culture whose understanding of reason comes close to what we would now comprehend as unreason? Kant and Hegel set the tone for the German prioritization of idealism over realism when they characterized rationality (and thereby progress or modernization) as freedom from empirical necessities. In this context Adorno has dubbed "Kant's ethics . . . an ethics of conviction" and has contrasted the latter with "an ethics of responsibility in which empirical conditions have to be taken into account."[9] This Kantian ethics of conviction does not pay any attention to "the effects of my actions."[10] Herein consists its "purity."

Kant in fact saw in the Jews the opposite of reason's purity: they embodied the impurity of empirical reality, of "matter." If we take our own bodiliness into account, this binary opposition between those who are pure (rational by virtue of having gained independence from the empirical) and those who are impure (that is, dependent on the empirical) seems to represent unreason rather than reason. It does so, of course, from the perspective of a contemporary understanding of what it means to be rational, as has been clearly laid out by Langmuir (see above). That is to say, if we accurately follow our empirical observation, we cannot but conclude that the exclusive equation of Jews with bodiliness is a fantasy and is thus irrational.

Some readers might turn suspicious at this point and accuse the author of doing injustice to the past (Kant and Hegel) by interpreting it from a contemporary perspective. They might furthermore denounce me as a writer who distorts history and philosophy by seeing the nineteenth and the early part of the twentieth century from the perspective of the Holocaust. The conception of the present study was indeed influenced by a German Jewish response to the Nazi genocide (see "Conclusion: Elias Canetti, Franz Baermann Steiner, and Weimar's Aftermath"). Does this impinge on the objectivity of its scholarly findings? This essay traces the dissemination of a disturbing image and its relation to ethical, aesthetic, and political ideas in the work of Kant, Hegel, and Wagner. Clearly this account emerges from the particular contemporary setting of its author. This location within a specific historical context does not, however, preclude objectivity. The observer may well be implicated in the observed, but an awareness of this implication helps address possible issues of distortion and simplification. I am therefore not concerned to pass judgment on or to ridicule Kant, Hegel, and Wagner. Rather, I am trying to understand why they wrote what they wrote and what kind of historical, aesthetic, theological, sociological, and ethical consequences followed from their writings.

The second part of this study analyzes the social, political, and intellectual significance of the interrelation between anti-Semitism and philosophy, the subject of part 1. It does so by attending to German Jewish responses to German idealist thought. Although this essay traces various historical and philosophical developments, it does not "collapse all distinctions, including that between present and past."[11] As the present has a relation to the past, certain aspects of a bygone historical period undergo various revisions in future periods. In a sense this essay traces and analyzes these revisions.

What was latent in the eighteenth and nineteenth centuries need not become manifest in the twentieth century. Thus Berel Lang has analyzed forms of affiliation between Kant's conception of enlightenment and acts and ideas of the Nazi genocide. Lang sees a universalism that is totalizing to the point that it cannot tolerate difference as being affiliated with the Nazi attempt to eliminate all who were seen to contradict a racist concept of what constitutes "the human."[12] He makes clear that this affiliation "does not amount to inevitability."[13] In the same way, Kant's and Hegel's prejudicial writings about Judaism did not necessarily result in Wagner's obsessive and paranoid concern with a Jewish conspiracy to "rule the world." Nevertheless, it means to turn the Holocaust into a metaphysical entity if one denies that those who conceived of it had no relation to a historical past. Nazi "assertions of particularism were characteristically formulated in the terms of unversalist principles."[14] According to Lang, these "universalist principles" mirror the formal logic of Kant's categorical imperative. By disregarding specific historical contexts, the categorical imperative remains indifferent to the particular differences between a majority and a minority culture.

In this essay I do not so much focus on the problems associated with Kant's notion of universality. Rather, I analyze the interrelation between Kant's and Hegel's anti-Semitic fantasies and various aspects of their philosophy. Clearly Kant and Hegel had a past, which influenced them, as much as they, in turn, became past, as their thought underwent various revisions in the nineteenth and twentieth centuries. Where, then, did Kant and Hegel pick up the stereotypes about Jews that they rework in their writings?

One could explain the persistent presence of anti-Semitism throughout history with reference to the concept of transformation. Thus, in the Middle Ages the Jews were identified with the Antichrist. This figure belongs, of course, to the realm of apocalypse. Within the German context, the Jews were pictured in the color red. These "Red Jews" denoted the red peril "that would devastate Christendom at the end of time."[15] The sixteenth century witnessed the stereotype's divorce from its ascription to apocalyptic time. The transformation in anti-Semitic stereotyping, which was taking place during the transition from the Middle Ages to the Age of Reformation, thus shifted the focus of attention away from the the end of days to the here and now.

Against this historical context, Kant and Hegel developed their respective social theories. As we will see, the Kantian and Hegelian body politic is one in which heaven takes the place of a contingent and imperfect earth. The Jews, however, represent this earthly remainder of incompleteness, of imperfection. The anti-Semitic stereotypes thus no longer fill the space of apocalypse. Instead, they now embody all that which hinders the construction of a perfect body politic in the here and now. They come to symbolize the worldly, which resists an immanent and imminent transformation into the other-worldly.

Worldly redemption does not necessarily imply an improvement of worldly life. Kant's and Hegel's philosophies did not accord priority to the melioration of material destitution. Kant downplayed the significance of worldly goods, with which he associated the Jews. Hegel celebrated dialectics as a way in which the autonomous mind can reshape and thereby beautify the poverty of the real. Yet both philosophers seem to have equated the social status of German Jews with their ethical conduct. During the eighteenth and early nineteenth centuries, the majority of European Jews were poor; most made their living from trading cattle and lending money to the peasants. Thus between 1780 and 1847 the Jewish community substantially constituted a part of poor and rural Germany:

> The peasants received hardly any loans from Christian moneylenders in the cities since they were a bad credit risk, while Jews were permitted only these commercial activities. For better or worse, both parties were forced to maintain their dealings with one another. Moreover, the Jewish traders sought out the small farmers in their homes or met them at small local markets, offering them money and goods and buying agricultural products or lending money on the anticipated harvest or livestock production, thus responding quickly and flexibly to the peasants' needs. . . . Thus Jews were disproportionately poor, as were most of the peasantry, survival being the principle object of their economic activities.[16]

Kant no doubt had these economic conditions in mind (and not the philosophers Moses Mendelssohn and Solomon Maimon, whose social status did not reflect that of the German Jewish community) when he labeled Jews cheaters and Orientals. Thus Herder reports Kant as saying the following in his lectures on practical philosophy: "*Every coward* is a liar; Jews, for example, not only in business, but also in common life."[17] By equating Jews with cowards, liars, and cheaters, Kant associated them with a lack of ethical conduct. This lack bespeaks imperfection. The aim of Kant's ethical commonwealth, however, consisted in freeing humanity from any reliance on that which is unethical. He saw the roots of violation of the ethical in the desire for material well-being. Those who are cowards seem to fear for their bodily welfare. They lie so as to avoid the infliction of harm. Kant associated the Jews with precisely such conduct. This, of course, has ramifications for a larger set of issues in Kant's political and moral theory. Do the Jews, as he represenred them, point to the blind spots in his philosophical system? Questions such as this will drive the discussion in chapter 1.

Religion's Immutability

Kant's depiction of Jews as liars and cheaters does not coincide with Wagner's paranoid fear of Jewish world domination. Despite continuities, there are discontinuities between Wagner's, Kant's, and Hegel's perceptions of the Jews. Even though Kant and Hegel gave a rather prejudicial account of Jewishness (in which the Jews embody the body as materialism and therefore heteronomy), they did not perceive Jews as a threat. Wagner differed. He fabricated a binary opposition between Jews and the *Volksgemeinschaft* (community of the people). He politicized the German idealist division between Jewish realism and German idealism precisely because he saw the Jews as a threat. Wagner, however, could easily find support for his paranoid fear in Kant's, Hegel's, Feuerbach's, and Schopenhauer's opposition between the non-Jewish (Christian or Christian German) ideal of autonomy and the supposed Jewish reality of heteronomy. Indeed this very opposition between an idealistic conception of sameness and "otherness" as the embodiment of commonsense corporality permeates—from Wagner to Treitschke to Chamberlain—the German anti-Semitic contrast between German idealism and Jewish realism.

In Kant and Hegel, the Jews are not so much powerful as they are "unhappy," "deceitful," and "poor." Yet Kant and then Hegel brought the image of "Jehovah, the Jewish God" into the picture. At this point their anti-Semitic fantasies are on the verge of becoming paranoid. Thus Kant referred to the Jewish "possession of a deity who alone could rank as God, and for whose sake they believed themselves obligated to hate all other deities."[18] This image of an immutable tie between Jehovah and his people informs some of Kant's and Hegel's writings but holds the center of attention in Feuerbach's, Fichte's, and Schopenhauer's fantasies about the Jews.

In what follows, I focus on Feuerbach and Schopenhauer, because certain aspects of their work help us understand Wagner's writing about aesthetics, politics, and religion (see chapter 3). In this paragraph, I briefly discuss Johann Gottlieb Fichte's opposition between Judaism and the Jewish state, on one hand, and Christianity and the German Christian state, on the other. As we will see below, it is such opposition that Marx undermined in his analysis of secular pseudotheologies. According to Fichte, "the Jewish nation excluded itself . . . from us [the German nation] by the most binding element of mankind—religion."[19] As in Kant and Hegel (see chapters 1 and 2), religion makes for immutability: "It [the Jewish nation] separates itself from all others in its duties and rights, from here until eternity."[20] Fichte employed the horrid metaphor of chopped-off heads in order to drive home the ideational foundation of this eternal religion. With reference to an immutable religion Fichte attempted to justify the exclusion of the Jews from civic equality: "I see absolutely no way of giving them [the Jews] civic rights, except perhaps if one chops off all of their heads and replaces them with new ones, in which there would not be one single Jewish idea."[21] The fiction of an immutable Jewish religion, for Fichte, thus served to justify political anti-Semitism.

The permutations of similar idealist narratives will be discussed in what follows. This discussion prepares the ground for an explication of how Wagner attempted to popularize an idealist fantasy. He, in fact, held that the "immutable tie" between the Jewish God and his people was responsible for the impossibility of translating the body into the body politic. Crucially, Hegel set the stage for Feuerbach's and Wagner's focus on Jehovah as the source of the alleged immutability of all these elements, which do not belong to a peculiar notion of redemption. As we will see, German idealists attempted to pave the way for such redemption through the workings of "freedom" and "reason" (Kant's autonomy, Hegel's dialectics). According to Schopenhauer, an aesthetic transcendence of the world enacts Kantian rationality. In a further move Feuerbach attempted to translate Christianity's rationality into the anthropological. Finally, Wagner syncretized, in his total work of art *(Gesamtkunstwerk)*, "reason," politics, and "Christianity's anthropological essence."

According to Hegel's idealist narrative, the Jews became enslaved to the empirical world by theologizing immediate being. To this extent, religion shaped the core of a nation's political outlook. Indeed, history translates "the essence of Christianity" into the workings of the modern state. Hegel defined Christian essence in terms of a binary opposition to the Jewish. He saw Jews as the embodiment of heteronomy. Now Feuerbach took over, from Hegel, the idea that history is the realization of theology's ethical and political content. In keeping with the work of his transcendental predecessors, Feuerbach's revolution stopped short of questioning the perceived rational essence of Christianity: He did not set out to negate religion as such but only "the inhuman" *(das Unmenschliche)* aspects of it.[22] He located such inhumanity in the God of the Jews, who caused a rift between immanence and transcendence. Once again Jehovah functioned as the originator of a gulf between the empirical and the spiritual, which Hegel attempted to bridge by way of dialectics. Jehovah thus produced the divide between anthropology and theology that Feuerbach's "humanistic" thought set out to overcome. But, with Kant and Hegel, Feuerbach saw reason self-consciously grow out of a Gentile culture, which constructed the Judaic as its other. Therefore, he contrasted "Christianity's religion of critique and freedom" *(Religion der Kritik und Freiheit)* with "the Israelite who does not dare to do anything, except for that commanded by God."[23] Here we encounter the fear for "worldly goods" with which Wagner imbued his anti-Semitic stereotypes and which Hegel used to "unmask" the spirituality of Israel.

In this prejudicial fantasy the characteristic of timidity served to reveal an orientation toward the goods of this world, because fear in this case resides in fearing the loss of worldly goods. In this way Feuerbach, like Hegel, associated Jewish obedience to God's commandments (or revealed laws) with the principle of utility.The characteristic of heteronomy (enslavement to the objects of material life) immutably appertains to Jewish existence on account of what Feuerbach imagined to be the Jews' attachment to their God: "The Jews have kept their peculiarity [*Eigentümlichkeit*] up to the present day. Their principle, their God is the practical principle of the world—egoism, namely, egoism in the form of religion."[24] This conflation of the Jewish God with the imagined immutability of the Jewish people followed Kant's and Hegel's line of argument and found its way into Wagner's anti-Semitic imagination. Radicalizing Hegel, Feuerbach called the Jewish God a product of the egoism of the Jews.[25] The veneration of God comes down to an admiration of God's power, and Feuerbach contrasted this "desire for *earthly happiness*" *(Verlangen nach irdischer Glückseligkeit)* in Israel's religion with Christianity's "longing for *heavenly bliss*" *(die Sehnsucht himmlischer Seligkeit)*.[26]

I have traced the trajectory of a German anti-Semitic fantasy about the "immutable tie" between the Jewish God and his people. Let us now turn to Schopenhauer's anti-Semitism as another example of this way of thought, whose "universal" humanism excludes the Jews from a rational and free society. Significantly, Schopenhauer's critique of Kant's neglect of both the body and the will prepared the way for Wagner's paradigmatic shift, in which art occupied the place reason holds in German transcendental thought. Schopenhauer did not appraise the will and the body but conceptualized them in terms of the Kantian thing-in-itself: as the truth that lies behind the world of appearances. This fact makes his thought appear to be materialist, and yet the recognition of the world's nontranscendental foundations should prepare the ground for both the overcoming and the final destruction of the worldly.[27]

In what is significant for the discussion of Wagner's *Gesamtkunstwerk* in chapter 3, Schopenhauer developed a quasi-religious aesthetic theory. Art, especially music, traces the ways in which "the world itself is the judgment upon the world."[28] If art indeed works together with transcendental reason, in that it helps us recognize the guilty and utterly worthless constitution of the empirical world, then Schopenhauer's notion of religion exactly described this pessimistic view of the world. His thought was religious only insofar as it evaluated the world in terms of "guilt" and "redemption."[29] Certainly, reason, art, and religion meet in this epistemology, which results in an attitude of, rather than in the suicidal enactment of, a resigned form of pessimism. Schopenhauer thus introduced art into this transcendental paradigm, but, in contrast to his academic competitor Hegel, he paid little attention to the body politic. The only exception is that he defined the Jewish as the political and, in so doing, he radicalized Hegel's and Feuerbach's charge against an imagined Jewish God who represents nothing but the power over earthly goods.

Reason as philosophy coincides with religion. Philosophy reaches down to the kernel of the Christian and finds there its essence, in radical opposition to the Jewish. Following Kant, Hegel, and Feuerbach, Schopenhauer constructed a notion of Jewish immutability, focusing on the religion of the Jews. The social life shaped by the immutability of a religious worldview divides an otherwise universal notion of humanity. Schopenhauer, for his part, partitioned the world into two opposed religious ideologies: the Zend religion—epresented by Judaism and Islam—and the religion of the Vedas, of which Christianity partakes. Zend is driven by an optimistic attitude toward the world, taking appearances for reality *(der Erscheinung die höchste Realität beilegen)*,[30] whereas the Vedas recognize the world as a mere appearance and see the root of all evil in being *(Dasein)*,[31] the redemption from which is their highest aim. The Jews were Schopenhauer's main scapegoats. He did not discuss Islam in any detail but focused on the Jews, with a view to expelling the Judaic from Christianity. He accused Jews of having infiltrated and subverted Christian culture by introducing a realist, as opposed to an idealist, attitude. He argued that in Europe transcendental thought has validity only in Kantian philosophy and is, however, cut off from the life of the populace precisely because of the influence of "a Jewish realist way of thought" on social life: "In India idealism is—in Brahmanism as well as in Buddhism—part of the teaching of popular religion; idealism is merely paradoxical in Europe, due to the essentially and inevitably *[wesentlich und unumgänglich]* realist Jewish position."[32] Wagner attempted such a popularization of idealism in his art (see chapter 3).

Pseudotheologies

A study of anti-Semitism needs to address not only aesthetic, political, and sociological issues but also theological ones. Indeed, the shaping of secular versions of anti-Semitism in the West has been well documented, especially in the work of George Mosse, Jacob Katz, and Sander L. Gilman.[33] What has been largely overlooked, however, but warrants attention, is the need to trace the ways in which pseudoscientific and pseudotheological versions of anti-Semitism are mutually sustaining and reinforcing. This study explores these mutual, albeit negative, relations by attending to certain strands of writing within German transcendental philosophy. This is in order to show how both "Jewishness" and Judaism came to be associated with the profane, the material, and the bodily, with a view to excluding Jews and Judaism from an idealist type of body politic. The articulation of these real but unthematized relations is crucial. We have to examine how pseudotheological ideas informed and inspired pseudoscientific forms of anti-Semitism, as well as how the pseudoscientific forms of anti-Semitism have grounded and sustained its pseudotheological forms. Doing so will make us better able to understand (a) the impact that both have made, and continue to make, in generating the secularization and (b) the politicization of religious oppositions between the Christian and the Jew in the social and intellectual history of the past three centuries.

By *pseudotheology* I mean a secularized and politicized Christian theology (but in a broader context, it could be any form of fundamentalism) and by *pseudoscience* a theologized notion of the secular. Thus pseudoscientific racists refer to "religion" so as to give a spiritual or intellectual account of "blood." Racist ideologists such as Houston Stewart Chamberlain and Karl Eugen Duehring presented their worldviews not as derived from "biology" but as originating from a "spiritual" and "cultural" sensibility. By secularizing and politicizing the theological, racism conflates the worldly with the otherworldly or, in other words, the body with the spirit. In this conflation, an imperfect bodily life transforms itself into the building material of its own overcoming. For example, nationalist and racist discourse celebrates the Aryan body as healthy and strong. Taken at face value, this might strike one as essentially biologistic. This aggrandizement of the "Aryan" physique must not be confused with an espousal of materialism and "worldliness." On the contrary, what it glorifies is precisely the immanent overcoming of the body's immanence.

In racist depictions, the Aryan physique is so intrinsically strong and healthy that it is without any imperfections. Here the body has overcome its bodiliness. We cannot find any signs of frailty and contingency. In these representations of what it means to be fully human, the body has become a strictly symmetrical arrangement of muscle power that can be put to work for the production of gigantic schemes.

The Jew's body, on the other hand, represents frailty, illness, and contingency. Here we encounter the complete absence of muscle power and perfect symmetry. In the context of these racist representations, the Jewish physique resembles that of a prostitute who has fallen prey to sexual disease.[34] From the anti-Semite's perspective, the "Jew remains the representation of the male as outsider, the act of circumcision marking the Jewish male as sexually apart, as anatomically different."[35] This study analyzes how German idealism's pseudotheology made a precondition of such pseudoscientific opposition between the Jew and the Aryan. By attempting to lay the ideational foundations for the construction of a perfect, noncontingent world that has overcome its dependence on nature's imperfection, German idealists implicitly, and perhaps unconsciously, depicted human frailty as its "other." Significantly, the Jews represented this detrimental difference of worldly contingency. Embodying this reminder of incompleteness, Judaism and Jewishness signified that which had to be overcome.

Jews were confronted with pseudoscientific difference on an everyday basis. "The Jew's experience of his or her own body was," Gilman writes, "so deeply impacted by anti-Semitic rhetoric that even when that body met the expectations for perfection in the community in which the Jew lived, the Jew experienced his or her body as flawed, diseased."[36] Given this sociohistorical context, it is not surprising to see that German Jewish writers were sensitive to any kind of pseudotheology that could be amenable to pseudoscientific constructions. This is one reason why I attend to German Jewish responses to German idealism's account of "the rational." Moses Mendelssohn, Heinrich Heine, Heinrich Graetz, Franz Rosenzweig, and Sigmund Freud took issue with German idealism's expulsion of various types of empirical imperfections from an ideal type of rationality. Although they were all inspired by Kantian and Hegelian thought, they disputed the hegemony of German idealism's view of what constitutes reason. This hegemony all too easily gave way to various types of social and political discrimination. Thus proponents of German national culture in the nineteenth and twentieth centuries referred to the distinction between idealism and realism in order to emphasize Germany's superiority. Within the work of various German idealists, references to the Jews shed light on this almost unconscious succumbing to hegemonic ways of thinking. Here the Jews represented the opposite of idealist hegemony, since they were the realists. During the course of the nineteenth and twentieth centuries, the Jews' position was augmented by the presence of Germany's various European neighbors, the English and the French in particular—in short, by all those who were seen to be "realists."

Why, then, was the primary focus on the Jews? This question points to the inarticulate level of German idealist philosophy. My notion of pseudotheology describes the unacknowledged presence of quasi-religious ways of thinking in the work of Kant and Hegel and some of their followers. These thinkers attempted to bring specific aspects of traditional Christian thought into the realm of a thoroughly secularized modern state. By "dying away from" everything that contradicts positive law, the citizen of this state had to reenact Christ's death on the cross. The French and the English belong to the Christian world. The Jews, however, do not. As such, they were seen to embody fundamental difference—a difference that immutably pertains to their religious roots. Following the "wrong" religious script, they could not partake of this translation of religious into moral and political truth. By attempting to depict Christian and then, in turn, German essence as being independent of or, rather, completely removed from its Jewish roots, Kant and Hegel set out to orientalize Judaism. The European Jew thus surfaced as the Oriental other. Being immutably bound to his God, he could not make the transition to modernity.

I first focus on the pseudotheological paradigm of anti-Semitism in German idealism. How can we account for the concern about the supposed "essence of Judaism" in discussions relating to the "essence of Christianity"? I examine how in the work of Kant, Hegel, and Wagner, the Jewish appears as worldly whereas the Christian is conceived as overcoming the material world.

Hegel and Wagner referred to Christianity as a combination of the Christian and the German. I then analyze, in the work of Moses Mendelssohn, Heinrich Heine, Abraham Geiger, Samson Raphael Hirsch, Heinrich Graetz, Otto Weininger, Hermann Cohen, Sigmund Freud, Walter Benjamin, Franz Rosenzweig, Elias Canetti, and Franz Baermann Steiner, German Jewish responses to this line of thought.

This study thus examines how pseudoscientific anti-Semitism at the end of the nineteenth and the beginning of the twentieth century was informed by the German idealist fantasy of an immutable tie between Jehovah and his people. Furthermore, it discusses how German Jewish writers, from Heinrich Graetz via Hermann Cohen to Sigmund Freud, develop a critique of this pathological pseudotheology. Graetz returned to Mendelssohn's notions of both rationality and Jewishness at the end of the nineteenth century. By contrast, post-Mendelssohnian German Jewish thought in the nineteenth century attempted to cast Judaism into the conceptual mold of Kant's rational theology and moral philosophy. In so doing, Reform Judaism (Geiger) and neoorthodoxy (Hirsch) developed a counterhistory that can be compared to Heine's literary submergence of Jewishness into Germanness.

In this context, I complement David Biale's and Amos Funkentstein's notion of counterhistory with that of a counternarrative. By *counternarrative* I mean a reversal of a dominant *conceptual* narrative, whereas counterhistory focuses on a *temporal* (that is, historical) reversal. I discuss these various counternarratives by analyzing how Mendelssohn, Graetz, Cohen, Benjamin, Freud, and Rosenzweig developed a notion of reason that avoided the prejudicial aspect of a seemingly universal concept of enlightenment that obfuscates its own particularity and thus excludes that against which it defines its identity. Accordingly, this study addresses two major issues. First, it questions the frequently assumed break between modern anti-Semitism and theology. Second, it traces the ways in which modern Jewish thought, from Mendelssohn via Rosenzweig to Levinas, advances an understanding of what it means to be enlightened. This understanding, despite many similarities, substantially differs from that which was developed by Kant, Hegel, and Feuerbach.

Marx's Analysis of Pseudotheologies

Feuerbach's focus on the immutable tie between Jehovah and his people (see above) clearly represents the culmination of a specific German idealist identification of religion with immutability or "essence." The following discussion of Marx anticipates the second part of this study, which analyzes German Jewish responses to the hegemony of idealism in the Germany of the nineteenth and twentieth centuries.

In his famous essay "On the Jewish Question" (1843), Karl Marx held the discipline of theology responsible for the civic inequalities of the Jews in the German states of the nineteenth century: "In Germany, where there is no political state, no state as such, the Jewish question is purely *theological*. The Jew finds himself in *religious* opposition to the state, which proclaims Christianity as its foundation. This state is theologian *ex professio*. Criticism is criticism of theology."[37] Here Marx gives a lucid analysis of what I will describe in this study as the pseudotheology of anti-Semitism. The Jew can only stand in opposition to the state if the state has been defined in Christian terms. As we will see in chapter 4, German Jewish writers from Mendelssohn onwards emphasized the Jewish foundation of Christianity. They did so, not least, with a view to supporting with theological arguments German Jewry's political demand for civic parity. One aim of the present study is to examine how the plea for a division between state and religion, as most clearly announced by "the first secular Jew," Benedict Spinoza, actually eventuated in a pseudotheological construction of the body politic in Germany from the late eighteenth to the early twentieth century.

Kant and Hegel first developed a political theory in which epistemological, moral, and theological elements form a unity. Now the ideational content of Christianity informs the operation of the modern, that is, secular state. In the past, doctrinal creeds, such as the belief in Christ, seemed, by contrast, to determine an individual's moral worthiness. A studious reader of Kant, Hegel, and Feuerbach, Marx internalized many of German idealism's anti-Semitic stereotypes.[38] At the same time, however, he embarked on an analysis of the pseudotheology that prepared the ground for such prejudicial discourse.

Marx argued, on one hand, that the fight for the civic equality of the Jews only ceases to involve theology once "the state ceases to maintain a *theological* attitude toward religion."[39] He seemed to locate in Judaism, on the other hand, the beginning of the capitalist prioritization of value over social wealth. He thus appeared to reformulate Kantian heteronomy in terms of abstract value. Capital is the prime example of abstract value. With money, after all, one can gain both possession and enjoyment of the goods of this world. His critique of capitalism, however, did not anticipate the anticapitalism of anti-Semites such as Wagner. Neither did he revalorize a dichotomy between autonomy and heteronomy and between idealism and realism. Rather, according to Marx, economic value that ensures the unequal distribution of material goods (use-values) has an all-encompassing character, which cannot be attributed to one sphere (such as "the Jews," or "the realists") but determines society as a whole.[40] Judaism denotes religion as such and thereby describes humanity's estrangement from both itself and nature. Marx rewrote his essay on the "Jewish question" in the essays collected in *The Holy Family*, which he co-authored with Friedrich Engels. Here, as Sander L. Gilman has pointed out: "Judaism no longer stands as negatively emblematic for *all* religion. The focus of the essays in *The Holy Family* is not the nature of the Jews but the nature and expression of Bauer's perception of the Jews. Marx modified the idea that Jews are defined by their role within the system of exchange. Indeed, in *The Holy Family*, Marx attributed all of the negative qualities that he (following Bauer) had associated with the intrinsic nature of the Jew to the Young Hegelians."[41] In this way Marx seemed to anticipate a nonapologetic account of Jewishness.[42] He thus appears to be closer to the thought of Franz Rosenzweig (see chapter 8) than to the work of German idealists and their successors.[43] Indeed, Marx sporadically turned the tables on Kant and the Young Hegelians by arguing that German idealism reflects social reality—in a way similar to that in which a symptom reflects the presence of an illness—but refrains from critically engaging with it. Conversely, Marx analyzed capitalist production in terms of autonomy. "What characterizes capitalism," in the words of Moishe Postone, "is that, on a deep systematic level, production is not for the sake of consumption. Rather, it is driven, ultimately, by a system of abstract compulsions constituted by the double character of labor in capitalism, which posits production as its own goal."[44] Mirroring the Kantian universal, the capitalist universal moves from concrete specificity toward abstraction.[45]

As will be discussed in chapter 3, Wagner attributed to the ring of the Nibelungs the value by means of which one can heteronomously gain the enjoyment—as opposed to the simple possession—of the goods of this world (use-values). Marx, by contrast, examined how such "heteronomy" actually resembled the German idealist transcendence of a heteronomous relation to the "other." Marx defined money qua Kantian autonomy as indifference to material conditions. Such analysis has indeed a point of reference in Kant's *Metaphysics of Morals* (see chapter 1). The material possessions (use-values), which are acquired by means of money (value), preclude a meaningful relationship with the external world. They thereby close the individual in on itself in a kind of autonomy as isolation from the external world of other human beings and of nature, too. This is what Marx emphasized in his "Economic and Philosophic Manuscripts of 1844" when he wrote: "In place of *all* these physical and mental senses there has therefore come the sheer estrangement of *all* theses senses—the sense of having."[46] Accordingly, the "idealism" of private property does its work by means of "fantasy":[47] by the arousal of "imaginary appetites,"[48] members of a capitalist society are driven to buy the products of estranged and estranging labor.

The economics of capitalism, of course, proscribes the accumulation of goods (that is, property). It thus might appear as though Marx depicted the concept of property along the lines of the Kantian principle of heteronomy. Wealth, however, does not reside in the enjoyment of worldly things but rather in their accumulation: "Thus political economy—despite its worldly and wanton appearance—is a true moral science, the most moral of all the sciences. Self-denial, the denial of life and of all human needs, is its cardinal doctrine."[49] Within this context, Marx's use of the term "moral science" described a "moral society," which operates according to the Kantian principle of the autonomous indetermination by empirical, or "worldly," conditions. He went on to emphasize the Christian foundation of such secular (that is, economic) morals when he aligned capitalist value with the New Testament image of heavenly treasures: "The less you eat, drink and read books; the less you go to the theatre, the dance hall, the public house; the less you think, love, theorize, sing, paint, fence, etc., the more you *save*—the *greater* becomes your treasure which neither moths nor dust will devour—your *capital*."[50] This image of a heavenly treasure of course serves to underline the religious character of capitalist economics—a feature Benjamin took up in his fragment "Capitalism as Religion" (see chapter 10). In "On the Jewish Question" Marx similarly analyzed the pseudotheological foundation of the "secular" German state.

In this essay, this pseudotheology is both Christian and Jewish. So when Marx equated Judaism with power, he simultaneously drew the German Christian state into this equation: "In the German-Christian state the power of religion is the religion of power."[51] Religion as such denotes an economic principle of "saving goods" so as to be assured of an increase in power. Religion, economics, and history thus form a trinity because the capitalist system gradually comes to maturity within historical time. Accordingly, the essence of Judaism must not be separated from the essence of Christianity, as pseudotheological anti-Semites argued. Rather, both concomitantly establish an ascetic ideal and thereby create the individual's economic estrangement from his or her social and natural surroundings.

Anti-Semites associate Jews with profit-taking and with the materialist potential of abstract surplus value. The image of "the Jew's immutable tie to Jehovah" describes this anxiety about the materialism to which capitalism could give rise. According to Kant and Hegel, the Jews only obey the laws of "their God" in order to be rewarded by him. This obedience to an ethereal law denotes an abstract dimension, whereas remuneration with worldly goods unmasks such abstraction as "pure materialism." According to Marx, only an utterly new mode of production, in which all members of society could find material and spiritual fulfillment, would prove capable of taking the sting out of such discriminatory discourse. Only when the enjoyment of worldly goods became both socially acceptable and attainable would "the Jew" of anti-Semitic stereotyping cease to be "the Jew."

In Marx's analysis capitalism shapes an ascetic way of life. This is so because capitalist society revolves around what I call the "autonomy of production." Hence "the process of production of any given product is only a moment in a never-ending process of expansion of surplus value."[52] This endless cycle of production for the sake of production vilifies consumption, which becomes associated with the Jews. As a result, the "dream implied by the capitalist form is one of utter boundlessness, a fantasy of freedom as the complete liberation from matter, from nature."[53] This notion of freedom coincides with Kant's. Within this context, the Jews, in turn, represent matter and as such they are seen to undermine this kind of freedom. The end of capitalism would put an end to such a representation of Judaism. In a society based on material wealth rather than on value, everyone would be "the Jew," and thus Judaism would no longer be equated with the anti-Semites' concept of it.

Thus, religion, as such, helps institute a modern capitalist society. This state of alienation, however, constitutes an important point of departure for history's progress toward a communist state. In order to make this historical leap possible, Marx argued not for the abolition of religion but for a radical separation between church and state: "Against Bauer, who claims that to demand political emancipation as Jews in a Christian state is illusory because the modern state must free itself of all religion, Marx argues that the post-French Revolutionary state does not presuppose the *abolition* but rather the *privatization* of religion."[54] In this context, Marx clearly followed Mendelssohn, who, as we will see in chapter 4, attempted to justify Jewish civil equality by separating the state from religion.

Marx's writings therefore evidenced an ambiguous relation to Judaism. This ambivalence bespoke a critical engagement with German idealism's pseudotheology. That is to say, Marx took issue with a conflation between the religious and the sociopolitical. This differentiates his anti-Jewish writings from those of his German idealist predecessors and contemporaries.[55] Whereas Marx identified not only Judaism but also any form of religion with the power of ascetic accumulation, Fichte, Feuerbach, and Schopenhauer continued to narrate the rather repetitive German idealist fiction about the abstract but empirically oriented power of the Jews.

Postmodern Theory and the Autonomy-Heteronomy Divide

Marx's analysis of the pseudotheological foundation of capitalist economics has shaped the Frankfurt School's broad-based cultural critique of bourgeois society. Following Walter Benjamin's approach (see chapter 10), Adorno has emphasized the "highly theological matter"[56] that shaped Kant's understanding of autonomy. Kant's "rejection of empirical motifs corresponds to" a certain Christian dogma, which proclaims that "evil rules in the world, that this world is the realm of evil."[57] Developing and deepening Marx's, Benjamin's, and Adorno's analysis, this study examines the reactionary aspects of the Kantian autonomy-heteronomy divide.

Autonomy here denotes the refusal of the self to engage with the other. In the context of the present study, the autonomous does not describe the liberating potential of non-identity, or difference. Instead, this work draws attention to the rather disturbing social implications of autonomy, understood as reason's independence from embodied and, thereby, individuated life. The notion of autonomous subjectivity fulfills a necessary and important role in various critiques of collectivism and other forms of social domination. This work does not attempt to undermine the theoretical and practical priority of the individual's independence from the subjugation that various groups might want to force on him or her. Rather, it analyzes how the German idealist concept of autonomy paradoxically depended on the collective pressures of an emergent bourgeois society.

The present study discusses how German Jewish writers from Moses Mendelssohn to Sigmund Freud set out to question the ethical superiority of a type of autonomous selfhood that paradoxically depends on social domination. Major German idealists constructed a radical divide between Jewish and non-Jewish society. Whereas they saw in Christian German culture the enactment of autonomy, they despised Judaic culture as heteronomous. Kant, Hegel, and Wagner believed that Jewishness denoted the opposite of rationality. Their understanding of reason significantly coincided with a notion of freedom as independence from empirical reality.

In what sense has our understanding of rationality been shaped by this presupposition of self-sufficiency and autonomy? This is a question that Emmanuel Levinas and, most recently, Jacques Derrida in his critique of totalizing knowledge and "full presence," addressed. The present study attempts to examine this question within the wider sphere of intellectual thought (German idealism, German Jewish writing) and social history (anti-Semitism in particular and racism in general). In examining Levinas's oeuvre, Derrida referred to this topic when he spoke of the "heteronomous curvature that relates us to the completely other."[58] He traced this postmodern ethics of heteronomy back to the biblical prohibition against murder. He thus wrote, "we know that for Levinas, the prohibition against killing, the 'Thou shalt not kill,' in which, as he says, 'The entire Torah' is gathered, and which 'the face of the other signifies,' is the very origin of ethics."[59] Derrida goes on:

> [Levinas] breaks with both Kant and Hegel, with both a juridico-cosmopolitanism that, in spite of its claims to the contrary, could never succeed in interrupting an armed peace, peace as armistice, and with the laborious process—the work—of the negative, "with a peace process" that would still organize war by other means when it does not make of it a condition of consciousness, of "objective morality" [*Sittlichkeit*] and of politics—the very thing that the dialectic of Carl Schmitt, for example, still credited to Hegel.[60]

In this context, the ethics of autonomous self-sufficiency has a close relation to the politics of homogeneity. Carl Schmitt indeed defined democracy as the homogenous. He claimed that the "political power of a democracy turns out to be its ability to annihilate or to exclude the foreign, the unequal, that which threatens homogeneity."[61] In the same essay, Schmitt went on to develop his friend-enemy opposition with reference "to the inhuman [*das Unmenschliche*], which evokes with direct necessity the good and the absolutely human [*absolut Menschliche*] as its opposite."[62] Significantly, he then quoted from Hegel's phenomenology: "it can be said about the Jewish people that, precisely because it stands immediately in front of the doors of salvation, it is the most reprobate and the most worthy of rejection [*das verworfenste*]."[63] Despite semantic and conceptual differences, both homogeneity and autonomy refer to self-sufficiency and thereby to the indetermination by or exclusion or annihilation of that which is perceived as "other."

It is precisely that categorical opposition between "the same" (ethically, the autonomous; politically, the homogenous) and "the other" (the heteronomous, the law of that which lies "outside") that makes a specific conceptual field complicit with the enactment of violence, of murder. As Eric L. Santner recently pointed out: "What makes the Other *other* is not his or her spatial exteriority with respect to my being but the fact that he or she is *strange,* is a *stranger,* and not only to me but also to him- or herself, is the bearer of an internal alterity, an enigmatic density of desire calling for response beyond any rule-governed reciprocity; against this background, the very opposition between 'neighbor' and 'stranger' begins to lose its force."[64] Developing Derrida's concept of the remnant (*restance, différance,* or *revenance*), Santner sees in the unconscious an excess of life that has the potential to make us attentive to our own internal strangeness. From the perspective of the Freudian unconscious we are "bearers of an internal alterity."[65] Once the self sees itself as a stranger to itself, the very distinction between the homely and the foreign, the familiar and the uncanny loses its validity. Santner interprets the monotheistic conception of God in terms of such "pressure to be alive to the world, to open to the too much of pressure generated in large measure by the uncanny presence of my neighbor."[66] Given this presupposition, psychoanalytic practice enacts—be it consciously or unconsciously—the spiritual guidelines laid down in the biblical tradition. In this way the Freudian notion "fantasy" describes the forces that obstruct an opening to the spiritual that is nothing but the "remnant": the excessive alterity of life in both the self that has truly become the other and in the other that has truly become the self.

We are thus all strangers to ourselves. Conversely, with its opposition between autonomy and heteronomy, German idealism attempted to empower the self by freeing it from this internal strangeness and thereby projecting the "other" onto the exterior. The self is supposed to be in control of itself, but what does it need to control? According to Kant and Hegel, the self has to guard itself against being swayed by the arbitrariness of otherness. In short, it has to protect its posited sameness against the external world of "matter," of heteronomy.

Within German idealist writing—from Kant via Hegel to its romantic revision in Wagner's aesthetics—Judaism and Jewishness denote this otherness. This otherness is excluded either from a rational-idealistic or an aesthetic-idealist conception of the body politic. Autonomy, as idealist freedom from material motivations, thus defines both sameness and otherness (as its heteronomous opposite). Precisely because the Jews are perceived to embody the lack of what is perceived to constitute sameness, they are, at least theoretically, excluded from an idealist body politic. They have to lose their otherness in order to become members of a modern German state. This is the famous quid pro quo in the debate about Jewish emancipation in nineteenth-century German culture.[67] Emancipation would thus establish the "sameness" of what had been "otherness." According to Gilles Deleuze and Félix Guatari, racism works precisely by means of this erasure of difference:

> Racism operates by the determination of degrees of deviance in relation to the White-Man face, which endeavors to integrate nonconforming traits into increasingly eccentric and backward waves, sometimes tolerating them at given places under given conditions, in a given ghetto, sometimes erasing them from the wall, which never abides alterity (it's a Jew, it's an Arab, it's a Negro, it's a lunatic . . .). From the viewpoint of racism, there is no exterior, there are no people on the outside. There are only people who should be like us and whose crime it is not to be. . . . Racism never detects the particles of the other; it propagates waves of sameness until those who resist identification have been wiped out (or those who only allow themselves to be identified at a given degree of divergence).[68]

In a provocative move, Deleuze and Guattari see the face of Christ behind "the White Man himself."[69] As we will see, Kant and Hegel constructed in different but related ways an understanding of what it means to be rational along the lines of Christ's death to the world. In traditional Christian Scripture the fruits of this death are to be reaped in heaven. In the German idealist narrative, however, these fruits are to be harvested immanently. To this extent, German idealism establishes a notion of sameness along the immanent lines of autonomy. Autonomy in turn describes one's inability to be determined by outside influences. This literally constitutes the law of the self. It is a law, however, that the self cannot simply give itself. Far from being anarchical, autonomy requires a (secular) commonwealth that differentiates between "Yours" and "Mine." By being ultimately undetermined by the external world, the self has to accept an unequal distribution of the goods of this world. By contrast, as the embodiment of heteronomy, "the Jews"[70] are described in terms of an orientation toward the goods of this world. In this way, Kant stigmatized them as "cheaters." He thus excluded them, at least theoretically, from the ideal body politic. The Jews represented the lack of sameness. Therefore, they embodied the corporeal, which resisted transformation into a body politic. This transformation, with reference to the law of autonomy, would help enact the immanent secularized teaching of Christ.

The first section of this introduction focused on a contemporary understanding of reason. Chapters 1 and 2 examine the unreason within the type of reason propounded by Kant and deepened and developed by Hegel.

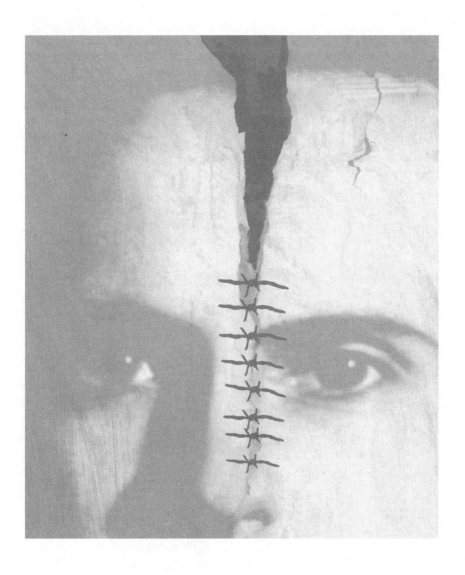

PART ONE

NARRATIVES

1 POSITING IMMUTABILITY IN RELIGION: KANT

Only nature can enslave man and only when the existence of each last entity is routed out and made to stand naked before him will he be properly suzerain of the earth.
— CORMAC MCCARTHY, *BLOOD MERIDIAN*

In the introduction I briefly examined the culmination of the German idealist fantasy about an immutable tie between Jehovah and his people. The following two chapters analyze how the construction of this prejudicial image grew out of Kant's and Hegel's respective philosophies.

In this chapter, I first discuss the epistemological foundations of Kant's moral and political philosophy. In his rational theology and moral thought, he gave a prejudicial account of Judaism. The adverse force of the charges Kant leveled against the Jews was intensified in his anthropology. How can we explain this intensification in the context of a more sociological (that is, anthropological) discussion? In his moral and religious philosophy Kant discussed mainly Judaism, but in his anthropological writing he focused on the "the Jewish nation." We will see in what sense these two entities, religion and nation, coincide in Kant's characterization of the Jews.

What could have caused such a conflation of politics and religion in the work of a philosopher who, one would have thought, took great care to differentiate between these two entities? Kant, following a one-sided reading of Spinoza, argued that Judaism is a religion without religion. He unmasked the essence of Judaism as a form of politics. However, Kant's moral philosophy incorporated a strong political—in the sense of public—agenda. Was it not concerned with the social validity of individual performances? After all, the famous categorical imperative demands the public applicability of each individual action. What did it mean when he wrote that Judaism is a religion without religion whose very essence consists of politics?

An exclusive focus on Kant's moral philosophy and rational theology does not suffice. Whereas critics have so far only examined the passages in which Kant discussed Judaism and the Jews, this chapter offers a hermeneutics of his prejudicial discourse within the context in which he developed it. Thus, an analysis of Kant's epistemological critique of traditional metaphysics helps us understand his redefined metaphysical perspective on social, moral, and political issues.

In Kant's view, a Jewish way of life could not transcend empirical conditions. This question as to the possibility of independence from material considerations formed the very heart of Kant's critique of traditional metaphysics. The *Critique of Pure Reason* set out to prove that we can neither recognize the intrinsic worth of any material thing nor ascertain the existence of some supernatural sign system that could bestow spiritual or intellectual value on it. The only way in which we can meaningfully deal with the external world is by imposing the laws derived from autonomous reason on nature. Natural appearance offers the material from which we can build a universe according to the free and consistent plans generated by rational operations.

In the second part of this chapter, I examine how Kant constructed this epistemological notion of an autonomous rationality with reference to traditional Christian rhetoric in his moral philosophy and rational theology. This will shed light on the way his reformulation of metaphysics went hand in hand with his attempt to do away with the Jewish foundations of Christianity. We will see that a secularized notion of Kant's image of Christ informed his account of autonomous reason. Autonomous reason, in turn, established the guidelines for rational action in Kant's enunciation of a noncontingent body politic. The politicization and concomitant secularization of the Christian plea for a transcendence of worldly interests points to the pseudotheology that manifests itself in Kant's prejudicial discourse about the Jews. In this pseudotheology Kant constructed the image of an immutable union between Jehovah and his people that informed German anti-Semitic discourse from Hegel via Feuerbach and Schopenhauer to Wagner. It is this pseudotheological discourse about the essence of Judaism that reappeared in pseudoscientific anti-Semitic fantasies at the end of the nineteenth century.

Kant's Refashioning of Metaphysics

In an idiosyncratic way, Kant and the German philosophers who followed him proceeded to define *freedom* in terms of liberation from one's inclination to depend on objects in the empirical world.[1] Kant's distinctive transcendental revolution consisted of precisely establishing a radical divide between "the world of nature and the world of freedom."[2] In his *Critique of Pure Reason* (1781), Kant laid the epistemological foundations for his moral and political philosophy. He did so as an apparently "empiricist" move. He debunked traditional metaphysics in that he called into question the certainty of any relation between a physical object and a metaphysical sign system that Western thought had so far attributed to it.

In this way, he criticized his philosophical predecessor Leibniz for "*intellectualizing* appearances" *(Leibniz intellektuierte die Erscheinungen).*[3] To some extent, Kant's notion of appearances denoted mere physical objects as they appear to our sensibility. Although this term did not necessarily imply a value judgment, it nevertheless referred to the empirical world in terms of a purely bodily constitution that lacks any inherently spiritual or intrinsically intellectual referent.

Whereas metaphysics before Kant assumed an underlying meaning, that is to say, a "thing in itself" behind "the thing," the *Critique of Pure Reason* radically broke with such a correlation between the physical and the metaphysical. We could not know anything about either the supernatural or the natural. Therefore we had to cease asking questions as to the hidden signification of empirical objects.[4] This seemed to indicate a philosophical affinity with materialism.[5] However, the introduction of epistemological limits was concerned with the perception of a spiritual world. An empirical world only fulfills the function of the first step on the long road toward making human reason the heir of a metaphysical tradition, a tradition that had been debunked in its "old," that is, correlating constitution. We are unable to recognize "things" as they exist "in themselves." This does not, however, eventuate in materialism. Rather, "reason" *(Verstand)* is not limited by sensuousness but, on the contrary, limits the sensuous precisely by calling things in themselves noumena and not phenomena or appearances.[6] Instead of pointing to the signification behind phenomena *noumena* goes under the name of "an unknown something" *(eines unbekannten Etwas).*[7]

This limitation concerning the perceptibility of both mere things (appearances) and things in themselves (noumena) liberates human reason from a reliance on both the natural and the supernatural worlds. We will see in the course of this chapter how Kant, via his discussion of a Jewish way of life, exemplified what he meant by such dependence on the external world, namely, heteronomy. Here it is important to emphasize that he set radical limits on human epistemology so that it would not circumscribe the capacity of human knowledge. The human inability both to understand the meaning of the empirical world and to ascertain the existence of a supernatural one instead enthroned "reason itself" as "the source of natural laws" *(der Verstand ist selbst der Quell der Gesetze der Natur).*[8]

Kant introduced a radical split between being (ontology) and meaning (morality) not because he wanted to shut the door on a moral order in its entirety. Rather, he set fundamental limits on human epistemology with a view to freeing human autonomy from a dependence either on the external natural world or on a thus far metaphysically assumed transcendent world that endowed the immanent world with meaning. Whereas traditional metaphysics mediated between immanence and transcendence so as to be able to assure a meaningful relation between humanity and its place in nature, Kant redefined the metaphysical in terms of human autonomy. Autonomous reason uses the contingent empirical world as the basic material by means of which it, in an a priori manner, constructs a new rational world that gradually progresses toward immanent perfection.[9]

Thus, for Kant, "the whole of philosophical knowledge based on pure reason in systematic coordination . . . is called metaphysics" *(die ganze . . . philosophische Erkenntnis aus reiner Vernunft im systematischen Zusammenhang . . . heißt Metaphysik).*[10] Therefore, Kant's epistemological critique set the stage for his metaphysical redefinition of the body and the body politic. Given that we do not know the possible meaning of bodily objects, it also could not be said with certainty that these contingent entities have any relation to a transcendent ground that would bestow on them some form of value. Our nonempirical, that is to say, rational, activity operates as the true and only source of moral validity.

The Politics of Metaphysics

In what way does this critique of metaphysics precondition Kant's exclusion of the Jews from his definition of an "ideal" body politic? The political dimensions of a Kantian epistemological revolution consisted in the demand for a social reconstruction of our sensuous inclinations—that is, of everything that pertains to our bodily constitution according to the moral law as laid down by autonomous reason. Mere reason *(Verstand)* synthesizes the variety of empirical objects by means of the imagination *(Einbildungskraft).*[11] Pure reason *(Vernunft)* does its work along the lines of the metaphysical, as redefined by Kant. It overcomes any dependence on empirical objects, which are, apart from their mere material existence, nothing but products of representation.

As we shall see, the political dimension of Kant's metaphysics of autonomous reason has important implications for his fantasy about the Jews as the embodiment of heteronomy. Within the discursive enunciation of a body politic operating according to the rationale of Kantian metaphysics, the body constitutes an entity that has to fall under the control of autonomous reason. Kant defined the epistemological as well as the political aspect of "freedom" as the independence of reason from one's corporeal inclinations. Kant's revolutionary wager consisted in the claim that the autonomy of reason from the body may be practiced within the context of the modern state. It is within this political context that a secularized Christian paradigm determined his discourse concerning Jews and Judaism. As Dieter Henrich has pointed out, Kant defined rational practice as the transcendence of practical interests:

"Only a practical reason which sufficed to determine the will to action for it-self alone, and without regard to other, external, impulses, would be pure. It is Kant's thesis that such reason really exists. Kant set the *Critique of Practical Reason* the task of refuting those who think that our reason can be practical only if it is at the same time empirically conditioned."[12] In this chapter I examine the pseudotheological paradigm behind this claim about practical reason's freedom from material interests. This paradigm comes clearly to the fore when Kant focuses his discussion on the Jews as a community. The mere body was incapable of participating in a body politic whose idealist stake resided in the overcoming of corporeal conditions. Crucially, it is this divide between the body (nature) and the body politic (freedom) that has political implications. To this extent, nature can only be overcome by an identification of bare life with politics. What describes the workings of this idealist body politic is that it subjects a totality of bodies within a specific group to its sym-bolic order. The rules of this order are valid but not meaningful. Instead, they are significant only insofar as they are able to utterly change the very nature of the empirically constituted body. In this way, the laws of the body politic are "being in force without significance." Citing Gerschom Scholem on Kafka, Giorgio Agamben has pinpointed in Kant the theoretical foundations of this modern law whose significance paradoxically consists in being nonsignifi-cant: "In Kant the pure form of law as 'being in force without significance' ap-pears for the first time in modernity. What Kant calls 'the simple form of law' *(die bloße Form des Gesetzes)* in the *Critique of Practical Reason* is in fact a law reduced to the zero point of significance, which is, nevertheless, in force as such."[13] The law of reason coincides with the reason of the law that is in force without significance. Kantian rationality, with its unbridgeable gulf be-tween the realms of freedom and nature, sets out to demonstrate the worth-lessness of bare life. Reason therefore dominates and overcomes nature by humiliating desires for objects in the external world. Kant's law of autonomy helped enact such a subjugation of the body to the forces of the body politic. The next section examines the secularized and politicized Christian paradigm behind Kant's account of freedom, reason, and the body politic.

Translating the "Otherworldly" into the "Worldly" Body Politic

Kant's peculiar attempt to make a scientific explanation of the world compat-ible with the overcoming of the worldly set the stage for much of the tension that is characteristic of nineteenth-century German thought.[14] As Yirmiyahu Yovel has recently pointed out, "the German *Aufklärung* differed from the French *Lumières* in that it did not oppose religious truth but tried to make it as rational as possible."[15] In contrast to the French deists, who "attacked re-ligion in the name of reason, German Enlightenment thinkers tended to *rec-

oncile reason with revelation, and did so mainly by having reason prove itself, on its own authority, the existence of God, free will, the immortality of the soul, and a moral order governing the world."[16]

But how did Kant attempt to reconcile the essence of Christianity with the rational? In his notion of autonomy he tried to harmonize secular reason with one element of Christian doctrine that prescribes the Christ-like dying away from the worldly. Kant maintained that the modern state acts according to the rationale of ethical autonomy when it forbids its subjects to give in to their inclinations toward "worldly goods" if these inclinations interfere with the commandments of its legal system. How are we able to explain this fusion of ethics with the politics of modern nations? Here it is worthwhile recalling that Kant separated concepts from intuitions. This separation causes some contradictions in his transcendental account, for it begs questions such as the following: If we are free from empirical necessities as rational beings who by virtue of their conceptual way of thinking can order the chaos of experience and legislate it in an autonomous manner, why then do we still need to be governed by laws of civil society that regulate the way we act in the world as intuitive beings, that is, as human beings who may be swayed by desires aroused by our perception or intuition of the empirical world?

As a consequence of this tension between concept and intuition, Kant constructed two different social models. One represents heteronomy, or a form of social interaction that is the reverse of the transcendental and conceptual and is therefore inclined to the empirical and toward the positivity of religion. In this type of society, a direct, intuitive response to particular empirical objects and likewise an intuition of received divine commandments shape the mental outlook of the people concerned. Whether intuition relates to empirical objects or to the objects produced by a religious imagination, it leans mainly toward positivity with respect to that which is outwardly and heteronomously given. Kant's description of a Jewish way of life, as we will see, fulfilled a function in his philosophy that at first seems to be marginal but is in fact related to the paradox that arises from the apparent discrepancy between his moral and his political philosophies. Robert Pippin has drawn attention to this conflict by asking, "[W]hy doesn't Kant, as a moralist, worry only about the moral permissibility of the exercise of state power; why does he try to establish that entry into a *Rechtstaat* is *obligatory*?"[17] We are free and can establish rules legislating the natural world in an autonomous manner. In order to do so, we have to subscribe to the rules of a civil society. Here we happily abrogate our right to intuitive happiness, as aimed at in a heteronomously legislated society. We willingly follow the restrictions imposed on our empirical and material desires by obeying a strict "Mine-and-Yours" ownership and property distinction. Thus, the autonomy of the individual paradoxically presupposes a political system that enforces the idea of holding objects "intelligibly" rather than being determined by their sensible conditions.[18] This paradox becomes less contradictory if we take into account

Kant's notion of freedom as liberation from reliance on empirical conditions. Indeed, the monetary and property laws of the early capitalist state helped enact Kant's understanding of autonomous rationality and did so in a way that combined the societal and the metaphysical. Thus the morality that informed the workings of post-Reformation nationhood prescribed, in Kant's view, a forgoing of "worldly" inclinations.

According to Kant, the body politic seems to reenact in a secular manner a somewhat Christian paradigm that proclaims salvation with a view to the renunciation of material interests. As early as the *Groundwork of the Metaphysics of Morals* (1785), Kant defined ethics as being "completely purged of anything empirical."[19] He attributed unquestionable authority to laws and insisted that these must not be "reasoned against" *(zu vernünfteln)*[20] precisely because they had no relation to the empirical and therefore contingent, to the bodily and therefore imperfect. Rather, they had an a priori foundation in the autonomy of pure reason: "[A] law, if it is to be valid as morality, i.e., as grounds for compulsion, must command absolute necessity; . . . the grounds of compulsion must not be sought in the nature of humanity, or in the conditions of the world in which it is placed, but in an a priori manner in terms of pure reason."[21] How does compulsion avoid a contradictory tension with freedom? If the force of the state proscribes a dispassionate relation to the material world, then it does not contradict but instead enacts Kant's definition of both freedom and autonomous reason.

It is against this background of a fusion of politics, ethics, and a secularized understanding of post-Reformation Christianity that in his famous *Response to the Question: What Is Enlightenment?* Kant demanded of his "enlightened" readers: *"[R]eason as much as you want and about whatever subject matter you choose, but obey!"*[22] In an important essay, Michel Foucault examined what the German word *räsonieren* means in the context of Kant's critical philosophy. It does not refer to the specific use of reason in relation to specific objects in the external world. Instead, it denotes the workings of autonomy: "Humanity will reach maturity when it is no longer required to obey, but when men are told: 'Obey, and you will be able to reason as much as you like.' We must note that the German word used here is *räsonieren;* this word, which is also used in the *Critiques,* does not refer to just any use of reason, but to a use of reason in which reason has no other object but itself: *räsonieren* is to reason for reasoning's sake."[23] This absence of an object describes the autonomy of reason. Political struggles are mainly concerned with the distribution of wealth, comprising an assembly of material objects. Kantian reason, however, proved its autonomy by being indifferent toward the external world. This indifference conditions the obedience to the commandments issued by political rulers. In this way, the word *räsonieren* differs from what Kant meant when he used the expression "to reason against" *(vernünfteln).*

To this extent, Kant paid attention to violence not as a threat to material bodies but rather as a subversion of the rational order of things. His law attempted to preclude the revolutionary violence of those who rebel against a post-Reformation, capitalist state founded on the rationalization of money and property. It therefore acted against a violent return to what Kant called a "natural" state in which the earth was everyone's possession. The *Metaphysics of Morals* (1797) characterized the primordial society as a kind of communism: "The whole of humanity originally enjoys the collective possession of the land of the whole earth (communio fundi originaria)" *(Alle Menschen sind ursprünglich in einem Gesamt-Besitz des Bodens der ganzen Erde).*[24] This collective society does not know the autonomy of reason.

Indeed, Kant made it clear that the introduction of the bourgeois Mine-and-Yours property and ownership distinction resulted from an autonomous rationality that decided about the distribution of wealth in an a priori manner. This was done without any regard for the corporeal well-being of specific members of its society: "But the distributing law of the Mine and Yours [*das austeilende Gesetz des Mein und Dein*] with regard to the individual's possession of land can . . . issue from nothing else but an *original* and in an a priori manner united will [*einem ursprünglich und a priori vereinigten Willen*], and can therefore only result from a bourgeois state of affairs [*nur im bürgerlichen Zustande*]."[25] This first "originally" and a priori united will of a bourgeois society contrasts with the "original" state of a "natural" collective community whose members are mainly anxious about the equal distribution of land. The introduction of autonomous reason goes hand in hand with the foundation of an early capitalist state. We will see that, in a manner similar to that whereby Hegel (see chapter 2) stigmatized Judaism as reenforcement of religious naturalism, Kant depicted the "Jewish nation" in terms of a "natural" society that did not distinguish possessions according to a bourgeois Mine-and-Yours ownership and property distinction.

As a result, the laws issuing from autonomous reason counteract such a "natural" state of happiness by introducing the nonempirical notion of property. According to Kant, "happiness [*Glückseligkeit*] comprises everything (and nothing more than that), which nature has given us; virtue [*Tugend*], however, means that which humanity can either give itself or take away from itself."[26] Happiness thus refers to corporeal well-being, whereas ethics, as Kant pointed out in his first *Critique,* has "nothing else" as "motivation [*Bewegungsgrund*] but the *worthiness of attaining happiness* [*Würdigkeit, glücklich zu sein*]."[27] This state of worthiness does not coincide with the experience of happiness. We will see how Kant associated this wish for the actual welfare of the body with the "Pharisees," an expression that in eighteenth-, nineteenth-, and early twentieth-century German discourse came to describe metonymically the essence of Jewishness.[28]

In what is important for Walter Benjamin's reading of Kant's moral philosophy as the theoretical foundation of a "religion of capitalism" (see chapter 10), autonomous law justified the unequal distribution of land. Crucially, the evaluation of money in the *Metaphysics of Morals* illustrates this fusion of ethical and political concerns. Kant depicted money as a convincing illustration of the metaphysical as the formal and nonempirical. Here we have reached the point where morality, politics, and epistemology meet. As we saw in the first part of this chapter, Kant redefined metaphysics as pure reason's independence from both empirical and supernatural conditions. First, Kant rejected forms of exchange involving empirical objects such as gifts. Second, Kant evaluated money as constitutive of the metaphysical doctrine of law *(metaphysische Rechtslehre)*[29] because it transcends any material transfer and operates in purely formal terms: "the notion of *money* [*der Begriff des Geldes*] . . . abstracts away from the material of economic traffic [*von der Materie des Verkehrs . . . abstrahiert*]."[30] Thus, the monetary economic constitution of an early capitalist society upheld, in Kant's view, an ethical system founded on autonomous reason. Just as money abstracts away from the particular quality of objects in the external world, virtue should disregard any empirical conditions that might interfere with the commandments of autonomous reason. To this extent, the monetary system of an early capitalist society helps the work of a type of practical reason that directs the will to action away from all the sensuous impulses to which it has been inclined in the first—"natural"—place.

Kant thus established a binary opposition between law and inclination *(daß er wohltue, nicht aus Neigung, sondern aus Pflicht).*[31] The Kantian ideal of autonomy has a significant bearing on this opposition between "duty" *(Pflicht)* and "inclination" *(Neigung)*. He defined autonomy as abstract movement away from the worldly, in radical polarity to heteronomy as the movement toward empirical objects. Receptivity to the particularity of different material entities constitutes the law of heteronomy. As we have seen, the first critique set out to prove that we were unable to perceive the distinctive character of things, since the "thing in itself" did not lie behind or hidden within the thing, as traditional metaphysics had claimed. Rather, it belonged to the sphere of human self-consciousness. On the epistemological level, which determines the moral one, heteronomy therefore amounts to self-deception.

Within this epistemological and sociopolitical context, Kant targeted the Jew as the embodiment of the heteronomous. As the manifestation of heteronomy, the Jew was not only the opposite of the Christian, who was defined in terms of autonomous reason. More important, he also represented the stranger in a Kantian civil society, whose very laws presupposed an autonomous state of indetermination by objects of empirical reality (see below). How did Kant arrive at such a derogatory equation between heteronomy and Jewishness? On one hand, he seemed to focus on what he perceived to be Judaism and, on the other, he employed the term *nation,* thus referring to the

Jews as a social and ethnic community. As we will see, this concern with the religion of the Jews had a political dimension. Indeed, Kant came to the conclusion that Judaism was a religion without religion.

Before he aligned the Jews with the political, an odd notion of censure in a philosopher so much concerned with the body politic, Kant maintained that Christianity does not have Jewish foundations. This pseudotheological move went in tandem with his attempted secularization and politicization of Christianity's otherworldly elements. To this end, the following analysis traces the extent to which Kant implicitly secularized and politicized the Christian ideal of overcoming the worldly. At the same time he enunciated a transcendental body politic in which the individual had to renounce the principle of heteronomy precisely by forsaking any heteronomous relation to the material basis of the external world. This was made abundantly clear when, in *Religion Within the Boundaries of Mere Reason,* he proclaimed Jesus to be a revolutionary hero who devalorized Judaism's priests and ceremonial statutes, thus introducing both a "moral attitude" *(moralische Gesinnung)* and a "public revolution" *(eine öffentliche Revolution).*[32] Jesus brought about "in his own lifetime a *public* revolution (in religion), by overthrowing a morally repressive ceremonial faith and the authority of its priests."[33] What did Kant mean by the phrase "*public* revolution (in religion)"? He underlined *public* and put *religion* in parentheses so as to emphasize the political significance of this "religious" revolution.

In this context, Christ's body on the cross stood in for the body that had been translated into the body politic. Kant depicted Jesus as a revolutionary whose truth consisted not in the particular and exemplary form of his life but in the rejection, symbolized by the cross, of all worldly existence. The cross functioned as an example only in the sense of a transcendental idea, since his death opened the door to freedom for everyone who, like Jesus, wanted to die away from any orientation to earthly life. This sacrificial understanding of freedom impinged on the moral constitution of the body politic. Kant cited the Christian notion of "the freedom of the children of heaven and the bondage of a mere son of the earth"[34] only to secularize and politicize this otherworldly principle as follows:

> However, the good principle [that of the freedom of the children
> of heaven] did not descend among humans from heaven at one
> particular time but from the very beginning of the human race, in
> some invisible way . . . and has precedence of domicile in humankind
> by right. And, since the principle appeared in an actual human being
> as example for all others, this human being "came unto his own, and
> his own received him not, but as many as received him, to them he
> gave the power to be called the sons of God, even to them that

believe on his name"; that is, by exemplifying this principle (in the moral idea) that a human being opened the doors of freedom to all who, like him, choose to die to everything that holds them fettered to earthly life to the detriment of morality.[35]

Kant quoted John 1:11–12 only to appropriate the image of a divine human being for his political and moral theory. Christ showed that the "freedom of God's children" could be realized within the immanent realm of a body politic that functioned along the lines of a secularized principle of world-transcendence. Kant used the "moral idea" of Christ's sacrifice as an explanation for the absolute authority of autonomous reason. Like Christ, everyone should "die away" *(absterben)* from the happiness of the sensuous, which interferes with the commandments of a completely detached rationality.

Thus, in Kant's understanding, religion preconditioned both the moral and the political mind-set of a nation. This had major implications for the debate about Jewish civil equality that became quite intense in German-speaking culture at the end of the eighteenth century. Indeed, in his treatise *Concerning the Amelioration of the Civil Status of the Jews* (1781), Christian Wilhelm von Dohm made religion the touchstone by which state officials could judge the moral character of the Jews: "It would have to be clearly proved that the religion of the Jews contains such antisocial principles [that is, as alleged by anti-Semites], that their divine laws are contrary to the laws of justice and charity, if one were to justify before the eyes of reason that the rights of citizenship should be withheld entirely from the Jew, and that he should be permitted only partially to enjoy the rights of man."[36] Dohm equivocated on the issue of Judaism's possible moral deficiency: "Either his [the Jew's] religion contains nothing contrary to the duties of a citizen, or such tenets can easily be abolished by political and legal regulations."[37] Dohm's treatise exemplifies how in the sociopolitical context of late eighteenth-century German discourse religion served as touchstone by which one could assess the moral worth of a specific "national character."

If Dohm (and his fellow reformers)[38] either seemed to argue for the moral implacability of Judaism or appeared to have conceded to anti-Semites that there are some immoral but easily amended aspects of it, Kant wholeheartedly embedded both morality and rationality within a secular culture that obfuscates its Christian foundations. In an unacknowledged but implicit mode, he argued in *Religion Within the Boundaries of Mere Reason* that Christianity prepared the ground for a body politic in which autonomous reason set the standard for a moral system based on the demand for the realization of the otherworldly in this world. He opposed this otherworldly principle of freedom to "the prince of this world" *(Fürsten dieser Welt)*,[39] whom he equated with "*Jewish* theocracy":

[I]n this government [Jewish theocracy] the subjects remained attuned in their minds to no other incentive except the goods of this world and only wished, therefore, to be ruled through rewards and punishments in this life—nor were they in this respect capable of other laws except such as were in part imposed by burdensome ceremonies and observances . . . and the inferiority of the moral disposition was in no way at issue—so this institutional order did no substantial injury to the realm of darkness but only served to keep ever in remembrance the imprescriptible right of the first proprietor.[40]

Kant's equation of both Judaism and "the Jewish nation" with theocracy, of course, appropriated the main tenet of the third chapter in Spinoza's *Theological-Political Treatise*. Spinoza "makes Jewish history—and, following it, human history at large—a thoroughly *secular* phenomenon determined by rational and natural causes alone."[41] Spinoza in fact wrote that in return for the Jews' "obedience" to God's commandments "the Law promises them nothing other than the continuing prosperity of their state and material advantages."[42] He did not, however, pass judgment on such worldly considerations. On the contrary, he went on to point out that these are "not surprising, for the purpose of an organised society and state . . . is to achieve security and ease."[43] As we have seen, Kant secularized Christianity's otherworldly orientations, thus turning the Christian into the foundation stone of a rational body politic in which all members strive to enact their freedom from empirical conditions. Spinoza, on the other hand, did not argue for a secularization of religious values. Rather, he maintained that Judaism in its first phase, in which the state was clearly separated from religion,[44] set an example for the rest of humanity. When Kant used the pejorative term "goods of this world," he implicitly referred to Spinoza's conception of a secular society.[45]

What has so far been overlooked, however, is that Kant embedded this critique of a thoroughly secular state in a secularized, that is, pseudotheological discourse. Kant's writing about Judaism as "religion without religion" had a highly prejudicial tone mainly because he made the "right religion," Christianity, the cornerstone of a rational body politic. In this way, he deprived Spinoza's political discourse of any ethical foundation. Indeed, he depicted "the Jewish nation" in terms of a primordial, "natural" state, in short, as "a realm of darkness." The reference to the "first proprietor" in the quotation above of course was to the "old Adam," that is, to a "primitive" stage of humanity.

Kant drew on Paul's theological concept of the old and the new Adam by casting it into a moralistic and, at the same time, political mold. Whereas "old Adam" traditionally referred to the Jews' disbelief in Christ, Kant secularized this image when he quoted Colossians 3: 9–10. Here he turned the "new

Adam" into the politico-ethical notion of justice: "Now conversion is an exit from evil and an entry into goodness, 'the putting off of the old man and the putting on of the new,' since the subject dies unto sin (and thereby also the subject of all inclinations that lead to sin) in order to live unto justice."[46] At this point Kant clearly engaged in a move from the theological (old versus new Adam) via the moral (evil versus good) to the political (justice). Crucially, he employed the phrase to "die away from" *(absterben)*, an expression that belongs to the cognitive field to which the notion of euthanasia appertains. Pointing to *The Conflict of Faculties* (1798), he infamously wrote about the "euthanasia of Jewishness" *(Euthanasie des Judentums)*.[47] A purified form of morality would bring about such a dying away: "The euthanasia of Judaism is pure moral religion, freed from all the ancient statutory teachings, some of which were bound to be retained in Christianity (as a messianic faith)." *(Die Euthanasie des Judentums ist die reine moralische Religion, mit der Verlassung aller Satzungslehren, deren einige doch im Christentum [als messianischen Glauben] noch zurück behalten bleiben müssen.)*.[48] Judaism as a messianic faith points to the Kantian and, as we will see, German idealist conflation of the Jewish religion with the Jewish nation. In *Religion Within the Boundaries of Mere Reason*, he advanced the strange claim that "Judaism as such, taken in its purity, entails absolutely no religious faith."[49] Having no religious faith, "Judaism . . . would still be left with the political faith (which pertains to it by essence)" *(der [wesentlich zu ihm gehörige] politische Glaube)*.[50] Christianity's "immutable, pure religious faith" *(unveränderlichen, reinen Religionsglauben)*[51] stood in stark contrast to the "religion of the Jews," which, as pure politics, defined their "essential and immutable" national character.

We thus arrive at a notion of immutability via a pseudotheological discussion about the essence of Christianity, whose construction seems to depend on its oppositional correlation to a fantasized image of a Jewish national character. Indeed, Kant went so far in his belief in an immutable Jewish national character that he disinherited the Jews of the complex ethical systems and narrations developed in the Hebrew Bible: "The *Jewish faith,* as originally established, was only a collection of merely statutory laws supporting a political state; for whatever moral additions were *appended* to it, whether original or later, do not in any way belong to Judaism as such.[52] The verb *anhängen* ("to append") describes a process by which something alien is attached to another entity. Thus, an ethical kind of commonwealth constitutes the immutable opposite of Kant's posited Jewish national character.

How did Kant try to verify his fantasy about Jewish immutability? Significantly, Kant, and Hegel as well (see chapter 2), used the term *race* only to make little of its significance. True to his Enlightenment and modernizing aspirations, he emphasized the common source of the whole of humanity and thereby explicitly rejected a potential focus on racial difference. In this respect, Kant disregarded the divergence between different people *(unerachtet ihrer Verschiedenheiten)* by emphasizing the common root from which every ethnic group develops *(einen einzigen Stamm).*[53] He clung to a cultural (in the sense of pseudotheological) notion of immutability that disregarded environmental factors: "Though Kant emphasized the common origin of all men, to avoid attacking the biblical account of creation, he nevertheless formulated a concept of race which would remain constant. Racial make-up becomes an unchanging substance and the foundation of all physical appearances and human development, including race."[54] In this way, Kant developed a notion of racial immutability without reference to pseudobiology. He set out to substantiate his notion of a "Jewish essence" with recourse to the image of an inseparable tie that bound the Jews immutably to Jehovah.

This is what he meant by the expression "messianic (or political) faith." It described the Jews as "a people especially chosen by Jehovah for himself" *(als ein besonders vom Jehovah für sich auserwähltes Volk).*[55] In the introduction we saw how this topos of an immutable tie between the Jewish God and his people informed the pseudotheological notion of immutability in the anti-Semitic writings of Feuerbach and Schopenhauer. This pseudotheological notion anticipated the pseudobiological element of "racial contagion" insofar as it involved the image of Christianity at risk of being "infected" by a *"messianic* faith."[56] In order to emphasize his fear of scriptural infection, Kant interpreted Mendelssohn's refusal to convert to Christianity as an exhortation to the Christians, functioning as a red flag warning of a potential loss of "Christian essence." Kant stated, "[B]y [the refusal to convert, Mendelssohn] apparently meant to say: Christians, first get rid of the Judaism in *your own* faith, and then we will give up ours."[57] This is precisely what Kant set out to do in his moral philosophy and rational theology. He attempted to remove Christianity's Judaic foundations. He did so by endowing Christian scripture with a radically anti-Jewish meaning.

As I have shown elsewhere, Kant reversed Paul's spirit-letter opposition so as to define Christianity as a revolution, as a conception that breaks radically with Judaism.[58] This reversal has major implications for the perception of both the corporeal and the Jewish. Kant often conflated the two, as we have seen. Kant's definition of morality as a dispassionate relation to the external world was a precondition for this reversal. It is the letter that became, in Kant's interpretation, devalued as the contingent, the material, the changeable, and the impure. In Kant's reading the letter signified, accordingly, the materially concrete, whereas the spirit denoted freedom from the corporeal as autonomous reason. Of particular importance in relation to Wagner's equation of Jewishness with his operas' narrative foundation (see chapter 3) is that Kant equated the letter with narrativity and concrete, empirical, and everchanging "actions" *(Handlungen),* whereas the spirit denoted abstract and static "attitudes" *(Gesinnungen).*[59] Thus, the Pauline spirit, that which gives life, turned into the letter that kills. This is so because Kant's *Geist* commanded complete separation from material life. In his *Religion Within the Boundaries of Mere Reason*, Kant argued that the letter signified any "motivating force" *(Triebfeder)* external to the unquestionable and static laws established by pure reason, be it "charity" *(gutherziger Instinkt)* or "compassion" *(Mitleiden)*.[60] The spirit, by contrast, denoted morality as the following of the law for the law's sake, free from any other motivating force *(er beobachtet es [das Gesetz] dem Geiste nach . . . darin, daß dieses allein zur Triebfeder hinreichend sei)*.[61] In a further elaboration, Kant based his spirit-letter opposition in terms of a fundamental divide between the "physical" *(physisch)* and the "moral" *(moralisch)*,[62] thus radically rejecting the spiritual validity of the corporeal and contradicting Paul's notion of the spirit as taking care of the body.[63]

It becomes clear on examination that by reversing Paul's spirit-letter opposition Kant attempted to erase Christianity's Jewish origins. To demonstrate this development, I must mention a further Kantian dichotomy. A legality-morality opposition in the *Metaphysics of Morals* paralleled his spirit-letter polarity in *Religion Within the Boundaries of Mere Reason*.[64] Like the letter, the law is driven by motivating forces outside the sphere of a static understanding of law. Here, Judaism is situated reductively within the "legalistic." The target of Kant's reversal of Paul's spirit-letter opposition was in fact the oral law of the Pharisees, which he associated with the empirical, letter-like principle of happiness. In the *Metaphysics of Morals*, he criticized the Pharisean watchword according to which law could be reinterpreted if it would help save human lives:

> Woe to them who have crawled through the snaky curves of the doctrine of happiness [*Glückseligkeitslehre*] in order to find something, which through the advantage which it holds out as a promise, frees them from punishment, if only by a small degree, according to the Pharisean watchword: "it is better that one man dies than that the whole people perish." For if justice [*Gerechtigkeit*] decline, then there is no value in human lives on earth.[65]

Here Kant compared the political (in the sense of worldly or "messianic") principle of happiness with the politico-ethical notion of justice. The law follows the workings of autonomous reason. This kind of justice then forms the foundations of a secularized Christian body politic in which the otherworldly has turned immanent.

Radicalizing his argument, Kant interpreted Judaism as "materialistic" and so, according to his interpretative framework, Jewish law emerges as being oriented toward the "goods of this world" *(Güter dieser Welt)*.[66] Kant thus counterposed Christology as the purely spiritual, in the sense of the abstract, as a radical opposition to Judaism as the letter, in the sense of the material. As we have seen, Christ appeared as the revolutionary who attempted to overturn Judaism as the religion of "slavery." Here again Kant developed Pauline imagery only to subvert its connotations. As Daniel Boyarin has shown, in Paul, "'slavery' is the benevolent and beneficial slavery of the child. It is for his own good."[67] In Paul, slavery functioned as a metaphor for the paternal guidance with which God directs the Jews. In Kant, however, slavery meant oppression and bondage. Worse still, the word *Sklavensinn* has essentialist overtones meaning "the mind-set of a slave."[68]

To this extent, Kant's reversal of Paul's spirit-letter opposition spilled over into his anthropological thinking. In his *Anthropology from a Pragmatic Point of View* (1798), Kant labeled the Jews "Palestinians who live amongst us"[69] and thereby exposed their exclusion from his "universal" and "non-dogmatic" philosophy. As Slavoj Zizek has recently pointed out, "the basic operation of ideology is not only the dehistoricizing gesture of transforming an empirical object into the eternal condition (women, Blacks . . . are by nature subordinated, etc.), but also the *opposite* gesture of transposing the a priori closure/impossibility of a field into an empirical obstacle."[70] This has major implications for the analysis that I am advancing in the present study. If Kant labeled the Jews "Palestinians who live amongst us," he stigmatized them as "Orientals" who are literally living next door.

This unarticulated level of Kant's philosophy describes what I have called his pseudotheology (see the introduction). Kant did not explicitly articulate the fact that he developed his social theory in a quasi-religious mode. Instead, he secularized and politicized aspects of Christian theology without critically reflecting on his undertaking. This lack of self-reflection bespeaks a loss of consciousness. In order to fully define the formal structure of his philosophy (autonomy, reason, morality, and freedom), Kant almost unconsciously fantasized about the Jews as its opposite. In doing so, he posited Judaism as an abstract principle that does nothing else but, paradoxically, desire the consumption of material goods. Here Kant unconsciously articulated his anxiety about a growing capitalist society, which he consciously celebrated as social instantiation of rationality (the Mine-and-Yours distinction as social and political realization of the principle of autonomy). Capitalist modes of labor, in fact, operate along the lines of an autonomous paradigm. The worker produces goods for the sake of production.[71] Capitalist growth consists in this seemingly endless increase of productivity. In capitalism, value is constituted by this autonomous principle of "production for the sake of production." Value thus subsumes concrete labor under a general category that abstracts away from the social utilization of the fruits of labor. Kant associated the Jews with this consumption of worldly goods. In so doing he unconsciously voiced his fears about the potential corruption of capitalism into materialism.

Why did Kant orientalize European Jews? This question may be addressed by a brief discussion of the particular historical context in which Kant developed his moral philosophy. Attention to this discourse brings into focus the pseudotheology to which Kant referred in order to give content to his autonomy-heteronomy divide. Like many other philosophical systems, the Kantian autonomy-heteronomy divide at one level constitutes a purely formal aspect of his architectonic. Yet at another, more unarticulated level, Kant exemplified this universal formality with reference to a particular historical and religious context. He thereby developed a rather static and essentialist notion of the Jewish as the "heteronomous" in direct opposition to the "rational" as the secularized Christian idea of autonomy from empirical (worldly) determinations. Whereas this dehistoricizing gesture moved in an abstract sphere—correlated to the abstraction implicit in the autonomy-heteronomy opposition—Kant targeted the Jews as the empirical obstacle to the establishment of a rational order in which heteronomy would be overcome.

The political aspect of his pseudotheological exclusion of Judaism from both Christian religion and a "modern," that is, "rational" body politic comes clearly to the fore in his *Anthropology,* where he called the Jews "a nation of cheaters" (*eine Nation von Betrügern*). In doing so, he reconstructed a group of people who value their interests in empirical life more highly than approximating the conceptual truth laid down by civil society. The Jews, in Kant's view, did not respect the property and monetary regulations that proscribe material gain—as enacted by cheating. Indeed, he attributed the causes of cheating to the religion that shapes the mentality of the Jews. Hence Kant maintained that on account of their "superstition" (*Aberglaube*), they did not seek civil honor (*keine bürgerliche Ehre sucht*).[72] Instead, they tried to make up for such a lack by outwitting the people who offer them security (*sondern dieser ihren Verlust durch Vorteile und Überlistung des Volks, unter dem sie Schutz finden . . . ersetzen wollen*).[73] This may indicate that the connection between the rather essentialist definition of the Jews as cheaters in his *Anthropology,* his discussion of Jewish law in the *Metaphysics of Morals,* and *Religion Within the Boundaries of Mere Reason* is not as slim as it might first appear. Indeed, the anthropological account emphasized the focus on a social group. This is the same as in the larger corpus of his transcendental philosophy, where Kant depicted the Jews as a group that has followed not the path of transcendental freedom but that of enslavement to the material world.

The essentialist depiction of the Jews as a group is anti-Semitic insofar as it stigmatizes them as the nonmoderns in the sense of nontranscendentalists and insofar as it depicts them as corrupting the body politic. Kant's concern was not with a medical, pseudoscientific account of Jewishness. For example, he argued that the Jews had had a "moral epoch" (*das jüdische Volk in seiner gesitteten Epoche*) in which Moses—with a completely negative view of the empirical and the sensuous (*in Ansehung des Sinnlichen gänzlich negativ*)—introduced the prohibition against images.[74] Thus Kant's anti-Semitism had little in common with the pseudoscientific account in circulation at the end of the nineteenth century, or so it seems. He focused on social normativity rather than on the "biological." Yet it was this emphasis on the body politic that constituted a modernization of the old—more religiously focused—Jew-hatred. In his account of the body politic, Kant fantasized about the Jews as figures of corruption. In sociohistorical terms, Kant here unconsciously voiced his anxiety about capitalism's "descent" into materialism.

Thus Kant's philosophical anthropology anticipated political anti-Semitism, which the supposed objectivity of pseudoscientific writing served to substantiate. Although Kant did not engage in a crude discourse about bodily functions, he did depict the Jews as being socially—rather than medically—conditioned toward the material.[75] Kant's views concerning Judaism, whether in his *Anthropology, Metaphysics of Morals,* or *Religion Within the Boundaries of Mere Reason,* are consistent in a negative manner. By means of this construction of a group that chose to be heteronomous, he accounted for the fact that, although the ability to transcend the empirically intuited world resides in every human being, it needs to be socially enforced. It depends on social normativity and, as a result, autonomy presupposes a civil society that metaphysically prescribes freedom from materialistic inclinations.

In a further move, Kant linked the body politic to religion, arguing that the inability to participate in a bourgeois civil society based on the Mine-and-Yours property and ownership distinction was reducible to the superstition of the Jews.[76] Thus, *Kant grounded the immutability of the Jews in their religion.* But what exactly did he mean when he labeled the Jews superstitious? Crucially, he defined superstition in terms of reason's subjection to external facts *(die gänzliche Unterwerfung der Vernunft unter Facta),*[77] that is, to the principle of heteronomy. In Kant's view, superstition is irrational because it does not restrict the use of reason to reason's (autonomous) self-rule but instead orients rational activity toward that "which it can justify by *objective grounds* and dogmatic conviction."[78] Thus, by calling the Jews superstitious, Kant defined rational autonomy as freedom from both the empirically and the religiously given, over and against the Judaic, which he characterized as the heteronomous, as the superstitious and the irrational. In this way, Kant excluded the Jews from his transcendental scheme.

It was owing to the heteronomously oriented religion of the Jews that their bodies could not be transformed into a body politic grounded in autonomy. As we have seen, in *Religion Within the Boundaries of Mere Reason,* Kant posited the goods of this world *(Güter dieser Welt)* as the motivating force behind the "mental disposition" *(Gemüter)* of the Jews.[79] According to Kant, cheating resulted from their religion, which served as a justification for barring them from entry into a civil society whose laws prescribed transcendental independence from determination by worldly motivating forces. As has been discussed in this chapter, the Kantian notions of reason and freedom modernized the old Christian Jew-hatred in philosophical-religious as well as in political-anthropological terms.[80] Thus, according to Kant's anti-Semitic fantasy, it was the religion of the Jews that positioned them as the immutable other of a body politic based on the transcendental indifference to empirical objects. Significantly, it was only such indifference that enabled rational will's acceptance of the Mine-and-Yours property and ownership distinction.

What was revolutionary about this distinction? It was not the distinction as such. Rather, it was the transcendental turn with which Kant imbued it. He did so in such a way that it prepared the ground for a "modernized" notion of the body politic. Now an unequal distribution of wealth made the members of bourgeois civil society implicitly subscribe to autonomy insofar as they respected the regulations that did not make the earth everyone's possession and thereby arbitrarily restricted access to "the goods of this world." Kant's transcendental paradigm could likewise be used as the theoretical underpinning of a communitarian and socialist body politic, as was the case in the work of Feuerbach and the young Hegelians whom Wagner read in his revolutionary period, shortly before writing his infamous "Judaism in Music" of 1850.

2 THE METAPHYSICS OF EATING: JEWISH DIETARY LAWS AND HEGEL'S SOCIAL THEORY

The image of philosophical thought as atemporal and undramatic, as itself non-representational, has been very much taken for granted in the historiography of philosophy since the nineteenth century; it has in certain respects been part of the profession of philosophy since its origins.
—BEREL LANG, ANATOMY OF PHILOSOPHICAL STYLE

Introduction: The Trajectory of Kant's Opposition Between Autonomy and Heteronomy

In what ways did Hegel develop Kant's political theory? As we saw in the previous chapter, Kant defined the body politic not in terms of the secular but in terms of secularization. The ethical commonwealth should translate the otherworldly into the language of the worldly. Following Kant, Hegel perceived in Judaism the exclusive reign of the worldly (that is, pure politics disguised as religion). This chapter examines how Hegel's Kantian view of Judaism shaped his understanding of both dialectics and the modern state.

Although most readers have realized the ways in which Hegel developed transcendental philosophy, they do not understand that this development went in tandem with a shift in the interpretation of Judaism. This movement encompasses Kant's writings from the *Metaphysics of Morals* to *Religion Within the Boundaries of Mere Reason*. Kant's philosophy, in turn, shaped Hegel's writings about history and dialectics from the *Spirit of Christianity* via the *Phenomenology of Spirit* to his later works. The way in which both idealists perceived Jewishness is in fact bound up with the way in which they interpreted empirical reality. As we have seen, Kant defined rabbinic Judaism in terms of an orientation toward the material world, and Hegel, while elaborating on Kant's idealism, maintained that the very positivity (of the empirical world), which supposedly shapes rabbinic Jewish culture, actually turns out to be illusory.

This chapter investigates how it came to be that Hegel's interpretation of Judaism informed his social and aesthetic theory. Grounds for such discussion can be found chiefly in his *Lectures on the Philosophy of Religion*, where he defined his political theory, in aesthetic terms, with reference to both Judaism as the religion of sublimity and Greek antiquity as the birth of beauty and happiness. Hegel perceived the latter as being in direct opposition to the unhappiness of Israel. First, however, a brief discussion of the importance of Hegelian topics such as dialectics, the history of different peoples, and the related notions of race and culture serves to locate the idealist writer in a sociohistorical and philosophical context. An inquiry into the meaning of various eating metaphors in Hegel's *Philosophy of Right,* in the *Lectures on the Philosophy of Religion,* and in the *Phenomenology of the Spirit* helps explain the role of Judaism within this sociohistorical context. As a result of this investigation it will emerge that Judaism plays a vital role as a figure of thought signifying the opposite of Hegel's dialectics. This helps us address the question that recent research on Hegel and the Jews perceived as an unsolvable riddle: Why did Hegel write in a prejudicial manner about European Jewry and Judaism in his philosophy of history and nevertheless argue for the political integration of Jews into contemporary German society?[1]

As regards Hegel's position within German philosophy, recent research by Dieter Henrich and Robert Pippin—among others—has clearly shown how he radicalized and developed Kant's "antiempiricist, antinaturalist and antirationalist strategies."[2] Hegel reinforced Kant's antiempiricism by arguing as if idealism "*could have no realist competitor,* and so can be construed as itself constitutive of 'reality as it is (could be) in itself.'"[3] If Hegel deepened Kant's idealism by arguing that intuitions are conceptually constituted, then we do not need a civil society that asks us to submit to laws that might conflict with our intuitions, because these are themselves conceptually shaped. In order for this conceptual view of intuitions to be valid, we need to know that being, as it is perceived by us intuitively, has the truth of nonbeing inscribed on it. This perception can, however, only be gained through speculative dialectics. For there the destination of being in nonbeing is terminated by death (and then the dialectical process further unfolds through the workings of becoming). In this way Hegel bridged the Kantian gap between heteronomy and autonomy, between understanding and reason, between intuition and concept, and yet Judaism still played the role of a scapegoat in his philosophical system. If in Kant's transcendentalism Judaism had the function of illustrating the heteronomous and the intuitive, which are not ruled by concepts that transcend the naturally given, why did Hegel also refer to scapegoating after having apparently done away with the dichotomy between the empirical and the transcendental?

The answer has to do with his development of Kant's idealism. Although Hegel claimed to have overcome the dichotomy between materiality and spirituality, the closing of this gap depends on a deepening of transcendental tendencies to the point where the empirical turns out to be the spiritual. The real is the rational, and those who perceive being as materiality live in a world of illusion *(Schein)*. Strikingly, Hegel targeted the Jews as a social group that lives in this illusory world. The main point of Hegel's charge against Judaism focused on positivity, and he radicalized a transcendentalist vilification of rabbinic Jewish culture that was in keeping with his radicalization of Kant's idealism. As a corollary of this, the heteronomy of a Jewish way of life turns into an illusory existence, because that which Kant attacked as deceptive *(Blendwerk)* but nevertheless empirically constituted *(Güter)* poses as an illusion.

Against this background, Slavoj Zizek's account of Hegel's supposed conflation of Kant and Jewishness goes a bit too far and ignores the congruency between a Hegelian development of transcendental idealism and a radicalization of a transcendentalist charge against Judaism. Rather than being in conflict with each other, both movements followed similar lines of thought. Instead of arguing that Kant and the Jews remain "prisoners within the field of representation,"[4] Hegel argued that the Jews do not realize that the empirical, which a Kantian view also associates with the deceptive, is in fact nothing but a phantom. In summation, Kantian transcendentalism and its Hegelian development discussed Judaism as that which deviates from an idealist account of the world. Hegel embedded Judaism in a narrative of history, although he intensified the charge of positivity to the point at which the empirical turns out to be not only the heteronomous but an illusion. In this historical narrative it occupies the place of an ideational story among a variety of others (those of Oriental natural religions, of Greek and Roman culture, and of Christianity) that are all sublated, overcome, and preserved, in the absolute knowledge informing the workings of modernity. This begs the question whether the main contention of Hegel's discourse about Judaism concerns a historical perspective or a dialectical one. Did Judaism belong to a dead past in Hegel's speculative account, or did it still play a significant role?

If Hegel took issue with Judaism, considering it the reverse of dialectics (similar to the Kantian account, in which as heteronomy it represents the opposite of transcendental autonomy), it would nevertheless be something of a negatively motivating force within the self-understanding of a Heglian modernity. Nathan Rotenstreich has pointed out that Hegel excluded Judaism from dialectics.[5] Recently, however, Yirimiyahu Yovel has shifted the focus of attention from dialectics to history by arguing that the Hegelian approach relegates Judaism to a historic past, depicting it as a relic that has no value for and within modernity.[6] One might question Yovel's interpretation by mentioning that Hegel treated all religions as remnants that were to be remembered in a transparticular and transreligious modern world for specific reasons that are bound up with the distinctive ideational contents to be gathered from them. A further weakness of Yovel's concentration on history results from his neglect of dialectics, which, as the above discussion has preliminarily established, cannot be relegated to a question of minor importance as regards Hegel's reading of rabbinic Jewish culture. In Rotenstreich's interpretation, on the other hand, historical issues do not receive sufficient attention, and consequently he does not accurately analyze the role of Judaism in Hegel as the opposite of modernity understood as secularized Christianity.

A clear understanding of the historical position of rabbinic Judaism in Hegel's narrative does help us comprehend its contrasting relation to Hegelian dialectics. Hence, a detailed discussion of Hegel's historical account of Christianity as the basis for his notion of modernity may contribute to a comprehension of the sociohistorical dimension of his dialectics. Secularized Christianity, as the basis for both Hegel's dialectic and his modern state, has received a rather confusing analysis in Rotenstreich's interpretation. This is especially the case if, as this chapter attempts to show, Hegel accused the Jews of making the natural absolute by not being able to see the "nothingness" that lies behind immediate being. Rotenstreich rightly sees Hegel's criticism of a Jewish way of life as dependent on his understanding of Christianity. However, Hegel did not define the Christian as the pantheist. On the contrary, he criticized Spinoza's pantheistic philosophy, arguing that it does not acknowledge the limits of empirical existence and, by not knowing these, conflates the finite with the infinite.[7]

Rather than arguing for the intrinsic compatibility between spirit and matter, which a pantheistic deification of the natural world pushes to an extreme, Hegel attempted to translate the immediacy of the empirical into the mediacy of the spiritual. He did so by establishing an identity of object and subject, of immanence and transcendence.

As has been shown above, Hegel did not transcend Kant's transcendental philosophy by referring to a "pantheistic mysticism" (as Rotenstreich maintains). Instead, he radicalized it by way of politicization so that Kantian idealism could become "real," insofar as that which had been considered to be "reality" became revealed as an illusion (*Sein* is *Schein*).

If Judaism is constituted by an illusion, then how could Hegel depict it in essentialist terms, as Kant had done by stigmatizing the Jews as cheaters? Like Kant, he saw "Jewishness" emerging from rabbinic Judaism, and the two idealists focused their discussion of Judaism on its ideational content, as they saw it. This content depicts an unchangeable characteristic that served to reveal the essence of modern Jewry just as race signified immutability in the nineteenth and twentieth centuries. The words *Jew* and *Christian*, as Sander L. Gilman has argued, "may take on racial as well as religious significance from the eighteenth through the twentieth centuries."[8] As we have seen, Kant posited racial immutability by focusing on culture. Hegel, for his part, accounted for "racial difference" *(Rassenverschiedenheit)* by referring to "particular spirits of nature" *(besonderen Naturgeister)* as they are spread over all geographical areas of the world.[9] Race in the sense of Hegelian "local spirits" *(Lokalgeister)* had a biological as well as a cultural dimension: it embraced both spirit and nature. In Hegel, as in Kant, the cultural commanded greater importance than the biological,[10] for it is this cultural formation that played a vital role in their philosophical account, filling gaps in their otherwise universalist schemes.

This apparent focus on social constitution and culture (as opposed to pseudobiology) does not, however, diminish the prejudicial force of Kant's and Hegel's depiction of Jewish culture, because here the "cultural" is the immutable. As discussed in the previous chapter, the role of rabbinic Judaism in Kant's transcendental philosophy was that of an immutable "other," of the persistent nonmodern element within a modern world. Hegel argued for the emancipation of the Jews, although he developed the charge of positivity with which Kant stigmatized the Jews. Nevertheless his focus on religion has far-reaching consequences for the role of the Jewish in his ideational narrative because, from his perspective, the religious shapes the political and ethical disposition of a people.[11]

As noted at the beginning of this chapter, this contradiction between Hegel's support of emancipation within a modern state and his highly prejudicial account of the Jewish way of life in his philosophy has posed a riddle to Hegel scholars. It should, however, have been noted that his support of disenfranchisement makes sense in terms of his self-consciously "modern" thought, for there all forms of difference, if taken seriously, result in perceiving immediate being (that is, particular difference) to be "real," whereas it actually only exists as an illusion. To this extent, difference needs to be ignored and must not be discriminated against in a "modern," that is, "enlightened" state: "Insofar as abstract thought undermines the outward, it also turns away from difference as such" *(Indem das abstrakte Denken sich gegen die Äußerlichkeit überhaupt kehrt, wendet es sich auch gegen den Unterschied als solchen).*[12] Hegel, therefore, did not contradict himself when he spoke out for the integration of the Jews into modern German society. Critics such as Yovel separate Hegel's political commitment to emancipation from his "*non-political, quasi-theological study that reconstructs the history of the world Spirit.*"[13] However, this approach ignores the fact that Judaism was not only included, like all other particular "local spirits," but had a special role to play within a modern dialectical state, precisely because it was perceived to remain immutably outside of dialectics A discussion of various metaphors for eating in the following section will help explain the ways in which the "Jewish" appears to be on the outside of a self-consciously speculative movement. As we will see, Hegel referred to eating metaphors to illustrate his understanding of law and sacrifice.

Eating

To eat means to sacrifice and to sacrifice means to eat oneself.

—Hegel

Law as a way of governing society and the process of eating received a curiously congruous treatment by Hegel, and this finds a correlation in his focus on Jewish dietary laws. He defined law, *Gesetz,* in terms of positing, of *setzen.* As such, laws are the result of free movement that neglects any given empirical conditions. They are autonomous with respect to religious or natural determinations.[14] In this respect religion poses a greater threat than nature, because it often empowers members of a given society to disobey laws by claiming to have God's word on their side. Hegel called this split between the individual and the social—between the subjective and the objective—the characteristic of a state of affairs that is *moralische* (having a subjective view of morality), in contrast to *sittliche* (having an objective, sociopolitical view of morality), in which the subjective completely identifies with the objective. If Hegel praised Kant for having introduced into the history of ideas the concept of autonomy, of self-determination as freedom from material and religious determinations, he nevertheless criticized him for not identifying the autonomy of the individual with the autonomy of the state.

Thus, in order for there to be *Sittlichkeit,* the citizens must have transformed their free will by internalizing the autonomous will of the state.[15] The free will of the citizens and the autonomous will of the state must be congruous; otherwise, the laws are an empty formalism for the members of a given community and the sacrifices demanded of them are only unwillingly enacted. Thus Hegel radicalized Kant by arguing that Kantian moral freedom can only become a politically *(Sittliche)* binding one by means of an intrusion of spirit into matter. Spirit needs to encounter matter not to spiritualize but to destroy it. Hegel described this point in the *Phenomenology,* where he argued for a conflation of the transcendental and the empirical by means of which the latter turns out to be dead, thereby illustrating the truth of dialectical investigations as to the coincidence between being and nonbeing: "But the essential objectivity must be *immediate and sensuous.* The immediate and the sensuous is dead, for the bone is dead insofar as it partakes of life and the spirit must be posited in it as real." *(Aber die eigentliche Gegenständlichkeit muß eine unmittelbare, sinnliche sein, so daß der Geist in dieser als toten—denn der Knochen ist das Tote, insofern es an Lebendigen selbst ist als wirklich gesetzt wird.)*[16] Hegel employed eating metaphors in order to depict this speculative process by means of which the immediate being of objects, such as bones, dialectically turns into its opposite, nonbeing.

The connecting element between eating and the sphere of *Sittlichkeit,* be it law or other spheres of the political, resides in a notion of sacrifice. This notion describes how the immediate and the particular need to be annihilated in order to become the lifeblood of a "greater" mediated whole, which is the spirit. The spirit manifests itself in singular states, which in turn become consumed by the most general state thanks to the favors meted out by the workings of destiny. Hegel characterized sacrifice as a consuming process in which the empirical turns into spirit, and it is this sacrificial movement that he defined as "life, the highest idea in nature," which entails "only this, to sacrifice itself."[17] To sacrifice means nothing other than to "abolish the natural, which is otherness" (Opfern heißt, das Natürliche, das Anderssein aufheben).[18] Which entity does the natural stand opposed to as otherness, if it is not life in its real rather than its illusory form?

The concepts of life and sacrifice ultimately coincide in Hegel's discussion of eating. He read the act of eating as a metaphor for the workings of sacrifice. Food sustains one form of life and kills another. Leon Kass has recently pointed out the ambivalence inherent in the act of eating: "Eating is at once form preserving and form deforming. What was distinct and whole gets broken down and homogenized, in order to preserve the distinctiveness and wholeness of the feeder. . . . The danger and the glory of living forms is writ large in the fact of eating."[19] Kass's discussion of eating contrasts with Hegel's. As we will see, both philosophers focused on Jewish dietary laws and thereby established their different points of view concerning the value of empirical life. For Hegel did not regret the destructive dimension of the consumption of food. Rather, in keeping with his dialectical manner, he identified sustenance with killing, although the differences between these two entities still have a function. Only as immediate moments of time (that is, as distinct temporal units) does nurture differ from murder. In a speculative scheme of things, however, these immediate moments overlap so that the eater realizes that his own empirical (in the sense of bodily) constitution could also turn him into an object for consumption, or on a wider political plane, into an object for sacrifice. In this way eating makes man conscious of his nothingness, even while keeping up his (illusory) natural existence for a limited period of time. By virtue of this self-conscious process the eater turns out to be a sacrificer and the sacrificer an eater so that "to eat means to sacrifice and to sacrifice means to eat oneself" (Essen heißt Opfern und Opfern heißt Selbstessen).[20]

In depicting the activity of law, the metaphor of eating also fills in the political gap that Hegel criticized in Kant's account of autonomy. For in eating, man internalizes the autonomy of the state, and this occurs in two ways. First, he realizes his autonomy with respect to the empirical world by eating life. Second, he becomes aware of the similarity between himself and that which he is eating: he is as much part of the empirical world as the object has been that is now in the process of being devoured. In eating he self-consciously finds out that true autonomy can be achieved only by submitting his own empirical nature to be killed and devoured for the "greater good" of the generality in which he lives as a particular empirical member. Thus the citizen perceives his autonomy to be completely identical with that of the state. Just as he annihilates the empirically given by laying hold of it and finally eating it, he himself is in the possession of the greater autonomous whole, the state. According to Hegel, idealism manifests itself in possessing the external world so that the immediate becomes mediated. In this respect he called animals idealistic. They too have a "free will" that does not leave life as it is but seizes it and "devours things, proving therefore that these are not absolutely independent" *(denn es zehrt die Dinge auf und beweist dadurch, daß sie nicht absolut selbstständig sind).*[21]

Hegel developed his eating metaphor further by establishing a binary opposition between the plant and the animal-like. In the *Philosophy of Right* he gendered this difference, calling the plant feminine and the animal masculine. The plant preserves life, whereas the animal acquires knowledge by eating life, thus subordinating the particular to the general. He qualified this binary opposition by a further contrast between animal and man. Both man and animal are idealistic by virtue of their very destructive activities as regards the existing empirical world. What differentiates the two is that the former has a self-reflective will, whereas the latter acts on the impulses of its drives. Drives are naturally given. Human will, however, can channel these drives in the direction of autonomy, away from any empirical considerations.[22] Thus, in Hegel's view, rational will can decide to annihilate the materiality of its own being and thereby become infinite.[23]

The contrast between the human and the divine has many similarities with the plant-animal opposition and the associated one between the human and the animalistic. In the *Phenomenology*, Hegel compared humanity with divinity. As in the plant-animal opposition, gender plays an important role in his hierarchical construction of difference.[24] Significantly, however, the secularized agenda of Hegel's theology comes to the fore in this opposition between God and man, for his God has a secular manifestation in the state. In this context, he introduced the notion of different kinds of right: one is the terrestrial law of humanity, the other is divine on account of its general nature, which transcends empirical particularity. Thus God manifests itself in the generality of the state, whereas a simply human or retarded terrestrial *Recht* resides in the family. Masculinity defines the power of the state *(Staatsmacht)*, whereas femininity characterizes the gender of the family. This gendering recalls the plant-animal opposition: the feminine plant supports the survival of existing empirical life; the masculine animal, on the other hand, destroys creaturely life by eating it. Hegel abandoned the plant-animal comparison in his discussion of the state for an important reason. As we saw above, the animal does not have a consciousness of its destructive activities.

Man, however, does. This consciousness of both eating empirical life and his own empirical condition enables him to be used as food, as sacrifice, for the "greater good" of the state.

Yet Hegel did not exclude the family and the feminine from his scheme of a political kind of morality *(Sittlichkeit)*.[25] Woman functions as the included other: she helps produce life and also supports its growth. Like the plant, she has a "selfless nature" *(selbstlose Natur)* and feeds those who belong to her to fuel the consuming power of the state. Hegel called this process of being eaten "utility" *(Nützlichkeit)* and argued that by becoming usable as a source of food and drink, the feminine element achieved its "highest perfection" *(höchste Vollkommenheit)*. Woman gives food for the "spiritual and intellectual fermentation" *(geistige Gärung)* of the masculine principle. Thus Hegel defined "the feminine principle as that of nutrition" *(weiblichen Prinzips der Ernährung)* and the masculine as "the driving force of self-conscious existence" *(männlichen Prinzipe der sich treibenden Kraft des selbstbewußten Daseins)*.[26] *Self-consciousness* here means consciousness of one's own sacrificial nature. The Christian "mystery of bread and wine" *(das Mysterium des Brotes und Weins)* transforms itself into the "mystery of flesh and blood" *(Mysterium des Fleisches und Blutes)*[27] alone in the sacrifices demanded by the modern state.

This description of nutrition and destruction begs the question as to the content of these biological procedures. How can the state become endowed with divinity simply because of its transparticular power as regards devouring empirical life? Note that Hegel described a contentless process only: the one of being fed, nursed, and then eaten. Surely, the activity of eating cannot characterize Hegel's Christology. If it does, his Christian God may not be called innocent. Rather, evil and good are inseparable parts of his being. This exactly marks Hegel's dialectical point. According to his theology, God drives man into action and by acting man in turn becomes guilty. Thus Zeus's law also embraces transgression. Crime and law are in fact inseparable so that the lower region of the Erinnies and the higher of the Olympus hold sway from the seat of the same throne.[28] However, the closeness of law and guilt does not absolve the criminal of guilt. Rather than being revealed and "good," the point of Hegel's modern Christian law is its ability to incriminate, and it is formal insofar as its rule should be indifferent to the well-being of particular empirical objects.

Like law, God pushes man into action so that he becomes guilty and needs to die, and in courting death he realizes divine will. As a consequence of this, "his guilt remains even after his death, though he has been freed from crime" *(Freisprechung nicht von der Schuld . . . sondern vom Verbrechen)*.[29] The emphasis here lies on action that makes man guilty, and by doing so reverses his knowledge into its opposite, into incompetence, failure, powerlessness, and guilt. By eating life, man acts and hence becomes guilty. And thus he realizes his own nothingness as an empirical creature. As a result, he happily accepts his own death and suffering for a greater nonparticular entity such as the state. Thus, as destruction, eating makes man guilty, but by behaving in a violent manner man in turn becomes conscious of the ethical grounds for his own suffering and death. In this sense Kantian knowledge of the intellectual emptiness of all empirical life does not suffice. Rather, it needs to be experienced through action that turns the immediacy of being into material to be self-consciously shaped by human construction. This emphasis on transformation explains both Hegel's focus on the animal and his association of the animalistic and the masculine: in killing living objects, the animal doubts *(zweifeln)* the existence of sensuous beings and also despairs *(verzweifeln)* of their reality in the conviction of their nothingness *(Nichtigkeit).*[30]

As Hegel elaborated in his *Philosophy of Right,* however, animals cannot give themselves a set of laws, thus channeling their drives for destruction. They eat but lack a law of eating. In Hegel's modern society, the state has a set of laws that are built on the internalization of a metaphysics of eating, which results in the realization of transcendental philosophy by means of a sacrificial kind of politics. By compelling man to sacrifice his empirical well-being, the laws of the state—being indifferent to particular characteristics—also realize the absolute freedom of man from the material conditions of his empirical life. Thus, as in Kant, positive law supports rather than conflicts with transcendental philosophy as liberation from material existence.

Significantly, Hegel focused on war as the prime example of such realization of the transcendental by means of the political, for in times of war the state "puts its subjects into close contact with their master, death" *(in jener auferlegten Arbeit ihren Herrn, den Tod, zu fühlen zu geben).*[31] The state, which "normally protects the life of its members"—thus mirroring the nourishing aspect of eating—ultimately asks them to sacrifice their immediate well-being and thereby "realizes idealism in a curious manner."[32] By means of the sacrifice of "the otherwise lawfully existing particular members of the society," the idealism of the union between the generality of the state and the autonomy of the individual becomes a reality. This *"negative relation"* of the state to its members *(diese negative Beziehung des Staates)* as "absolute power poised against the singular, against the particular, against life and property and the right to the latter" *(als die absolute Macht gegen alles Einzelne und Besondere, gegen das Leben, Eigentum und dessen Rechte)* brings to the level "of being and of consciousness" *(zum Dasein und Bewußtsein bringt)* the "nothingness" of all these particles of immediate being.[33] In this way the metaphysics of eating results in a metaphysics of the state and its laws by means of which the latter curtails and, in the case of the law of war, annihilates the material existence of particularity. This is not to say that Hegel only tolerated eating as killing, for he clearly did not deny the necessity of nutrition as regards the existence of life as such. Hegel included the nourishing element of the "feminine" but as other to the spirit of the nonempirically defined generality that devours her grown-up children.

Thus, the feminine, as the nursing element, is included for the sake of raising life that eventually fulfills the sacrificial demands of the state. Note that, as in his anti-Jewish writings, Hegel discriminated against women on a pseudotheological basis. As Seyla Benhabib has argued, "although Hegel rejects that differences between 'men' and 'women' are naturally defined, and instead sees them as part of the spirit of the people *(Volksgeist)*, he leaves no doubt that he considers only one set of family relations and one particular division of labor between the sexes as rational and normatively right."[34] A construction of pseudotheological rather than pseudobiological immutability served to justify Hegel's writing about the "essence of women": "Most significant is the fact that those respects in which Hegel considers men and women to be spiritually different are precisely those aspects that define women as 'lesser' human beings."[35] Hegel thus implicitly constructed pseudotheological notions of immutability, while articulating his bias against both Jews and women. Whereas Jews, as representatives of rabbinic Judaism, were the excluded other of Hegel's dialectics, women were its included other. Being the other of dialectics, they played a vital role in a universalist modern state, for the self-understanding of the "modern" depends on an overview of world history. Here rabbinic Judaism, as in Kant's distinction between a heteronomously oriented society and one that functions on the principle of autonomy, symbolized an illusion of spirit on which the Hegelian notion of reality nevertheless depended. The complexity of this mutual dependence of exclusion and inclusion received a short but very illuminating treatment in the *Phenomenology,* where Hegel accused the Jewish people of being the most depraved *(das verworfenste)* for precisely the reason that they were closest to the doors of salvation. The verb *verworfen* emphasizes exclusion—the movement of being thrown out of some place in a rather violent manner—and at the same time it carries strong excoriating connotations. But how can a people who are closest to salvation be paradoxically the most reprobate?

Does this refer to the standard Christian narrative in which the Jews are cursed for the reason that they are closest to redemption and yet refuse to believe in Christ the redeemer? This does not make sense if one recalls that Hegel, even though his idea of modernity relied on Christian, or, to be more precise, Lutheran ideas, explicitly rejected any prioritization of the Christian faith, since this, as has been discussed above, would have been particularist. Indeed, his notion of spirit had little in common with the New Testament; rather, it grew out of a confrontation between transcendental philosophy and speculation.[36] So Hegel's moral language in the context of the Jewish people's closeness to salvation might be confused with this standard Christian paradigm in which the Jews have forfeited their place in the history of redemption *(Heilsgeschichte)* on account of their refusal to accept the particular figure of Christ as redeemer.[37] Hegel's ethics, however, were concerned with the state, with *Sittlichkeit*, and the legal and ethical aspect of modern politics took over the place that religion (including Christianity) had occupied in the past. This modern state is constructed along the lines of a somewhat Christian, secularized Kantian principle of freedom, and yet it cannot be called a "Christian political entity," for every religious definition would violate the demand of generality.[38]

Oddly enough, the word *verworfenste* has received little attention as a result of this focus on the notion of salvation. So far it has not been pointed out that Hegel used the word *verworfenste* for a religion that perceives the absolute within the finite.This was precisely his understanding of Judaism in his *Lectures on the Philosophy of Religion*. In these lectures he referred to the *Phenomenology* by employing the term *verworfenste* in his discussion of "the monstrous depression of spirit—namely despicability—to perceive the absolute in the most finite manner of existence, because the finitude of man is the most dry being for itself and insofar as it is only immediate, causes degradation, on account of its opposition to generality"[39] *(Es ist daher der ungeheuerste Kontrast und Depression des Geistes—eben Niederträchtigkeit—in der höchst endlichen Weise das Absolute zu schauen, denn Endlichkeit des Menschen das spröeste Fürsichsein, und insofern es nur unmittelbar ist, degradiert, in seinem Gegensatz gegen Allgemeines.)*[40] The religion that perceives the absolute in immediate being is the most reprobate and therefore the most rejected *(Dies ist unmittelbar die verworfenste der Religionen)*,[41] for it does not attempt to leave the mark of an autonomous, mediating human spirit on the external world but, rather, remains closed in itself *(Fürsichsein)*. This kind of religion appeared as people in the *Phenomenology*, where Hegel used the same terms *(das verworfenste [Volk])*. The Jewish people remain immutably caught in the immediacy of being *(innerhalb der Unmittelbarkeit des Seins stehengeblieben)*.[42] It is this, rather than their refusal to believe in Christ, that Hegel meant by using the metaphor of standing *immediately* in front of the door of salvation *(unmittelbar vor der Pforte des Heils stehe)*.[43] Yovel, who does not discuss Hegel's German original but only refers to A. V. Miller's English translation, neglects this crucial term, and we read only the following:

> "Just so, it may be said of the Jewish people that it is precisely because they stand before the portal of salvation that they are and have been the most reprobate and rejected: what that people should be in and for itself." The Jews reached the doors of salvation but refused to go through it; therefore they will be locked out of the gates of salvation forever, with no further evolution and no real hope. In other words, *they will no longer have a history.* As the most reprobate *(verworfene [sic])* people, all that remains of the Jews is an ongoing fossilized existence.[44]

Rather than quoting the whole sentence, Yovel cuts it short and presents his argument about Hegel's supposed traditional Christocentric view of the Jews. Hegel, however, focused on human autonomy, as the remainder of the sentence makes clear: "what that people should be in and for itself, this essential nature of its own self, is not explicitly present to it: on the contrary it places it beyond itself."[45] Instead of arguing that the Jewish people's identity consists in their refusal to believe in Christ, when others do so, Hegel denied that they have any "autonomous character" *(Selbstwesenheit)*.

The Jewish people of the *Phänomenologie* are heteronomous to the extent that they are completely at one with their environment and refrain from imposing their will on the external world. They are, Hegel argued, completely selfless to the point of being—by way of dialectics—completely selfish, and in this context he introduced the theme of dispossession, their *Entäußerung*, as the opposite of a metaphysics of eating. The term *Entäußerung* belongs to the ideational context that is opposed to that described by his eating metaphors, for it denotes a doing away with one's autonomy as regards the external world. As is more fully discussed below, Hegel differentiated *Eigentum*, the appropriation of some external object according to the self-determination of the human mind, from *Besitz*, the mere taking possession of something that goes without any self-willed transformation of the thing one is holding in hand. Significantly, he developed this distinction in his discussion of rabbinic Judaism. According to Hegel, the Jews are heteronomously bound to the empirical world *as a result of* an immutable attachment to their God, who truly possesses the earth. Further, and more important, God asks his people to divest themselves of any transformative relation to his creation, upon which they are allowed to live only as tenants, not as landlords.[46] By having the Jewish people relinquish their autonomy as regards their dealings with the external world, Hegel excluded them from his metaphysics of eating.

As a consequence of their religious imagination, Hegel's Jews value all life as spiritual and therefore refrain from eating blood (blood here denotes a substance that supports most forms of empirical existence). In his *Lectures on the Philosophy of Religion* he elaborated on this point. There he emphasized the role of "blood that must not be devoured for the reason that, according to the Jewish imagination, it incorporates the life of animals." He went on to stress that, therefore, "man must not devour and destroy the soul (of life) but has to respect it" *(Das Blut spielt vornehmlich eine Rolle, da es als das gilt, was nicht von Menschen verzehrt werden soll, indem darin nach der jüdischen Vorstellung das Leben des Tieres ist; also die Seele soll der Mensch nicht verzehren, vernichten, sie soll respektiert werden).*[47] It is precisely on account of this respect for existence as God's creation that Hegel focused on Jewish dietary laws, especially on the prohibition against the eating of blood, which, in his view, is the embodiment of absolutizing immediate being. Hegel might not be wrong in his analysis of Jewish dietary laws. Leon Kass has recently argued that "avoiding the blood of life does indeed show some respect for the life that one is nevertheless violating."[48] Thus, Jewish dietary law helps enact a creaturely theology in everyday life: "In all these ways the dietary laws build into daily life constant concrete and incarnate reminders of the created order and its principles and of the dangers that life—and especially man—pose to its preservation. In these restrictions on deformation and destruction, there is celebration of creation—and of its mysterious source."[49] Interpreting Jewish dietary law as helping set limits to the violence that life inflicts on itself, Hegel stigmatized Judaism as the opposite of his dialectics, which speculatively attempts to pinpoint the coincidence between being and nonbeing. Thus, by embodying life as God's creation, Jewish dietary law, in Hegel's view, absolutizes immediate being, whereas an idealist worldview sees in mere existence only the material by means of which human subjectivity shapes its autonomy. In a paradoxical manner, the very spirituality of the Jews causes an absence of Hegelian "spirit." At the end of the *Philosophy of Right* Hegel explicitly excluded Israel from his dialectics. Here German culture emerges in radical opposition to the Judaic: whereas Israel is separated from subjectivity as well as the world and its negativity *(Aus diesem Verluste seiner selbst und seiner Welt und dem unendlichen Schmerz derselben)*, the German peoples perceive in the suffering within finite reality the realization of infinitude *(erfaßt der in sich zurückgedrängte Geist in dem Extrem seiner absoluten Negativität, dem an und für sich seienden Wendepunkt, die unendliche Positivität dieses seines Inneren, das Prinzip der Einheit der göttlichen und der menschlichen Natur).*[50] By not eating life (blood) the Jews, in Hegel's view, do not exert violence and as a result do not become its victims. Thus the Jewish people were excluded from his supposedly all-embracing dialectics.

They were included, however, in his understanding of modernity. It is precisely for the reason that Hegelian idealism positioned itself as the opposite of a Jewish way of life that the Judaic played a special role in his historical narrative. This is because every particular culture—be it Roman, Greek, Christian, or Jewish—participates in the formation of Hegel's nonparticular modern state, whose constitution depends on indifference to difference. How this came about is discussed below. Here it is important to emphasize that such exclusion sheds light on the ideological presupposition of his logical inquiries, which he himself defined as metaphysical. According to Hegel, logic is the supernatural *(daß das Logische vielmehr das Übernatürliche ist).*[51] It is the natural that transcends itself in death. The Jews, on the other hand, figure as those who are natural insofar as they do not want to change empirical life: they do not eat the blood of life. Interestingly, Judaism appears as a way of life in which the world is defined as holy. As a consequence, Hegel's dialectics builds on a radical split between immanence and transcendence that he tries to overcome by means of a dialectical movement from negativity (life and its death) to the affirmation of the state as a secularized version of Christ's transcendence in the Resurrection. This divide is bridged in and through sacrifice, and it is from this secularized Christian position that he developed his idealist political theory. If Hegel derived from Judaism the ideational opposite of his modern state, what status have other cultures in his philosophy? In what sense has a rabbinic Jewish culture a singular place not only as a relic—like every other culture—but as an ideational figure of what the modern must not be, if it has truly idealist pretensions?

Beauty and Sublimity

> *But a Jewish butcher's knife cannot stab; only a practitioner of the more "modern" and "humane" form of butchery, the pig butcher of Kafka's nightmares, can stab the victim in the heart.*
> — SANDER L. GILMAN, *FRANZ KAFKA*

Above, I focused on how the ideological presuppositions of Hegel's dialectics informed the metaphors by means of which he attempted to illustrate the empirical relevance of his idealism. Here I treat the specific role of rabbinic Judaism within Hegel's social and aesthetic thought as regards his philosophy of history, in which he theorized certain particular cultures that either conflict with or form the basis of an idealist notion of modernity.

There are three stages in this historical account: (1) the "immediate religion" *(unmittelbare Religion)* of "oriental" and "primitive" peoples, (2) the religion of "beauty and sublimity" *(Religion der Schönheit und Erhabenheit)*—the first being Greek, the second being Judaic, and (3) the "religion of expediency" *(Religion der Zweckmäßigkeit)*. The third stage, the Roman, figures as the Hegelian precondition of Christianity.

The movement from the first to the third stage goes in tandem with an ascension from nature to spirit and from there to the absolute religion (Christianity), in which spirit and nature coincide. This penultimate position, which leads to the end of religion as fulfilled in the absolute knowledge of modernity, as Hegel understood it, has a curious similarity to the first, for it is in the first that a unity between spirit and nature becomes established. At first glance, this closeness between the religion of nature and Christianity might deceive the reader. Hegel, however, maintained that the natural religion lacks freedom *(insofern ist sie [die bestimmte Religion] die Religion der Unfreiheit)*[52] insofar as the consciousness shaped by it imagines itself to be at one with nature. On the other hand, Hegel understood a free society—the conditions for which are laid down in Greek, Roman, and Christian culture—to function according to the transformation of the natural by an autonomous human spirit. The natural or immediate religion, on the contrary, does not have a notion of spirit (as Hegel makes clear in his discussion of the Eskimos).[53] In Hegel's evolutionary scheme unhappiness and suffering seem to be absent from the first stage, where, as he argues in his account of Persian culture, "the good in its generality has a natural form" *(das Gute in seiner Allgemeinheit eine natürliche Gestalt hat).*[54]

Hegel first introduced the notion of suffering in his version of Judaism, although he established a similarity between the immediate religion of Persia and the Judaic. However, the Persians imagine God to dwell in the whole of nature, whereas the individual of Hegel's Jewish culture attempts to please a divinity who, as one God, possesses the earth but is infinitely removed from it and demands submission to his commandments of those who wish to find happiness within the empirical world over which he rules. Thus the movement from immediate religion to the religion of sublimity entails a shift from generality to individuality: in the former divinity and nature are at one, whereas in the latter monotheism introduces the notion of subjectivity, of a God who is not nature but who possesses and dominates it. In the natural religion of the "primitive" and the "Oriental" everything has autonomy, because there exist as many divinities as there are natural beings. In Hegel's ideational fiction about Judaism, on the other hand, nature itself depends on its creator and therefore (1) must not be interfered with and (2) consequently lacks any right of self-determination. Now the only autonomy resides in God alone: "The only determination of things is then simply that they are creatures, that they have entered the categories of the outward, the non-autonomous, or, the nature of natural things here turns prosaic; it has become despiritualized and they are the non-autonomous in themselves. All autonomy is concentrated in the One."[55] Although nature learns to face spirit in Judaism, the Judaic God nevertheless enforces immediacy, so that Hegel, as we have seen, calls the religion of sublimity the most reprobate and rejected one for the reason that it sees the absolute in the immediate. In this way Judaism actually reinforces the making absolute of being implicit in natural religion by having introduced the notion of an abstract spirit who, by virtue of his omnipotence, promises immediate fulfillment to those who are most dependent on him, that is to say, who are most obedient to his rule and that, crucially, with a view to achieving happiness in empirical life. Thus natural religion pictures nature in its various forms as essentially good and divine. Judaism, in Hegel's view, however, centers on the individual, who does well within nature under the condition that he follow God's laws, which proscribe any willful interference with immediate being. In this way Hegel accused Jewish law of precluding human autonomy.

At this point, Hegel's differentiation between *Eigentum* and *Besitz* helps explain the triangular relation between God, man, and nature in this narrative of Judaism. *Eigentum* presupposes that the owner has autonomy as regards his possessions; *Besitz,* on the other hand, means the nonautonomous holding of objects turned over by God to man. Those who attempt to depict

Hegel as a "critic of all property forms" have to acknowledge that "his central notion of a free and equal political relationship is inexplicable without concepts of property."[56] A discussion of the historical context in which it is placed helps explain this aspect of his social theory, for these concepts of property have no independent location within a political philosophy but are part of an ideational framework in which Judaism represents the empirical, as opposed to the Greek, Roman, and Christian, whose principle resides, according to Hegel, in the transformation of immediate being.

The autonomous transformation of empirical objects and the consequent consciousness of one's own participation in this material existence (which finally issues in the internalization of a politics of sacrifice, in which man, having realized his own empirical limit, transcends it by willingly risking his life for a greater general good) adequately describe Hegel's notion of freedom, as he himself makes clear in his differentiation between *Eigentum* and *Besitz:*

> The source of *Eigentum* is personality, that is, the freedom of the singular individual and man is *Eigentümer* insofar as he is a person, but *Besitz* as such, this empirical side of property, is completely free, and exposed to chance happenings . . . ; this empirical, singular possession is willed by God and it is this possession which is valid as such. Thus arbitrariness is infinite, constructed as the divine. (Das Eigentum hat die Persönlichkeit, diese Freiheit des einzelnen Individuums zu seiner Quelle, und der Mensch ist wesentlich Eigentümer, insofern er Person ist; aber der Besitz als solcher, diese empirische Seite des Besitzes ist ganz frei, dem Zufall preisgegeben . . . ; dieser empirische einzlene Besitz ist von Gott gewollt, und dieser Besitz ist es, der als solcher gelten soll. Die Willkür ist unendlich, zum Göttlichen gemacht.)[57]

Here there are two opposed notions of freedom: that of the autonomous human mind and that of the arbitrary reign of chance, which drives the free movement of immediate being. In the first case the human mind determines life and in the second the objects of empirical life heteronomously determine the mind of the individual. Hegel in fact took up Kant's charge of heteronomy and a "slave-like mindset" *(Sklavensinn)*[58] with which he targeted rabbinic Judaism (see chapter 1).

In his radicalization of Kant's position Hegel linked social and aesthetic theory by connecting the notion of freedom with that of beauty. By theologizing immediate being, the Jews, in this idealist fantasy, become enslaved to the empirical world. They fear God as the power that either destroys their particular and material interests or who furthers them if they obey his rules. Hegel imagined "the God of the Jews" in terms of material power: the fear of God comes down to the fear for material possessions. Israel's God either destroys empirical life or he sustains it on the condition that his laws are followed. Thus, Hegel praised the Jewish religious sensibility only to place it on a materialist plane. Just as he depicted Israel's fear of God as ultimately a concern for material possessions, he maintained, having earlier called the "faith" of the Jews "admirable" *(Diese Zuversicht ist das Bewunderungswürdige),*[59] that this trust in God ultimately turns out to be hope attached to the happiness that can be found in empirical life. If these hopes are met, faith increases. This, however, only constitutes the first step, for the happiness found in empirical life has only a temporal value: "the intuition of absolute power changes into absolute trust. This trust is only a beginning, but it causes temporal happiness" *(die Anschauung der absoluten Macht überschlägt in die absolute Zuversicht. Diese Zuversicht ist das erste, hat aber die Folge des zeitlichen Glücks).*[60] Being temporal, this kind of happiness is both short-lived and, seen from the speculative perspective of Hegelian dialectics, illusory, for the temporal trajectory of finitude is suffering as such *(der Schmerz ist überhaupt der Verlauf der Endlichkeit).*[61]

Hegel's Greeks, on the other hand, are free, beautiful, and happy. By contrast, the Jewish God prevents freedom, beauty, and happiness in that he declares nature to be his true possession, which must not be transformed or shaped according to the will of human self-consciousness. Hegel, as Yovel has pointed out, "does not say that the Jewish religion is sublime; he says only that it is the religion *of* sublimity: namely it pictures God as sublime and man as his opposite."[62] This opposition engenders fear and unhappiness insofar as the religion of sublimity means fear for both material possessions and one's survival. Greek culture—one of the cultures that help shape modernity as idealism—remains free of fear and its consequences. To which constructions did Hegel refer in order to substantiate his binary opposition between the Jewish and the Greek? First of all, "the Greek principle resides in the subjective freedom of the spirit" *(das griechische Prinzip ist vielmehr die subjektive Freiheit des Geistigen).*[63] The religion of sublimity "lacks precisely this moment of freedom within subjectivity" *(Moment der Freiheit der Subjekte, welches dem betrachteten der Religion der Erhabenheit fehlt).*[64] Whereas in Hegel's understanding of Judaism, God, as master, enslaves both man and nature as nonautonomous entities, in ancient Greece nature itself has autonomy. The latter point violates the Hegelian ideal of the complete submission of the natural to the autonomous human mind (this becomes changed in Roman antiquity). However, in Greek antiquity the very autonomy of nature with respect to any creaturely account gives rise to the autonomous human mind, which finds true happiness in constructing beauty out of immediate being and thus proves its independence from both God and the unmediated natural: "Spiritual subjectivity only exists as triumph over nature, as a self-created product, as overpowering nature" *(Die geistige Subjektivität ist nur als Triumph über das Natürliche, als Resultat, das sich hervorgebracht hat, als überwältigend das Natürliche).*[65] The spiritual subjectivity of the Greeks makes nature beautiful by mastering, deforming, and even destroying it (as illustrated in the act of eating). The subjective spirit of the Jews, by contrast, respects immediate being as God's true possession *(Eigentum)* and hence perceives the absolute in the natural rather than following the mediated path of autonomous construction that leads to beauty, freedom, and true happiness.

Following the commands of their God, the Jews, in Hegel's view, try to find fulfillment in the material world. This longing for happiness in immediate being causes suffering, and Hegel interpreted this agony as the logical consequence of trusting the divine in temporal terms rather than speculative ones. In sum, it is the outcome of self-deception, which results from imagining the wrong kind of divinity. Insofar as, according to Hegel, the Jewish God forbids any human autonomous activity to be exerted on the external world, he condemns his people to an exile from reality. Thus, they are confined to a nondialectal and therefore unhappy, illusory existence. A life without impact is unreal, for Hegel defined reality not as that which appears to us in present sensuous forms at specific moments of time. Rather, his notion of *Wirklichkeit* (reality) derives from *wirken* (having an impact), that is to say, it describes forms of change, forces that influence objects throughout time, throughout a process.[66]

Thus, those who construct beauty enact Hegelian dialectics: the transformation of plain natural objects presupposes knowledge of the ultimate coincidence between being and nonbeing. Hegel's notion of beauty describes the construction of outward, heteronomous being by the free, autonomous human mind. In this way man shapes nature according to his inward image of the beautiful, and in doing so he gains both freedom and happiness:

> This, however, we call the beautiful, where the outward is filled with character, with meaning, where it is determined by free-reigning inwardness. The outward is a natural material so that its shapes are only witnesses for the spirit that is in itself free. The outward moment has to be overcome completely, so that it only serves as expression, as a revelation of the spirit. (Dieses aber nennen wir eben das Schöne, wo alle Äußerlichkeit durchaus charakteristisch, bedeutsam ist, vom Inneren als Freien bestimmt. Es ist ein natürliches Material, so daß die Züge darin nur Zeugen sind eines in sich freien Geistes. Das natürliche Moment muß überhaupt so überwunden sein, daß es zur Äußerung, Offenbarung des Geistes diene.)[67]

If the beautiful utterly transforms immediate being and thereby proves its autonomy and gains its sense of happiness, then the sublime causes suffering owing to its lack of such dialectical movements, which are pertinent to Hegel's notion of reality: "The other form is the religion of sublimity, that namely the sensuous, finite, spiritual, as well as psychic natural is not going to be absorbed and transfigured through a free subjectivity." (Die andere Form ist die Religion der Erhabenheit, daß nämlich das Sinnliche, Endliche, geistig und psychisch Natürliche nicht aufgenommen, verklärt ist in der freien Subjektivität.)[68]

In sociohistorical terms, this transformation of immediate being into constructions established by the free and autonomous human mind had a wider impact on society in general at the end of the nineteenth century. Sander L. Gilman traces the origins of cosmetic surgery, for instance, to Kant's notion of human autonomy as follows: "Kant divided 'nature' into 'physiology,' i.e., the way that 'nature made man,' and 'anthropology,' i.e., 'what man made of himself.' The latter became the space were aesthetic surgery could be imagined."[69] In this chapter I have shown how Hegel's radicalization of Kant's concept-oriented philosophy of human autonomy issued in an aesthetic as well as in a social theory whose various revisions at the end of the nineteenth century could then influence political and pseudoscientific theories.

As an outward expression of an autonomous mind, however, the beautiful only represents a step on the road toward modernity. The beauty of Greece "makes the natural appear to be autonomous" (auch das Natürliche erscheint als sebstständig).[70] So Hegel imagined a kind of suffering different from that which he found in Judaism, a kind of suffering that imperial Rome willfully exerted on its subjects. Crucially, however, both Roman and Greek antiquity are characterized by autonomy, that is, by the mastering of immediate being. This may be the transformation of the natural toward the image of beauty as constructed by the free human mind (Greece), or it may consist in the overpowering of empirical life by violent forces that self-consciously inflict pain (Rome).

What makes for this priority of pain over beauty in Hegel's ideational fiction about the precondition of the "modern"? He was ultimately interested in a social theory that justifies the suffering of individuals for a "greater good" (the state, or the world spirit that triumphs in the election of one state that commands more influence than its competitors). This ultimately results in a secularized version of a Protestant Christianity that also informed Kant's transcendental philosophy. Hegel saw Rome—and not, as has been argued, Israel—as the foundation of Christianity and that precisely for the reason that the Roman enjoys inflicting pain on immediate being. The Roman religion of expediency figures as the true transition to the absolute religion that, in its secularized and nonparticular form, provides the basis of absolute knowledge, which informs the workings of modernity.

Hegel used the same word, Schmerz, for the suffering in the Roman and the Judaic worlds. In the former, pain is an outcome of self-consciously exerted imperial power, whereas in the latter man becomes unhappy because he cannot find the satisfaction in the material world that he seeks (as a result of following God's heteronomous laws). Thus in Hegel's account there are radically different approaches to immediate being in the two cultures: Israel values life as God's possession and tries to recover happiness within the natural (as promised by its creaturely theology), which cannot be found there, since empirical existence is only temporal, whereas Rome willfully devalues the natural and enjoys its suffering. Thus in Rome suffering and happiness coincide, for the pain inflicted on empirical life causes enjoyment: the killing in the gladiatorial games "serves as a feast for the eyes of the observers" *(Das kalte Morden diente ihnen zur Augenweide)*.[71] By contrast, in Hegel's representation of Greek and Judaic antiquity, suffering and happiness remain two separate entities. However, only Christianity gives meaning to the suffering of the "general unhappiness of the world" *(allgemeine Unglück der Welt)*[72] and thereby fully reconciles it to a notion of happiness.

In this way Christian theology, which proclaims the self-conscious sacrifice of an individual for the ultimate redemption of humanity, turns into the spirit of the state, according to which happiness resides in the sacrifice of the particular for the sake of the general. Hegel's account of Judaism as a way of life that immutably follows a God who promises happiness in the illusion of immediate being stands in direct opposition to his notion of a collective self-consciousness wherein happiness and suffering dialectically concur. Hegel's devaluation of the differences between all particular cultures, religions, and peoples might diminish the prejudicial force of his fiction about rabbinic Judaism, but his attempt to translate the religious into the language of secular social theory made his anti-Judaism open to political and pseudoscientific revisions. Hegel's concern with religion rather than with pseudobiology does not lessen the adverse effect of his depiction of Jewishness, for, as has been shown in this chapter, as with Kant so with Hegel: it is the Jewish God that spuriously serves to prove the immutability of the Jews. In chapter 3 we will see how such a religious and cultural notion of immutability informed Richard Wagner's anti-Semitic imagination.

TRANSFORMING THE BODY INTO THE
BODY POLITIC: WAGNER AND THE
TRAJECTORY OF GERMAN IDEALISM

*The ideas of philosophy, in other words—its mind—do not only constitute
a history; they appear always within* history, subject to the same
constraints that any form of action or making is subject to and mirroring
those constrains in the ideas themselves.
—BEREL LANG, *ANATOMY OF PHILOSOPHICAL STYLE*

Schopenhauer's and, to a lesser extent, Hegel's attempt to correlate the beautiful with the rational paved the way for Wagner's fusion of art, politics, and
religion. This chapter discusses how Wagner defined his political and aesthetic ideals in terms of the Kantian notion of freedom as the subject's independence from empirical conditions. The first part examines his theoretical
writings about art, religion, and politics, and the second discusses how Wagner literally put onstage a Kantian autonomy-heteronomy divide in the *Ring
des Nibelungen*. Symbolizing heteronomy, that is, value that helps one gain
possession of use-values, the Ring functions as a character-defining device, in
relation to which the protagonists of this music-drama cycle establish their
respective personalities. Accordingly, the Ring denotes the heteronomous
qua an orientation to the enjoyment and power yielded by material objects,
whereas Kant's ideal of autonomy consisted in freedom from any external determinations. What is missing so far—an examination of Wagner's revision
of key concepts developed by Kant, Hegel, Feuerbach, and Schopenhauer[1]—
would contribute to an understanding of how simplified and rather eclectic
versions of Kantian moral philosophy entered German "national culture" via
Wagner's dramatic and theoretical writings.[2]

The next question, then, is why did Kant, as well as Hegel, Feuerbach,
Schopenhauer, and Wagner, focus on the Jews as the empirical impediment to
the construction of an idealist type of body politic? In the historical context of
Germany in the eighteenth and nineteenth centuries, the Jew represented the
Oriental who lives in the West but does not essentially belong there. As "Orientals" they were seen to embody fundamental difference. This otherness
accentuated the perceived lack of continuity between the Christian and
the Judaic. The image of an immutable tie between the Jewish God and his

people quasi-allegorically defined the Oriental origins of the Jews. Incapable of separating himself from Jehovah, the Jew could not but represent "the Oriental in our midst." Seen in this light, as the uncanny within the homely, the Jews are easy targets for the internal contradictions of a secularized and politicized version of Christian moral thought. That is to say, they bear the brand of the tension between the ideal (autonomy in Kant's case, dialectics in Hegel's, the total work of art in Wagner's) and the real (heteronomy, the non-dialectical, social-political life that has not become part of "total art").

Wagner's almost obsessive contrast between idealism and realism, as well as the concomitant move by which he blamed the Jews for precluding a realization of the ideal, partly developed out of his intense studies of German transcendental philosophy. Radicalizing Schopenhauer's revision of Kant's rational theology, Wagner tried to reconcile art with the essence of Christianity. Thus Wagner's aesthetic sensibility involved an attempt to replace the transcendental conception of the rational. Ultimately, both concepts attempted to transform the essence of Christianity into a contemporary intellectual matrix: they focused on the transformation of the individual and contingent body into an autonomous and all-embracing entity. To this extent, they shared a concern with the transformation of the body into the body politic. However, this does not alter the fact that Wagner also reinvested a German transcendental paradigm with an aestheticism that claimed to make out of contingent materiality a spiritual unity akin to the attempts of Kant and some of his followers to see reason as the touchstone of a civil society that is defined by secularized Christian-Lutheran values.

Religion, Art, and Politics in Wagner's Theoretical Texts

> *In beiden [Hegel and Wagner] wird der mythische Ursprung des deutschen Idealismus offenbar: in Hegel's Geschichts-Mythologie nicht anders als in Wagners Mythenopern, deren Mythologie gerade an ihrer vollendeten Scheinhaftigkeit als echt sich bewährt. (Both [Hegel and Wagner] reveal the mythical origin of German idealism: Hegel's mythology of history does this no differently than Wagner's mythological operas, whose mythology proves itself as authentic precisely in its illusionary quality.)*
>
> —T. W. ADORNO, "MUSIKALISCHE APHORISMEN"

As German Enlightenment philosophy attempted to reconcile reason with religion, so, too, Wagner set out to make art compatible with a rationality that has its grounds in a secularized understanding of Christianity. In his essay "Concerning State and Religion" (1864) he let the artist proclaim Christ's "my realm is not of this world."[3] Wagner went on to ask how this transcendence of empirical life can be realized, taking into account that this "extra-worldly realm stands within this world."[4] Crucially, he argued for a combination of aestheticism and politics in order to create a body politic in which the body can truly be transcended—in Schopenhauer's terms, overcome and destroyed.

Wagner employed a Hegelian argument in his description of such a transformation of the body into the body politic while abandoning a philosophy of the state. For the state does not overcome egoism but rather reinforces the individual's egoistic desire for survival. On account of this worldly element, "religion is in its essence completely different from the state."[5] Nevertheless, religion can only turn the worldly into the otherworldly by means of an alliance with the state. It is precisely here that Wagner then referred to Hegel, proclaiming that "the highest and purest religion only appeared in the world [*in die Welt getreten*] exactly at the point at which it completely separated itself form the state and sublated the latter into itself [*und in sich diesen vollständig aufhob*]."[6] Wagner thus drew on Hegel's *aufheben* to characterize the dialectical relation between religion and the state in which the former abolishes and, at the same time, incorporates the existence of the latter. Wagner conceptualized religion as a means for overcoming an egoistic will to power. Religion thus seems to occupy the place that Kant and Hegel reserved for reason. In Wagner's theoretical writings, we encounter an obsession with Jewishness as the embodiment of egoism. Making use of Feuerbach's pseudo-theology, he attributed the immutability of race to the Jewish God, who turns out to be the principle of power. As the discussion of the infamous essay "Judaism in Music" will make clear, Wagner conflated political power with the immutable "essence of Judaism."[7] He proceeded to contrast his construction of a Jewish politics of power with Christianity's politics of religion.

Accordingly, by negating the world *(Verneinung der Welt)*,[8] religion abolishes the egoistic desire for both comfort and survival that propels individuals to live together in statehood. How can religion destroy the egoism implicit in the old state and, at the same time, found a new one that negates the will for earthly power? Addressing this question, Wagner theorized art in terms of the mediation between the body and a redemptive kind of body politic. He did so by evaluating the religious-political role of "delusion" *(Wahn)*. One example of such delusion is patriotism, for the patriotic citizen abandons self-interest in the delusory belief that his selfhood and that of the state are identical. He is thus "overpowered by the delusion that lets the danger to the state appear to be infinitely intensified personal danger for whose aversion he sacrifices himself with a zeal that is equal to the intensity of his identification" *(ein Wahn sich bemächtigt, welcher die Gefahr des Staates ihm als unendlich gesteigerte persönliche Gefahr erscheinen läßt, für deren Abwendung er sich dann mit ebneso gesteigertem Eifer aufopfert)*.[9] This identification of the individual with the cause of the state radicalizes the Hegelian idea of totality, in which the particular loses itself in the general.[10]

Hegel made the individual's consciousness of his own empirical and particular and, therefore, illusory existence a precondition for such a political sacrifice.

He referred to a metaphysics of eating in order to drive this point home (see chapter 2). By means of his eating metaphors, he attempted to illustrate that by eating the blood (that is, the life) of dead bodies, the one who eats recognizes her own empirical constitution. Thereby she is predisposed to be eaten, to be consumed by a greater, more general force than herself: the state. It is no coincidence that Wagner employed Hegel's famous term *aufheben* in a discussion about the relation between religion and the state. Wagner indeed radicalized the Hegelian position. Hegel acknowledged the egoistic reasons for which individuals come together and found states. But he did not explicitly condemn these motivations. Rather, he only emphasized the idealism that lies behind such social foundations. This comes to the fore in the extreme case of war, a time at which the rulers of a political entity are able to teach their subjects "their master—death" *(ihren Herrn, den Tod)*.[11]

Wagner criticized the "normal" case scenario in which the members of a given state go about their business. Because of their optimistic trust in earthly activities they evidence "egoism" and thereby the absence of "Christian essence." With respect to this Schopenhauer kept repeating that it consists in the pessimism fulfilled only in the overcoming and the eventual destruction of the world. The monarchical state, which has been conflated with the essence of Christianity, in fact politicizes this Schopenhauerian pessimism, which remains no longer pessimistic insofar as Wagner believed in the attainment of autonomy, gained by such enthusiastic acceptance of suffering for the sake of a general entity. The member of this religious state makes himself or herself "independent from the world" *(von dieser Welt unabhängig zu machen)* by virtue of his or her "voluntary renunciation and suffering" *(freiwilliges Entsagen und Leiden)*.[12] Thanks to a redemptive kind of body politic, the body can transcend itself even though it remains in this world.

According to Wagner, Kant's autonomy (independence from the world) can be realized by exercising a strong feeling of patriotism. In this way, a member of the *Volk* does away with all concerns about his or her own welfare and offers his or her life as a sacrifice for the "non-egoistic" good of a redemptive body politic. Patriotism turns the potentially egoistic structure of statehood—if understood as a community of people who work together only to mutually further their own interests—into a body politic that helps realize the Kantian autonomy from all inclinations to the goods of this world. This theory of patriotism and independence from the worldly has an important bearing on the development of Wagner's anti-Semitism. For, in keeping with the transcendental matrix discussed above, here "Jewishness" denotes Kantian heteronomy—the dependence of the self on objects in the empirical world. By the middle of the nineteenth century, the economic exchange system of capitalism stood as a trope for enslavement to the material world (even though Kant, as discussed in chapter 1, exemplified autonomy in the acceptance of a Mine-and-Yours ownership and property distinction).

Wagner radicalized Kant's notion of autonomy in a political manner, for it now described independence from any form of exchange and contract. The autonomous member of the *Volk* gives her life without any form of contractual agreement and without any wish for any kind of return in exchange for her sacrifice. Consequently, Wagner did not reject the state *in toto;* he only condemned the forms of exchange that precondition an inorganic modern state. As Zizek has pointed out, in a path-breaking paper, "antisemitism does not stand for antimodernism as such, but for an attempt at combining modernity with social corporatism, which is characteristic of conservative revolutionaries." Accordingly, the "opposition of German true spirit versus the 'Jewish' principle is not the original one: there is a third term, modernity, the reign of exchange, of the dissolution of organic links, of modern industry and individuality."[13]

What has so far not been discussed in the critical literature is that Wagner's anti-Semitism is closely related to his revision of a transcendental paradigm. If reason was the medium through which humanity could attain "freedom" in terms of autonomy from empirical reality in the eighteenth century, then by the middle of the nineteenth century it was art that promised to link the individual to the organic unity of the *Volk*. Art thereby enabled a patriotism that made the individual independent of the fear for the goods of this world. This paradigm shift from reason to art, as media of redemption, goes hand in hand with the change in anti-Semitic stereotyping. When reason represented the "modern," the Jews were stigmatized as the nonmoderns, the "primitives." Judaism was labeled "superstitious" and "irrational."[14]

With the advance of industrial society, the focus started to shift, and the Jews were blamed for the injustices that were perceived to accompany modernization.[15] Within this context Wagner blamed the Jews for the "egoism" of modern bourgeois society and defined the capitalist exchange system as Kantian heteronomy. By rejecting the materialism of modern society, Wagner, as Zizek has pointed out, did not abandon modernity as such. More specifically, he did not reject the "modern" transcendental paradigm as introduced by Kant's philosophical revolution. He only shifted the focus from the medium of reason to that of art. Thanks to the public impact of art, a redemptive body politic can found the otherworldly within the world. The Jews are still phantasmic representatives of the worldly. The way out of this world, however, is no longer seen to reside in the rational capability of abstraction but in artistic sensibilities that appeal to the emotions and direct the individual to autonomy. Autonomy is understood, here, in terms of independence from any inclinations to the empirical world, independence that is finally realized in patriotic self-sacrifice.

Does art not generate a delusory state of being and in doing so create spurious identifications, in which the concerns of the particular (the individual) and the general (the state) coincide? It is this kind of rhetorical question that Wagner posed throughout the corpus of his theoretical writings. Art replaces the contemporary world of exchange and egoism with the conscious delusion of idealism. Wagner spoke of artistic achievement *(Dieses leistet die Kunst)*[16] in the context of this medial work, which helps transform the body into the body politic. "The conscious delusion" *(den bewußten Wahn)*[17] created by the work of art helps do away with the contemporary reality *(Realität)* and thus works for an idealist future.

Wagner wanted to lay the ground for "the realization of the ideal"[18] that is accomplished only in the transformation of the body into the body politic (and thereby the body's self-negation). In order to speak to a mass of bodies art must become popular—it must be *Volk*-centered. Here Wagner saw in Schiller's theater "the attempt at its [theater's] elevation to a popular-idealist art" *(Versuchs seiner Erhebung zu einer popular-idealen Kunst).*[19] This popularization of idealism turns the people into protagonists of an idealist narrative and thus does not abandon Kantian autonomy but, on the contrary, widens its sphere of influence thanks to the appeal of art (theater). Indeed, the notions of art, autonomy, and the German people formed a unity in Wagner's thought. *German* became the synonym for idealism, for the word *German* "means to do what one does for its own sake" *(Deutsch sei, nämlich: die Sache die man treibt um ihrer selbst willen treiben),* whereas the principle of worldly gain, that is, the "essence of utility" *(Nützlichkeitswesen),* describes anything that is opposed to the sphere of idealist power.[20]

In contrast to Schopenhauer, Wagner believed in the possible investment of idealism with real power, a hope akin to Hegel's attempt to bridge the gap between the spiritual and the empirical. In this context, he discussed art as the medium that could help close the divide between the state and religion. Art could mobilize the people for a patriotic loss of individuality, which, as a result of this loss, partakes of statehood. Yet, this transformation cannot be enacted without the support of a political system that sets out to incorporate the state into a religious apparatus of suffering. This politico-religious structure works for one's complete independence from worldly concerns. This, in turn, is precisely why Wagner asked for the help of political rulers and, even in his revolutionary period,[21] argued for a corporatist monarchy. That is to say, he celebrated an ideal monarch who decrees the sociopolitical measures by which the heteronomy of particular bodies is changed into the autonomy of the general body politic. The monarch represents the autonomous body and as such gives body to the Wagnerian body politic.

Here Wagner conflated the two bodies of the king—one the king's physical body, the other his metaphysical body (traditionally representing Christ and here representing the principle of auonomy)[22]—and makes out of the body politic a union of Christ's and society's lifeblood. As representative of autonomy and politics, as the realization of the otherworldly within this world, the monarch enacts the "negative freedom" *(negative Freiheit)*[23] from heteronomy (as described by the Kantian notion of autonomy), for he "is already and totally" *(vornherein für je und alle Fälle)* "unbound by the law of utility that binds the whole of the state" *(den ganzen Staat bindenden Zweckmäßigkeitsgesetzes entbunden)*.[24] Untouched by the principle of heteronomy that is implicit in the question regarding the use of empirical objects for the welfare of the self, the king is completely autonomous and thus "completely liberated" *(vollständig befreit)*.[25]

There is, however, a more realistic dimension to Wagner's glorification of the monarch as the embodiment of the autonomous body politic. The king can potentially provide the element of real power that could erect such an autonomous political system, in which art would popularize idealism, or rather, would confirm the idealism that is already inherent in the *Volk*. Wagner in fact argued that the German prince should become like the German artist. He should dwell close to the pulse of the German people and their alleged idealism, because he yields the crucial ingredient of power that is lacking in both the idealism of art and that of the *Volk*. German politics founds "an order of world-redemption" *(Ordnung in diesem erhabenen, welterlösenden Sinne)* on the precondition that Germany's princes acquire as much German, that is, idealist-Christian, essence as its artists have in the past *(Deutschland's Fürsten mußten ebenso deutsch sein, als seine Meister es waren)*.[26]

Following Feuerbach, Wagner accused the Jews of holding this power for selfish and therefore heteronomous ends. Wagner claimed that by contrast, in the hands of the German people and their artists, power would be self-consuming. It would transform any member of the *Volk* into the body politic, which is autonomous to the point that it operates for its own sake, instead of being bound to the practical concerns of utility. In Wagner's anti-Semitic imagination, as in Kant's, Hegel's Feuerbach's, and Schopenhauer's, the Jews exemplified the principle of heteronomy—be it called utilitarian or egoistic. It is always the Jews who are blamed for an orientation toward the "goods of this world." Even though the paradigm of world redemption shifts its focus from reason to art, the anti-Semitic aspect of German transcendental thought also determined Wagner's racism and, here too, the immutable resides in religion rather than in biology. In his infamous essay "Judaism in Music," he posited Jewish immutability in the Jewish God: "But the Jew has stood quite apart from this community [the historical community of European nations], alone with his Jehovah in a dispersed and barren stock, incapable of real evolution, just as his own Hebraic language has been handed down as something dead."[27] This passage shows how Wagner connected the immutability of race to the "inseparable link" between the Jews and their God. The inability to undergo evolution *(alle Entwicklung aus sich versagt bleiben mußte)*[28] originates in the consecration to Jehovah, in the fixed "standing quite apart and alone with Jehovah" *(Der Jude aber stand außerhalb . . . einsam mit seinem Jehova).*[29]

If Kant saw the origin of the Jews in their superstition, if Hegel made the Jewish God responsible for the fear for material possessions, and if Feuerbach called Jehovah "the principle of power," then Wagner equated the God of the Jews with heteronomy as such. One of the crucial differences between Wagner and the German philosophers has to do with his increasing politicization of anti-Semitism. He attempted to mobilize a mass movement against the integration of the Jews into German civil society precisely because he stigmatized them as a threat to the realization of an idealized homogenous *Volksgemeinschaft.* Paradoxically, he equated Jewishness with power and, at the same time, set out to mobilize power against the Jews. This paradox ultimately comes down to the absence of power, which, as discussed above, Wagner associated with both art and the German people. The Jews possess that which is lacking in Wagner's idealistic Germans. In "Elucidations on Judaism in Music," he pointed out to the *Volk* that "the power, which we were lacking, belonged to the Jews" *(Jene uns fehlende Macht gehörte aber den Judentum).*[30] Why did he employ the past tense instead of speaking in the present? Wagner saw his art in terms of a revenge on Jehovah that consists in taking power away from the Jews, thus outdoing their God,who originally gave it to them, first in the Old Testament and then through what Wagner imagined to be "the Jewish infiltration" ("Jewification") of Christian culture (following Fichte and Schopenhauer, he believed in an Aryan Christ).[31]

Indeed, Wagner took up Hegel's fantasy about obedience to rabbinic law, which allegedly preconditions God's help in securing worldly possessions. However, he radicalized the Hegelian charge when he argued that the "tribal God, of this small people, promised those who belong to him the future domination of the whole world, including everything that is alive and active as long as they strictly keep his laws" *(der Stammgott eines kleinen Volkes den Seinigen, sobald sie streng die Gesetze hielten, . . . die einstige Beherrschung der ganzen Welt, mit allem was darin lebt und webt, verhießen).*[32] Wagner blamed Jehovah and the Jews for Christianity's rise to political power, and thus he feared the Jew behind the Christian—an anti-Semitic figure of thought to which Nietzsche referred too, albeit it in a different context.[33] The "corruption of Christian religion" *(Verderb der christlichen Religion)* originates in "the inclusion of Jewishness in the constructions of its dogma" *(Herbeiziehung des Judentums zur Ausbildung ihrer Dogmen).*[34] The inclusion of what Wagner imagined to be "the principle of power" (Jewishness) paradoxically threatens to weaken Christian culture and society such that the emergence of the Jew as an influential force within contemporary society points to the illness of the body politic. Wagner, in fact, employed the metaphor of the body to drive home the point that society is in state of "corruption": "Only when a body's inner death is evident can outside elements gain entry, and then only to destroy it."[35] In this way, anything that has fallen prey to the power of corruption reveals the face of the Jew, so that Jewishness signifies the "defaming conscience of our modern civilization,"[36] as an example of which Wagner singled out the popularity of Heinrich Heine's works.

As we have seen, Wagner followed Kant, Hegel, Feuerbach, and Schopenhauer in attributing the racist notion of immutability to the Jewish religion. This religion turns out to be a religion without religious content—what Kant called "superstition"—insofar as the "true religion" emerges from the wish to gain independence from any reliance on the material world. In trying to gain power over empirical life, the Jew as Christian still follows Jehovah, for "he [the Jew] has in truth no religion, but only the belief in certain promises of his God, which, unlike in every true religion, are not at all related to extemporal life, which transcends real life, but exclusively refers to contemporary life on earth, on which the tribe indeed remains assured of its domination over all living and lifeless objects" (denn in Wahrheit hat er keine Religion, sondern nur den Glauben an gewisse Verheißungen seines Gottes, die sich keineswegs, wie in jeder wahren Religion, auf ein außerzeitliches Leben über dieses sein reales Leben hinaus, sondern auf ein eben dieses gegenwärtige Leben auf der Erde erstrecken, auf welcher sein Stamm allerdings die Herschaft über alles Lebende und Leblose zugesichert bleibt).[37]

Most significantly, Wagner praised Schopenhauer for having followed Kant in his attempt to free Christianity from Jehovah. After having established in his essay "Recognize Yourself" that self-knowledge results in the recognition of the "Jew within," Wagner called Schopenhauer the "enacter of Kant" *(dem Ausführer Kants)*,[38] since both philosophers "prepared the ground for a true ethics" in which "the Christian world is cleared from its over thousand year long confusion with the Jewish notion of God" *(tausendjährige Verwirrung zu lichten, in welcher der jüdische Gottesbegriff die ganze christliche Welt verstrickt hatte)*.[39] This statement is linked to Wagner's striking assessment of the progress in the history of philosophy: "there has not been any real progress [*eigentlicher Fortschritt*] from Plato to Kant."[40] It appears that, in Wagner's view, Western philosophy had been corrupted by Jewish influences, until Kant liberated it from such infection.

Wagner's focus on Kant sheds light on the sociohistorical situation of German intellectuals in the latter half of the nineteenth century. Until World War I, "academics necessarily held an unusually eminent place in their nation, as long as higher education was an important factor in German social stratification."[41] To be part of the educated German society meant to be idealistic. Wagner set out to widen the influence of idealism and thus to educate the lower classes. His obsession with the Jews yields evidence of, among other things, his anxiety about a kind of modernity that could descend into materialism (as Kant fantasized about the Jews as agents of materialism who could corrupt capitalism's autonomy of production). If the philosophers of the German Enlightenment constructed a notion of universality based on humanity's endowment with reason (an endowment that is absent in "superstitious" people, thus limiting the supposed universality of the "rational"), Wagner imbued art with humanist associations by making it speak to the whole of the people, regardless of class difference. Yet his art stops short of speaking to the Jews and thereby follows the trajectory of German transcendental reason. Wagner indeed discussed the dilemma of the German humanists at the beginning of "Judaism in Music," when he wrote in the voice of the "Enlightenment liberator," identifying with the "we" who "proposed the freedom for the Jews with no knowledge of the race."[42]

Race, as we have seen, turns out to be the inseparable union between the Jews and Jehovah's power. The fight for universal emancipation thus stops short of including the Jews, since it is Jewishness from which the people must be emancipated: "it is we who [must] fight for emancipation from the Jews . . . the Jew is more than emancipated . . . he is the ruler."[43] In this way Wagner's "all-inclusive art" comes down to the unification of the people against their rulers, who are posited to reside outside the universality of the people rather than within it, such that it is no longer the princes or the factory owners but the Jews who are the exploiters.[44] Indeed, the power of the real rulers (monarch and capitalist) should be united with that of the worker.

Wagner tried to secure this power through his art, which addresses both the German rulers and the German people. In his essay "What Is German?" he demanded that "the princes must found their new alliance with the people,"[45] and it is by means of such an alliance that idealism, as Wagner understood it, gains power. Power, as discussed above, is the element that Wagner associated with Jewishness. In the hands of the Jews power is heteronomous; it is the power over the goods of this world, which are used (according to the principle of utility) for selfish ends (according to the principle of egoism). In the hands of the Germans, however, power enables the "redemption of the world," achieved by overcoming the worldly in a state of autonomous indifference to one's position in empirical reality. Thus, the prejudicial exclusion of the Jews from the German has its ground in the transcendental opposition between autonomy and heteronomy, spirit and matter, worldly power and idealist powerlessness.

At the conclusion of this chapter I examine how the binary opposition between the fearless but (in earthly terms) stupid hero Siegfried and the Nibelungen, who desire "immeasurable power," refashions a Kantian polarity between autonomy and heteronomy. In his Ring cycle, Wagner indeed put this transcendental divide onstage. He consciously set out to popularize this opposition in order to mobilize the people against the Jews. Thus, "art has passed judgment on the Jewish God" *(Jener Gott wurde durch die Kunst gerichtet),* whereas "Jehovah has not much to say to the faithful soul of the people" *(der Johovah . . . der gläubigen Seele nicht viel zu sagen)*.[46] Wagner triumphed over Jehovah, who cannot compete with homogenous "people-power," which is mobilized by means of the translation of an anti-Semitic paradigm into the emotional language of the *Gesamtkunstwerk,* which "resolves the tension between concept and sentiment" *(Zwiespalt zwischen Begriff und Empfindung aufhebt)*.[47] How this translation unfolds on the Wagnerian stage is briefly discussed in the following paragraphs.

Putting the Autonomy-Heteronomy Divide Onstage

In the Ring cycle, Wagner portrayed contemporary society in terms of a heteronomous bondage to the material world. In this section I wish to draw attention to the ring as a symbol of enslavement to the enjoyment derived from objects of empirical reality. Indeed, it is their relation to the ring that divides the protagonists into embodiments of either autonomy or heteronomy. As we will see, this transcendental divide may be summarized in terms of Siegfried, the Rhinemaidens and Brünnhilde's binary opposition to the Nibelungen, Fafner and Fasolt, and Wotan. Siegfried's disregard of threats to his life and body imbues him—like the "pure fool" *(reiner Tor)* Parsifal,[48] who is not afraid even of the sorcerer Klingsor—with the aura of autonomy. Crucially, his relation to the ring brings out his opposition to heteronomy, for he is the only character who does not attach any use-value to the ring. The neglected dialogue between Siegfried and the Rhinemaidens warrants analysis. At the beginning of *Götterdämmerung*'s third act, the ring turns into a symbol of the transcendence of the body, rather than constituting a means for "selfishly" securing its welfare. A comparison of this scene with Alberich's surrender of the ring, in the fourth scene of *Das Rheingold,* nicely underlines this autonomy-heteronomy opposition.

Wagner indeed equated "the tragic ring of the Nibelungs" with the "stock-market portfolio [*der verhängnisvolle Ring des Nibelungen, als Börsenportefeuille*] that brings to completion the horrid picture of world-domination."[49] A few pages after this quotation, in his essay "Religion and Art," he painted the anti-Semitic image of "the Jew with the prosy stock-market bell" *(der Jude mit der papiernen Börsenglocke)*.[50] The ring turns out to be a symbol of capitalism's heteronomy in the same way the Jew symbolizes enslavement to selfish enjoyment, gained by means of domination over both "lively and lifeless objects" of the empirical world.

It is against this background that the illuminating analysis of the Nibelungen as anti-Semitic stereotypes could be extended to all the characters who want to keep the ring in order to raise the prospect of progress in the material world.[51] Except for Siegfried, and possibly Brünnhilde and the Rhinemaidens, all the protagonists of the Ring cycle depict Wagner's racist fear of a

European society that has been infiltrated by "Jehovah's principle of power." The gods are called "light-elves" in order to bring out their relation to the Nibelungen, who are called "black-elves."[52] Significantly, Wotan's first appraisal of his mighty new castle (scene two of *Das Rheingold*) follows Alberich's theft of the ring.[53] Critics who want to shift the focus of discussion away from Wagner's anti-Semitism and concentrate on the social criticism of the Ring take Wotan's possessiveness to be the revolutionary critique of a politics of power.[54] This undoubtedly holds true but leaves out of account an analysis of Wagner's theoretical writings. Here, as discussed above, he made the Jew responsible for a politics of material power, against which he sets the idealist power of art, backed up by the patriotic idealism of the *Volk*.

Wotan "is what he is only through contracts"[55] and thus exemplifies the contractual or utilitarian principle within modernity, for which Wagner made the Jews responsible in his essays. But Wotan also desires possession of the ring and thereby evidences his heteronomy. Tellingly, Wagner employed the same word for Wotan's and Alberich's inclination to depend on the goods of this world, as symbolized by the ring: the dwarf commands that "you should lust for [*gieren*] gold" in *Das Rheingold*,[56] and the curse has in fact come true in *Die Walküre*, in which Wotan confesses that "he has lustfully [*gierig*] held the gold in his hands."[57] Indeed, Wotan wants the ring as soon as he hears about its use-values, about its promise of "world-domination," and he hears this before Alberich utters his curse. After Loge informs Wotan of the ring's magic, which makes its possessor gain possession of the world, he explodes: "I must have the ring!"[58] How did the ring become the ring? This question lies behind Wotan's, Fafner's, and Fasolt's sudden obsession with the gold. The issue of causation brings us to the beginning of the cycle, where, as David J. Levin has shown, representation gives way to narration.[59]

Narration, however, implies movement and action within the material world, in which plots unfold with respect to desires for specific empirical objects, such as the ring. Alberich's theft of the ring kicks off narration and thereby introduces the principle of heteronomy. Kant indeed saw heteronomy in the very constitution of the narrative element that he equated with Paul's letter (see chapter 1). It is Alberich's inclination to depend on the goods of this world that makes him lust for *maßlose Macht* (power beyond any measure). His desire is always bound to the enjoyment derived from objects within material reality, be it sexual desire *(Lust)* or the joys gained from social domination. Alberich does not turn the ring into a medium of transcendental freedom from the empirical (as is the case with Siegfried), since he values his life more highly than the mere possession of the gold.

If Alberich lost his life, he would also lose the use-value yielded by the ring. For this reason he bows to Wotan's demands near the end of *Das Rheingold* in a scene that stands in striking contrast to Siegfried's intransigence when confronted by the warnings of the Rhinemaidens at the beginning of *Götterdämmerung*'s third act. Alberich does not forsake his "life and body" for the principle of autonomy, for which Siegfried willingly forgoes his life and—true to Wagner's definition of "German essence" in "Was ist Deutsch?"—keeps the ring for its own sake. In contrast to Siegfried, Alberich "frees his life and body" *(Leib und Leben)*[60]—as we shall see, Siegfried makes use of the same words when he refuses to hand the ring over to the Rhinemaidens—even if this means the loss of the ring.

This illustrates that, for Alberich, the gold is only a means that enables the enjoyment of the goods of this world. Siegfried, by contrast, does not know and is not interested in the use-value of the ring, which is in his possession. As he makes clear to Hagen, he is "ignorant of the power within it [the ring]" *(unkund seiner Kraft)*.[61] Alberich emphasizes this point in the dialogue with his son Hagen:

Denn nicht weiß er	Because he does not know
des Ringes Wert,	the worth of the ring,
zu nichts nützt er	He does not make use
die neidische Macht.[62]	of the enviable power.

Clearly, for Siegfried, the ring has no use-value; rather than using it as means to enhance his position within the empirical world, he paradoxically uses it to put an end to all use-values.

A few scenes before the actual enactment of the apocalyptic twilight of the gods, the Rhinemaidens entreat Siegfried to hand the ring over to them. At the moment at which Siegfried offers the ring to the maidens as a present, he is warned of the catastrophe that would await him were he to keep the ring. This is enough to reverse "the hero's" generosity. In stark contrast to Alberich, who hands over the ring when he is forced to choose between it and his life, Siegfried refuses to hand it over, precisely because it endangers his position within the material world. Thus, Siegfried emphasizes his autonomy with respect to concerns for his welfare:

Doch bedroht ihr mir Leben	But with the threat to my life
und Leib:	and body
Faßte er nicht	Even if it were not
Eines Fingers Wert	Worth a trifle
Den Reif entringt ihr mir nicht.[63]	You could not wrest the ring from me.

Wagner dwells on his hero's transcendental freedom, for Siegfried goes on to illustrate his disregard for life and body with a gesture:

Denn Leben und Leib . . .	For life and body . . .
seht!-so	Look—just like that
werf ich sie weit von mir![64]	I throw them far away from me!

Siegfried throws a piece of earth far away from himself, thus illustrating his distance from the "earthly." By willingly endangering his life and body, Siegfried proves his transcendental freedom from empirical conditions and material interests. With Siegfried, the ring symbolizes the eschatological redemption from the world and thereby from heteronomy, that is, from the orientation to the goods of this world.

As we have seen, Wagner placed the transcendental divide between autonomy and heteronomy, between the body and a redemptive kind of body politic, onstage. By willingly endangering his life and body by refusing to return the ring to the Rhinemaidens, Siegfried sets the path for the "night of annihilation" *(Nacht der Vernichtung)*[65] with which the Ring cycle ends. The ending coincides with the beginning so that narration again gives way to representation. The plot, which is driven by heteronomous desire, outdoes itself thanks to the fearlessness of its hero.[66] As the material basis of its construction, narration embodies the foreign element of Wagner's art, denoting it as the Jewish principle of power, otherwise defined in the conceptual designation "heteronomy." The concept and its related characteristics constitute anti-Semitic stereotyping in German transcendental philosophy. By celebrating, in an intentionally popular mode, the destruction of a society shaped by heteronomy, Wagner set out to pass judgment on Jehovah, whom he believed to have infiltrated the core of contemporary European society. Thus, not only are the Nibelungen anti-Semitic stereotypes, but so, in short, are all those who lust for gold as a means of enjoying worldly goods.

By freely disregarding any threat to his own life and body, Siegfried points to the transformation of the body into the body politic. Wagner perceived the idealism of such "selfless" transformation most clearly in the patriotic identification of the individual with the *Volk*. Politicizing German idealist thought, Wagner excluded the Jews from the *Volk* by stigmatizing them as the opposite of the idealist principle of autonomy. Siegfried's autonomous attitude, which consists in his refusal to return the ring *in exchange* for his life and body, thus lays the cornerstone of Wagner's attempted popularization of the anti-Semitic stereotype, implicit in the German transcendental divide between autonomy and heteronomy.

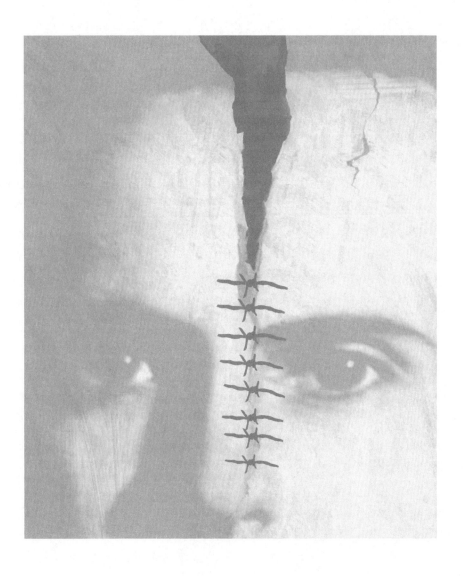

PART TWO

COUNTERNARRATIVES

4   Moses Mendelssohn's Other Enlightenment and German Jewish Counterhistories in the Work of Heinrich Heine and Abraham Geiger

In part I of this study I analyzed Kant's, Hegel's, and Wagner's philosophical narratives. In each of these narratives Judaism represents the lack of a specific kind of rationality. According to Kant and Hegel, the Jews are immutably bound to their God, who holds out the promise of finding fulfillment within the empirical world. The posited inability to abandon the lure of such a promise constitutes unreason. As we saw in chapter 3, Wagner politicized and thus attempted to popularize this prejudicial view of "the true, the beautiful, and the good" when he constructed his dramatic narratives around the conceptual kernel of an idealist-realist opposition. In part II of this study, I examine various German Jewish counternarratives to this paradigm. In different but related ways, Moses Mendelssohn, Heinrich Heine, Heinrich Graetz, Sigmund Freud, Franz Rosenzweig, Walter Benjamin, Elias Canetti, and Franz Baermann Steiner examined the unreason at the very heart of Kant's, Hegel's, and Wagner's understanding of reason.

This chapter first focuses on Mendelssohn's *Jerusalem, or On Religious Power and Judaism.* In this book, he developed an interpretation of rationality that did not set out to imitate Kant's Copernican revolution as propounded in the *Critique of Pure Reason* (1781). On the contrary, he distanced himself from "Kant, who destroys everything" *(alles zermalmenden Kants)*[1] and distinguishes his version of the Enlightenment from a Kantian fusion of morality and epistemology. This comes most clearly to the fore in his plea for separation of state and religion. In the second section of *Jerusalem,* Mendelssohn delineated a conception of reason's heteronomy that clearly contrasts with Kant's notion of autonomy. He did not see his version of rationality in the all-comprehensive terms in which Kant described the validity of autonomous reason, precisely because his differentiation between the moral and the epistemological allowed for a multiplicity of epistemologies and moral ways of acting that may differ from one culture to another.

As we have seen in the previous chapters, German idealism to a large extent defined Jewishness in terms of a radical lack of rationality. Mendelssohn did not engage in an apologetic discourse in which he argued for the intrinsic unity of the Jew and a modern Christian state. Rather, he developed another version of what it means to be enlightened. According to Mendelssohn, a Jewish way of life was more reasonable and rational than the speculative flights that issue from the modern, written culture of autonomous reason. Indeed, he saw in this split between the spiritual and the empirical the prime cause of idolatry and therefore superstition. In this way, Mendelssohn anticipated Cohen's, Rosenzweig's, Freud's, Benjamin's, Canetti's, and Steiner's attempts at turning the tables on an Enlightenment philosophy that stigmatized the Jews as superstitious and irrational.

The second part of this chapter discusses how Mendelssohn's immediate heirs engaged in a somewhat apologetic discourse with which they set out to further the cause of Jewish civic equality. I discuss Abraham Geiger's theological and Heinrich Heine's literary works as examples of counterhistories. In these accounts, Jewish civilization figures as the birthplace of modern culture, instead of offering a critique of some of its shortcomings.

Moses Mendelssohn, or Reason's Heteronomy

Jerusalem, or On Religious Power and Judaism (1783) by Moses Mendelssohn (1729–1786) set the stage for much of German Jewish writing and thought in the nineteenth and twentieth centuries.[2] German Jewish writers in the first half of the nineteenth century, most explicitly Heinrich Heine, read his work along lines that helped further the image of a natural affinity between the Jewish and the German. Mendelssohn thus figured as an illustration of a kind of elective affinity that bound Berlin and Jerusalem into an almost indistinguishable union. This apologetic reading of Mendelssohn's struggle for civil parity neglects the fact that he never gave in to the call for a regeneration of both Judaism and the Jewish people that, with the exception of Wilhelm von Humboldt,[3] supporters of emancipation demanded. In contrast to Franz Rosenzweig and to some extent Hermann Cohen, as we will see, Mendelssohn avoided the confrontation with Christian prejudice on the "public battlefield" *(öffentlichen Kampfplatz).*[4] He did not advance an apologetic account of Judaism. In the words of Amos Funkenstein, "he was not a forerunner of the reform, nor was he 'der jüdische Luther' (Heine)."[5] Crucially, Mendelssohn gave an account of both the Enlightenment and of reason that clearly differed from that which the German transcendental philosophers understood by the terms *rationality* and *morality*. In what follows, I mainly examine Mendelssohn's separation between epistemology and morality. It is this differentiation that links the first section of *Jerusalem,* which establishes the distinction between state and religion, to the second, in which Mendelssohn differentiates between Judaism as revealed legislation and Christianity as revealed doctrine. The state mainly enforces actions that are not necessarily underwritten by an epistemologically cohesive view of the world. Religion, on the other hand, influences attitudes or convictions *(Gesinnungen)* of specific individuals. More important, the epistemologies that form these attitudes are as divergent as the multiplicity of individuals who live in any given social unit.

Accordingly, Mendelssohn's distinction between epistemology and morality, in *Jerusalem's* first section, prepares the ground for the plea for diversity with which the book closes. In this way, *Jerusalem* paradigmatically articulated German Jewry's "struggle to live with a plurality of indentities and cultures—which is increasingly recognized to be a salient feature of Western modernity."[6] Ironically, Kant's version of the Enlightenment supposedly established the foundation of modern liberal thought. This has been often proclaimed.[7] Kant's version of the Enlighenment had rather reactionary implications insofar as it defined itself over against Mendelssohn's separation between the moral and the epistemological. To this extent Mendelssohn's twofold differentiation of state and church, on one hand, and action and theory, on the other, developed and deepened Spinoza's notion of a liberal kind of politics as defined in the *Theological-Political Treatise.* By arguing that Moses did not reveal a universally valid theory but only a particular outline for a context-specific form of action, Mendelssohn reflected certain arguments that Spinoza, in his discussion of Judaism, pronounced a social and political theory.[8]

In contrast to Kant, who developed a universally valid interpenetration of an exclusive epistemology with a concomitant moral theory that, as we saw in chapter 1, obfuscated its foundations in a particular—that is, Christian—tradition, Mendelssohn emphasized the distinctiveness of God's revelation to Moses:

> The voice which let itself be heard on Sinai on that great day did not proclaim, "I am the Eternal, your God, the necessary, independent being, omnipotent and omniscient, that recompenses men in future life according to their deed." This is the universal *religion of mankind,* not Judaism; and the universal *religion of mankind,* without which men are neither virtuous nor capable of felicity, was not to be revealed there.[9]

Mendelssohn subjected Kantian claims to universality to an ironic treatment. Indeed, he detected not inclusion but exclusion in this "universal religion of mankind": "Judaism boasts of no *exclusive* revelation of eternal truths that are indispensable for salvation, of no revealed religion in the sense in which that term is usually understood. Revealed *religion* is one thing, revealed *legislation,* another."[10] In shifting the emphasis from religion to legislation, Mendelssohn underlined the sociopolitical aspect of Judaism, as he understood it. This aspect describes a particular way of life that does not purport to be a sine qua non for the salvation of the rest of the world. As we have seen, Kant demoted as the will to power over the goods of this world that which Mendelssohn, and to some extent Spinoza, interpreted as a particular form of social organization.

Mendelssohn, on the other hand, argued that Jewish laws circumscribe power precisely because they are revealed. How can revelation impose limits on political power? God as the unknown giver of the law interdicts any absolutist claims as to the exact and immutable meaning of a revealed legislation. What has so far been ignored in the critical literature is that revelation, in the Mendelssohnian usage of the word, has one meaning when it qualifies the law and a slightly different one when it describes religious doctrine.[11] How can we explain this difference in connotation? Some readers might wonder if it really exists. The context, however, in which Mendelssohn described what he meant by revealed legislation clearly establishes that revelation here implied a split between epistemology and morality. To be sure, he did not deny that the law consists of writing. However, the written statutes are deliberately vague so as not to allow an idolatrous identification between signs and things. Mendelssohn thus described revelation in terms of writing; he qualified differences between a revealed doctrine and a revealed legislation. Whereas the text of a revealed doctrine purports to be complete, that of a revealed legislation does not do so. This incompleteness prevents revealed law from falling prey to idolatrous worship. Thus Mendelssohn argued that Mosaic "laws were revealed, that is, they were made known by God, through *words* and *script*."[12] However, "only the most essential part of them was entrusted to letters; and without the unwritten explanations, delimitations, and more precise determinations, transmitted orally and propagated through oral, living instruction, even these written laws are mostly incomprehensible, or inevitably became so in the course of time."[13] A revealed legislation thus only indicates how a moral actor should conduct herself, but it leaves uncertain how to apply this teaching to the ever-changing contexts of everyday life. Accordingly, it does not offer an epistemology but only circumscribes a mold that helps shape the course of particular actions. A revealed doctrine, on the other hand, lays claim to completeness, at least in Mendelssohn's view. It purports to offer a fully consistent epistemology that preconditions every form of moral action. On account of a split between the epistemological and the moral, Mendelssohn saw in Israel's revealed legislation a way of precluding idolatrous assumptions of immanent self-sufficiency and also an admonition against the intolerance, religious and political, that accompanies presuppositions of a universally valid way of perceiving the world.

It is this split that provides argumentative consistency to his apparently rather distractive meditation about the oral and the written law. Significantly, Mendelssohn linked the doctrinal to immutability and therefore to a full disclosure of meaning, which he associated with writing. In ancient Judaism, however, the doctrinal was not a matter of revelation and was thus in need of constant reinterpretation:

> Doctrines and laws, convictions and actions. The former were not connected to words or written characters which always remain the same, for all men and all times, amid all the revolutions of language, morals, manners, and conditions, words and characters which invariably present the same rigid forms, into which we cannot force our concepts without disfiguring them. They were entrusted to living, spiritual instruction, which can keep pace with all changes of time and circumstances, and can be varied and fashioned according to a pupil's needs, ability and power of comprehension. . . . The ceremonial law itself is a kind of living script, rousing the mind and heart, full of meaning, never ceasing to inspire contemplation and to provide the occasion and opportunity for oral instruction.[14]

As a living script, revealed legislation avoids the rigidity that Mendelssohn criticized in the pronunciation of a revealed doctrine. What makes for the ever-changing and ongoing life of such scripture is precisely its not-to-be-fully-known "revealed doctrine." Because the meaning of the law is a matter of interpretation, revealed legislation, as Mendelssohn understood it, needs to be rewritten, reinterpreted, and thus readapted to new social and political circumstances. To this extent the law does not offer a valid epistemology. Instead, it offers a particular moral system, that is, a guideline for actions within the empirical world. By commanding action or the avoidance of action, depending on specific life contexts, the ceremonial law appeals to our sense of moral practice and not necessarily to our epistemological or theoretical faculties. As David Sorkin has recently pointed out, this "distinction between practical and theoretical knowledge . . . may well have resulted from his [Mendelssohn's] view of Judaism."[15] Mendelssohn in fact perceived in this differentiation between the moral and the epistemological the most striking characteristic of Judaism: its purity.

Mendelssohn described this "original" type of Judaism in terms of two unions. The first I have already touched on. It consists in the connection between teaching and everyday life. This combination goes hand in hand with the second, namely, the fusion of state and religion. How could *Jerusalem*'s second section so blatantly contradict the plea for a separation between state and church advanced in the first? According to Mendelssohn, ancient Israel's theocracy precluded any absolutization of a religious doctrine, precisely because it had a revealed legislation instead of a reveled doctrine, which underwrites the foundation of Christian politics. In ancient Israel, "faith is not commanded, for it accepts no other commands than those that come to it by way of conviction."[16] A split between the epistemological and the moral thus allows for a plurality of convictions *(Überzeugung)*. As we have seen, the revealed law does not have any all-inclusive epistemological pretensions. It only proscribes specific actions that are related to ever-changing empirical contexts. Its epistemology is fluid, so to speak. Nevertheless, it gives clear descriptions as regards an infinite variety of *particular ways of acting* that are always correlated to objects in the external world.

A correlation between teaching and life makes for this epistemological fluidity. The meaning of the law, that is, its ongoing application to ever-changing circumstances within empirical contexts, is a matter of continual interpretation. This is precisely because a not-to-be-known—that is, transcendent—deity has revealed Israel's legislation, and not a ruler or a ruling family who could be the fully present epistemological source of legal meaning. Accordingly, in ancient Israel, politics consisted of the search for the never-present meaning of the law. This is what Mendelssohn meant when he spoke of "politics . . . as a deity, where the ordinary eye only sees a stone."[17] Politics resembles the rigidity of stone only when scripture loses its epistemological fluidity and functions as a full and ever-present revelation of meaning.

This ossifying move coincides with the discrepancy between religion and politics in ancient Israel. Now, rather than a not-to-be-known deity, a ruler or a ruling family dictates what the legislation "exactly" means, thus rigidifying the law by driving a wedge between ever-changing life and teaching. Israel's theocracy thus gave way to a monarchy:

> Already in the days of the prophet Samuel, the edifice developed a fissure which widened more and more until the parts broke asunder completely. The nation asked for a visible king as its ruler, a king of flesh and blood, perhaps because the priesthood had already begun to abuse the authority which it had among the people, as Scripture reports about the Sons of the High Priest, or perhaps because the splendor of a neighboring royal household dazzled the eyes. In any event, they demanded a *king such as all other peoples have.* The prophets, aggrieved by this, pointed out to them the nature of the human king, who had his own requirements and could enlarge them at will, and how difficult it was to satisfy an infirm mortal to whom one has transferred the rights of deity. . . . State and religion were no longer the same, and a collision of duties was no longer impossible.[18]

Mendelssohn described this move from a theocracy to a monarchy as the introduction of an idolatrous form of worship. Indeed, the monarch—a flesh-and-blood human being—arrogates the role of God. By following the example of other nations, Israel abandoned monotheism and subscribed to the idolatry of the Gentile world. This increase in state power went in tandem with the abuse of religious authority (the priests have inflated their political influence). Significantly, a fissure between state and religion occurs precisely at the moment at which spiritual leaders demand political power and thus promote the deification of politics. In an important essay, Emmanuel Levinas had argued that in Mendelssohn's view, "Israel . . . attempted to carry out the superhuman adventure that consisted—though only for a time—in upholding a political law regulated by the religious law. This was exactly the opposite of a political conditioning of the spiritual!"[19] According to Mendelssohn, ancient Israel realized the never-to-be-recuperated religious limitation of political power precisely because it was a theocracy. Consequently, it ascribed political might to an unknown source to which no one could claim to have access. With the abuse of religious authority, an immanent sphere of power emerged, and as a result, a monarchy replaced the theocracy. This, however, meant that religious teaching now conflicted with everyday political reality. Politics now represented that which ancient Israel considered to be the idolatrous abrogation of absolute power.

Within the boundaries of Israel's former theocracy, on the other hand, absolute power could not be grasped by humanity's limited epistemology, because it was thought to reside with a not-to-be-known transcendent deity alone. According to Mendelssohn, the alleged immutability of the written word promoted the establishment of an absolutist kind of epistemology. Similar to the way in which he described Israel's move from theocracy to monarchy in terms of idolatry, he thus related the replacement of the oral by the written word to the idolatrous: "the need for written characters was the first cause of idolatry."[20] What, however, did Mendelssohn exactly understand by orality? We have already seen that he associated it with fluidity over and against the purported immutability of written doctrines. Mendelssohn, however, did not primarily attempt to develop a linguistic theory. Rather, he linked his distinction between the written and the oral to a variety of other issues. As we have seen, he related it to the movement from the theocratic to the monarchical.

Furthermore, in Mendelssohn's view, ancient Israel's oral culture dwelled closer to the pulse of "things as they are in themselves." An absolutist regime, and the concomitant introduction of an immutable belief system, disrupted the flow of humanity's interaction with nature. Now written doctrine could not be questioned anymore—and thereby made fluid—because the representatives of the monarchy (priests and the monarch himself) functioned as the finite and fully present source of all knowledge, thus replacing God. Accordingly, in critiquing both "writing" and an absolutist form of politics, Mendelssohn called into doubt the validity of autonomous reason. In his view, nature offers a more reliable, though less comprehensive, source for practical action than the speculative truths generated by autonomous reason.

Mendelssohn thus articulated a version of enlightenment that radically differs from what Kant defined as freedom and rationality. As discussed in chapter 1, Kant's *Critique of Pure Reason* denied that we can know objects in the external world. Apart from an understanding of their quantitative, material constitution, we cannot have meaningful relationships with them. We can, however, impose the autonomous law derived from reason onto "things" in the external world and thus re-create the world according to the plans established by our rationality. Anyone who accepts things as they are in themselves, empirically constituted, falls prey to heteronomy. Kant associated such a heteronomous way of life with Jewishness. Hegel in fact saw in the emergence of Judaism a reenforcement of "natural religion" that, in his understanding, absolutized immediate being (see chapter 2). More important, in the Kantian as well as in the Hegelian philosophical system, the epistemological preconditioned the moral, which, in turn, determined political and economic actions: Because we cannot accurately perceive what the external world really is, our moral reflections must not take into account our context-specific and therefore contingent standing within the material world—this would enact the principle of heteronomy. Instead, we have to follow what the autonomy of reason prescribes as abstract and universally valid truths. Reason's autonomy can differentiate between right and wrong precisely when it disregards external circumstances. In this way, a wide gulf opens between nature, on one hand, and knowledge and morality, on the other. Accordingly, Mendelssohn's critique of writing questioned the hegemonic structure that informs such fusion of the epistemological with the moral. By attempting to undermine the hegemony of idealist philosophy in German intellectual culture, Mendelssohn anticipated the work of German Jewish writers (Heine, Graetz, Freud) in the latter half of the nineteenth century.

Mendelssohn's notion of writing thus resembles what Kant defined as autonomy. More important, Mendelssohn argued that heteronomous motivations constitute the driving force behind moral actions. Israel's revealed legislation instantiates such heteronomy, which leaves room for various epistemologies, that is to say, for various ways of perceiving the world, be they autonomous or heteronomous: "Commandment and probation, reward and punishment are only for actions, acts of commission and omission which are subject to a man's will and which are guided by ideas of good and evil and, therefore, also by hope and fear. Belief and doubt, assent and opposition, on the other hand, are not determined by our faculty of desire, by our wishes and

longings, or by fear and hope, but only by our knowledge of truth and untruth."[21] Here Mendelssohn clearly associated the epistemological (knowledge of truth and untruth) with autonomy (not determined by desire) and
revealed doctrine (belief). On the other hand, he correlated Israel's revealed
legislation with both morality (commandment and probation) and heteronomy (reward and punishment; hope and fear). As we saw in chapter 1, Kant
denied Judaism any moral and, for that matter, religious dignity with reference to its heteronomy, which, in his view, vitiates rational perception
(epistemology) and thus precludes the (moral) enactment of humanity's independence from any material conditions. Rather than being a sine qua non for
morality, Mendelssohn argued that matters of truth do not necessarily stipu-
late moral action. While being considered epistemologically deficient, outside
influences of hope and fear do nevertheless help to procure ethical endeavors.

In this way, Mendelssohn saw in Israel's revealed legislation not an appeal to the autonomy of reason, but rather an admonition to engage rationally with the social and the natural world. By interacting with the emotive
side of humanity, heteronomy thus does not fall prey to irrationalism. According to Mendelssohn, Israel in its purity did not follow immutable abstractions. Rather, it derived guidelines for moral actions not from human
knowledge—as laid down in written doctrines—but from the ever-changing
script of nature. Consequently, Mendelssohn's notion of orality described insights yielded by our interaction with the external world, whereas the written
represented a split between teaching and life: "Eternal truths, on the other
hand, insofar as they are useful for men's salvation and felicity, are taught by
God in a manner more appropriate to the Deity, not by sounds or written
characters, which are comprehensible here and there, to this or that individual, but through creation itself, and its internal relations, which are legible
and comprehensible to all men."[22] In contrast to Kant, who separated both
epistemology and morality from our material welfare, Mendelssohn connected truth with happiness *(Glückseligkeit)*. More important, the perception of the true does not depend on the tenets derived from reason's
autonomy—as proclaimed in spoken and written words—but rather issues
from the contemplation of the external world, which is understood to be
God's creation.

The fact that Mendelssohn did not differentiate between sounds and
written characters indicates that he had something in mind other than a linguistic theory. Indeed, he argued that the sign system of the original oral culture dwelt closer to "the things themselves"[23] than is the case in written
culture, wherein truth and morality proceed from doctrinal abstractions. In
Israel's "oral phase" the "truths useful for the felicity [*Glückseligkeit*] of the
nation as well as of each of its members were to be utterly removed from all

imagery."²⁴ Note that Mendelssohn traced the origin of words back to hieroglyphic scripts that resembled images.²⁵ The written thus described an imaginary world—the fantasized sphere of idolatry—whereas the oral bespoke a close correlation between teaching and life, between humanity and nature, which was understood to be the work of God's creation. Mendelssohn characterized Israel's revealed legislation as a bridge that connects teaching to life:

> Images and hieroglyphics lead to superstition and idolatry, and our alphabetic script makes man too speculative. It displays the symbolic knowledge of things and their relations too openly on the surface; it spares us the effort of penetrating and searching, and creates too wide a division between doctrine and life. In order to remedy these defects the lawgivers of this nation gave the *ceremonial law*. Religious and moral teachings were to be connected with man's everyday activities. The law, to be sure, did not impel them to engage in reflection; it prescribed only actions, only doing and not doing.²⁶

In this dense citation, Mendelssohn focused on the themes so far discussed in this chapter. Unpacking this passage involves establishing connections between the various arguments that are unfolded here in quick succession. Mendelssohn first associated images and hieroglyphics with writing in order to hold alphabetic script responsible for a speculative flight away from commonsense reality as it is constituted by the external world. In contrast to Kant, who asserted in his *Critique of Pure Reason* (1781) that we should forgo metaphysical reflection about the specific qualitative character of specific things, Mendelssohn argued that nature holds open revelatory vistas to the whole of humanity, regardless of different religious doctrines. Now by supplanting the world of nature with another man-produced fantasized world (a world of images), writing precludes a search for the revelation that dwells in God's creation. Note also that the German *Schreiberei* is a colloquial diminutive for *scripture (Schrift)*—comparable to the English *waffle*. It thus underlines the ironic tone of the citation. Second, Mendelssohn therefore maintained that a close connection between teaching and life helps bridge this gap between the spiritual and the natural. He questioned whether specific spiritual guidelines for everyday actions can be established in a universally valid manner but emphasized that as far as the particular case of Judaism is concerned, Moses' revealed legislation serves to fill precisely such a gap. Third, Mendelssohn argued for the separation of the epistemological and the moral. Although Israel's revealed legislation establishes a close connection between body and soul, that is, between the spiritual and the natural, it nevertheless separates the epistemological from the moral. Moses' law only describes how to act in the external world; it does not impose a specific epistemology on the members of a given society.

Abraham Geiger's and Heinrich Heine's Counterhistories

Mendelssohn's Enlightenment thus offers an alternative to that formulated by German idealist philosophy. Nevertheless, German Jewish writing and thought in the nineteenth century implicitly or explicitly set out to distance itself from such "another Enlightenment": "Whereas Mendelssohn has been concerned to show that Judaism was fully congruent with natural religion, Jewish thinkers after Kant were concerned to establish Judaism's status as a religion of morality and belief, an effort for which Mendelssohn's notions of 'divine legislation' and heteronomy were an impediment."[27] To be sure, Mendelssohn conceived of Enlightenment thought as an openness to multiple identities that could, each with different ways of perceiving the world, enrich the moral, religious, and intellectual life of the modern state. His version of the Enlightenment was therefore much closer to multiculturalism than Kant's or Hegel's. At the end of the eighteenth and the beginning of the nineteenth century it became increasingly clear, however, that modern German states followed the idealist attempt to build a modern nation on one particular principle of reason, namely, that derived from the Kantian version of a certain notion of secularized Christianity.

As we saw in chapter 1, the religion of the Jews and the nation of the Jews formed an indistinguishable unity in Kant's writings. At the beginning of the nineteenth century, one strand of anti-Semitic literature was likewise "more religious, the other more nationally orientated."[28] As a result, German Jewish thinkers of that time attempted to reduce Judaism to a confessional status, to a question of belief that had no impact on the political outlook of the respective believers: "Instead of learning the biblical and talmudic texts, they [German Jewish children in the nineteenth century] studied the principles of the Jewish faith, just as Christian children learned the fundamentals of their religion. . . . The most important value of Judaism was morality, without which there could be no religion."[29] The reform movement attempted to morally purify Jewish forms of worship: "This reform was—in keeping with the tendency in German liberalism to level out difference—intended to eliminate a number of integral elements of Jewish life: the ritual dietary laws, circumcision, use of Hebrew language, and the celebration of the Sabbath on Saturday. The Talmud would be subjected to a thoroughgoing expurgation."[30] Certainly, Samson Raphael Hirsch's neoorthodox movement did not attempt to reform Jewish law and the Jewish liturgy. However, reform and neoorthodoxy both set out to delineate a Jewish mission to the modern world.

Indeed, Hirsch criticized the reform movement in a mode related to the Kantian divide between freedom and nature. He ironically undermined the watchword "Religion allied to progress" by arguing that far from being progressive, the reform movement had fallen prey to what Kant stigmatized in

Judaism as materialism and therefore a heteronomous bondage to the goods of this world: " 'Religion allied to progress'—do you know, dear reader, what that means? Virtue allied to sensual enjoyment, rectitude allied to advancement, uprightness allied to success. . . . It means sacrificing religion and morality to every man's momentary whim."[31] Clearly Hirsch, following Kant's rational theology,[32] linked religion to a notion of the "moral," according to which the quest for "sensual enjoyment" and worldly success (in short, all elements that contribute to happiness) undermines the epistemological, moral, and political foundations of human autonomy. Whereas Kant claimed that Judaism embodies the opposite of such autonomy, Hirsch, in a counterhistorical move, described Judaism's mission in precisely the terms of a universal ethics from which it had been excluded in various works of German transcendental philosophy: "The more the Jew is a Jew, the more universalist will his views and aspirations be."[33]

Thus the various ideologues writing in the first half of the nineteenth century attempted to formulate Judaism's compatibility with a modern Christian state, rather than possible and salutary differences from it: "In their structure Hirsch's ideas resembled the reform theory of mission as well as Auerbach's theory of the regeneration of Germany."[34] Unlike Heinrich Heine, the German Jewish novelist Berthold Auerbach did not convert to Christianity. Both writers, however, were quite similar in their attempt to describe Germany as Israel's *doppelänger,* so to speak. In doing so, they engaged in constructing a counterhistory that conflicts with the idealist construction of a radical opposition between the Jewish and the German, on one hand, and the Judaic and the Christian, on the other. Amos Funkenstein has recently theorized the concept of counterhistory as follows: "Counterhistories form a specific genre of history written since antiquity; it is curious that they have not been identified as such in treatises in historiography sooner. Their function is polemical. Their method consists of the systematic exploitation of the adversary's most trusted sources against their grain—'die Geschichte gegen den Strich kämen.' Their aim is to distort the adversary's self-image, of his identity, through the deconstruction of his memory."[35] Geiger and Heine wrote cultural-political and theological counterhistories, respectively. Before turning to Heine's literary approach, I will first discuss Geiger's counterhistorical theology. What, however, are the differences between these counterhistories and versions of "another Enlightenment" as formulated by Mendelssohn? In this context, I would like to introduce a notion that is complementary to that theorized by Funkenstein in the quotation above. Counterhistories are certainly polemical, at least insofar as they revise the self-image of the majority culture from the perspective of the minority culture, which the former posits as a lack and contrasts with its own completeness (for example, absence of reason versus full acquisition of it). They do not necessarily undermine the ideational content of the predominant theoretical paradigm, however. Rather, they attempt to adapt the history of their own culture to the ideational content developed by that of the majority. This does not necessarily result in a christianization or germanization of Judaism. Indeed, counterhistories reverse the dominant *temporal* scheme of events: the progressive elements of modern Germany and Christianity figure as being derived from Jewish sources and are thereby deprived of jingoist notions of originality.

But counterhistories rarely deconstruct the concept of reason and progress as formulated in the majority culture's discourse. They only revise the most widely accepted temporality of ideas, not the ideas themselves or some aspect of them. In this regard, Funkenstein's notion of counterhistory could be complemented with that of a counternarrative. Mendelssohn's "other Enlightenment" is an example of such a counternarrative, for he deconstructs not only the memory of the majority culture but also the ways in which it *conceptualizes* rationality. We shall see how such deconstructions of what it means to be rational define the countertheories developed by Rosenzweig, Freud, and Steiner. Thus, counternarratives have a more direct conceptual impact than counterhistories. Whereas the former revises the temporality of progress, the latter lays its finger on the wound that gave rise to such revisions, namely, the prejudicial content that informs the ideational formations of certain conceptualizations of "progress" and of "reason."

By composing counterhistories, German Jewish writers and scholars stressed Judaism's social and moral mission, thus implicitly responding to certain strands in German idealist philosophy that had depicted the Jewish as the embodiment of naturalism and materialism. As we saw in chapter 1, the perceived immorality of the Jews—the equation of Judaism with superstition and materialism—had served, at least potentially, as justification for their exclusion from an otherwise "inclusive" modern state. Thus, Geiger's and Heine's focus on Judaism's ethical mission participated in the Jewish struggle for civic equality. Significantly, two striking elements shaped their respective literary and scholarly works: they both rewrote the dominant historical account of Christianity from the perspective of its Jewish foundation and concomitantly emphasized Israel's universalism and its ethical mission. In the following paragraphs, I will give a brief account of Abraham Geiger's theological counterhistory.

In his counterhistorical theology, Geiger made Judaism the point of origin for the achievements of the German Protestant majority culture of his day. To this extent he depicted the religion of the Jews as the exemplary model, according to which the Protestant Reformation could cast its intellectual outlook. "Whatever values the Reformation had acquired at its outset," he proclaims, "such as liberation from the rules of priestly caste and the clear recognition of the simple, literal meaning of Scriptural texts, had been attained by Judaism long before."[36] Geiger thus did not critique the Christian from the perspective of the Jewish. Rather, he argued for the compatibility of Christianity's modern, progressive elements with ancient Judaism.

To be sure, he criticized regressive elements in the Christian world as pagan. Do these critical moments within Geiger's counterhistory make it also a counternarrative? In an important study (to which my account of Geiger is heavily indebted), Susannah Heschel has recently argued that the Society for the Culture and Science of the Jews—with which both Geiger and Heine were associated—"is one of the earliest examples of postcolonialist writing."[37] She points out that nineteenth-century German Jewish historians "were the first to call into question accepted 'truths' about the history of the West and the respective roles played in it by Christianity and Judaism."[38] Here Heschel implicitly describes Geiger's work as that of a theological counterhistorian. To a large extent, his account attempted to revise the ideational self-understanding of Christian superiority: "The paganism within Christianity is the source of its dogma and intellectual rigidity, its intolerance and hostility toward Judaism."[39] What Heschel discusses here is an indirect criticism of the theological formation of Christianity.

Geiger, however, did not engage in a conceptual critique of notions such as progress and rationality. As we have seen, these were developed within pseudotheological translations of the Christian idea regarding each citizen's Christ-like "death to the world" into the "progressive" language of secular ethics and politics. Geiger in fact fashioned his image of Judaism along the lines of the concepts of freedom and of reason as formulated in the pseudotheological strands of German idealism. Indeed, he took up the Kantian notion of freedom from the heteronomous rules of Jewish ceremonies ("liberation from the rule of the priestly caste"). His criticism of Christian dogma retraced Kant's and Hegel's critique of positive religion. Within the context of nineteenth-century German politics and culture, Christian theology did not weigh as much as pseudotheological attitudes (Kant's *Gesinnungen*)—which were, as we have seen, keenly politicized by Richard Wagner and his followers—such as the "selfless" sacrifice of one's life for the greater good of the German people.

Against this background it is rather significant that, like Hirsch, Geiger seemed to cast "Israel's mission" into the Kantian mold of an otherworldly idea. He dissociated Judaism's ideational content from the materialist desire for "some earthly wealth"[40] that Kant attributed to the "religion without religion." Instead, the Jews are driven by "an idea that is being defended, an idea which they cherish as their chiefest treasure, one which raises them above all the other nations and which is destined to be broadcast throughout the earth by the people chosen for this purpose."[41] According to Geiger, Israel's mission thus consists of the proclamation of a Kantian moral idea. His counterhistorical account made Judaism compatible with the German transcendental concept of reason. Therein lay its subversive aspect: it freed Judaism from the prejudicial descriptions put forward by the main strand of German idealist philosophy.

Nevertheless, Geiger did not point to the immorality of the prejudicial discourse whose conceptual language he was adapting to make it precisely that against which the idealists leveled their charges. As discussed in chapter 5, we only see glimpses of such a critique in the counternarrative of Heinrich Graetz. In the following paragraphs, I discuss how Heinrich Heine's literary equation of the Jewish with the Christian, on one hand, and the German idealist, on the other, runs parallel to Geiger's theological subversion of Christianity's assumed historical and moral superiority.

In his discussion of Shakespeare's *Merchant of Venice,* Heine delineated an "elective affinity" *(Wahlverwandtschaft)* between Jews and Germans: "It is indeed striking to witness a deep elective affinity between the two nations of morality, namely, between the Jews and the Germans."[42] This notion of *Wahlverwandtschaft* has chemical associations as well: it denotes the mutual attraction of two chemical substances. Goethe in his famous—and in the nineteenth century rather infamous—novel *Wahlverwandtschaften* employed this scientific term in order to help explain the natural laws that underlie adulterous adventures. Significantly, Heine used this term—which, as a result of its Goethean usage, had rather immoral connotations for his contemporary readers—in order to describe the bond between two nations that supposedly epitomize morality per se. Goethe tried to describe the quasi-scientific lawfulness that makes someone fall in love with another in violation of a given society's moral order. The scientific objectivity of the term *Wahlverwandtschaft* fulfills a similar function in Heine's work, where it serves to describe the rationality of the Jews as an objective fact. The Jews, Heine argued, resemble German idealists.

Whereas Kant orientalized European Jews when he called them "Palestinians who live among us," and whereas Hegel saw in Judaism a reinforcement of "Oriental" natural religions, Heine germanized ancient Israel: "one could see the former Palestine as an Oriental Germany, just as one should consider contemporary Germany as the homeland of the holy word, as the mother-earth of prophecy and as the castle of pure spirituality/intellectuality."[43] In this way, Heine seemed to completely submerge the Jewish in the German. Like Geiger, Heine characterized Judaism as a religion of prophets rather than of priests. Both writers attempted to remove the Jewish from any associations with "primitive" heteronomy. Heine in fact argued that from "the beginning of history, the Jews carried in themselves the modern principle" *(die Juden trugen schon im Beginne das moderne Prinzip in sich).*[44] In so doing, Heine of course followed the ideology of the Society for the Culture and Science of the Jews, for he tried to undermine a colonialist account of intellectual history as advanced by Kant, Hegel, and some of their followers. As

Immanuel Wolf, the secretary of the society, wrote in 1822, "the relationship of strangeness in which Jews and Judaism have hitherto stood to the outside world must vanish."[45] Judaism figures as the primordial point of departure for the establishment of a modern Occident. Demolishing the image of an uncanny, strange "state within the state," Heine depicted the Jewish in homely (*heimisch* as opposed to uncanny, *unheimlich*), that is to say, familiar terms.

In an ironic move, he undermined the pseudotheological image of an immutable union between Jehovah and his people. As we saw in chapters 2 and 3, it was precisely by means of this image that anti-Semites such as Wagner tried to construct a radical divide between idealist Germans, on one hand, and the threat posed by powerful and materialist Jews, on the other. Heine universalized this pseudotheological stereotype and thus undermined the binary opposition between Jew and Gentile. To be sure, the Jews, he wrote in his novella *Schnabelewopski*, "are always the most obedient of Theists."[46] This attachment to their God, however, does not pose any supernatural threat to the outside world, since Jehovah has in the meantime become the universal God of humanity: "In political matters these [the Jewish theists] can be as republican as anyone; they can even roll in the mud like any old *sansculotte*— but when religious ideas come into play they remain humble servants of their Jehovah, that old fetish who wants nothing more to do with the entire crowd and has had Himself newly baptized as pure divine Spirit."[47] Here Heine revised the Hegelian image of the Jews as materialist people who expect worldly happiness to result from their theistic obedience to Jehovah's statutes. Instead of directing their eyes in a selfish manner to the possible prospect of finding fulfillment in immediate being, theistic Jews, in Heine's account, are true idealists. They are willing to sacrifice their life and body for the greater good of the republic. Their attachment to Jehovah has nothing to do with a nondialectical and therefore, in Hegelian terms, illusory hope for happiness in the empirical world. Rather, Jehovah himself has become Hegel's absolute Spirit that leads world history to immanent redemption!

In this way, Heine equated the Jewish with the Christian and with the ascetic kernel of German idealism, too. He in fact replaced the Christian-Jewish opposition with a new one: that between the Nazarene and the Helene. He first employed the term *Nazarene* in order to depict the writer Ludwig Börne. What have Jehovah, Heine, and Börne in common within the parameters of this Heinean narrative? As Jehovah underwent a baptism by means of which he turned into Hegel's *Weltgeist*, Louis Baruch converted to Christianity as Ludwig Börne. Similarly, Harry Heine turned into Heinrich Heine. Nevertheless, in Heine's view, Börne did not betray his Jewish heritage precisely because of the moral asceticism that defined his Christian and his political activities. Heine characterized the Nazarene as "narrow-minded" (*Beschränktheit*),[48] not, however, as regards a heteronomous orientation toward sensuous enjoyment. Instead, in his counterhistorical move Heine refashioned Christian otherworldliness as an intrinsically Jewish affair:

> I say Nazarene in order not to employ the expression "Jewish" or "Christian," even though both expressions are for me synonyms and are used by me not to denote a belief system but a disposition. . . . [A]ll human beings are either Jews or Hellenes, that is to say, those with drives that are ascetic, are hostile to images [*bildfeindlich*] and are addicted to sublimation [*vergeistigungssüchtig*], or those who have a personality that is full of the joys of life [*lebensheiterm*], full of the pride in human development [*entfaltungsstolzem*] and full of realism [*realistischem*].[49]

As we saw in the previous chapters, with the advance of German transcendental philosophy questions of belief (such as belief in Christ) had ceased to be an issue. Instead, attitudes *(Gesinnungen)* mattered. Kant and Hegel attributed to Jews a sensuous, materialist, and realist disposition, to which they contrasted a pseudotheological notion of reason that consists in realizing the nothingness of empirical life. This epistemological perception would then propel moral actions that show indifference toward one's corporeal constitution. In the passage quoted above, Heine reversed this binary opposition between Jewish realism and Christian German idealism. In a manner related to Geiger's counterhistorical theology, Heine argued that asceticism originated not with Christ but with Moses. As a result, Jews are not driven by materialism and realism. On the contrary, they have bequeathed these qualities to the Christians. Heine replaced the pseudotheological and sociopolitical opposition between the Jew and the Christian with a truly fictional one: that between ancient Hellenes and present-day Jews and Christians. As we shall see in the following chapter, Heinrich Graetz took up Heine's opposition only to underscore the historical importance of contemporary Jewry: the fact that the Hellenes are a dead people helps explain the vitality of modern Jewish life. With Heine, unlike Graetz, the historically removed sphere of ancient Greece now becomes the symbolic field inhabited by nonidealists. To this extent Heine reshaped Jewishness along the conceptual lines of German transcendental philosophy. In an unacknowledged manner, however, he did away with the prejudicial content of this philosophical paradigm by dissociating the Jewish community from any accusations of pursuing a materialist quest for power.

Nevertheless, Heine cast Jewish-Christian asceticism in a pathological mold, thus anticipating Nietzsche. In this way, he characterized Börne as a "slave to Nazarene abstinence" *(ein Sklave der nazarenischen Abstinenz)*.[50] Some critics have described this rather derogatory assessment of the Jewish-Christian heritage in terms of Jewish self-hatred.[51] Siegbert S. Prawer, on the other hand, has emphasized the "close connection between Heine's Judaism and his sympathy with the outcast, the underdog, and the apparently defeated whom a future time would vindicate and, where possible, raise again from the dust."[52] More recently, Roger F. Cook has argued that Heine not only sympathized with the discriminations Jews had to endure in nineteenth-century German culture—and which forced Heine himself to convert to Protestantism—but that he also developed a critique of some philosophical epistemologies: "[Heine] sees the age-old tradition of poetry as an invaluable tool for dismantling philosophy's claim to an epistemological privileged discourse that can determine universal and transcendental truths."[53] Although it is true that Heine played off poetry's playfulness against the conceptual rigidity of some philosophical discourse, he did not discuss the anti-Semitic content within German transcendental philosophy. But his counterhistory came close to developing a counternarrative when in his late writings he depicted the Jewish as an aesthetic equivalent of the Hellenic, thus offering an implicit contrast to some forms of Christianity as well as some strands within German idealism.

In his late poem "Princess Sabbath," Heine combined moral and sensuous elements in his description of Judaism:

Wo der Allerhöchste gleichfalls	On the very spot where likewise
All die guten Glaubenslehren	God revealed his moral doctrines
Und die heil'gen zehn Gebote	And the holy Ten Commandments
Wetterleuchtend offenbarte.	In the midst of flames and lightning.
Schalet ist des wahren Gottes	Schalet is God's bread of rapture,
Koscheres Ambrosia,	It's the kosher-type ambrosia
Wonnebrod des Paradieses,	That is catered straight from Heaven;
Und mit solcher Kost verglichen	And compared with such a morsel
Ist nur eitel Teufelsdreck	The ambrosia of the pagan
Das Ambrosia der falschen	Pseudogods of ancient Hellas,
Heidengötter Griechenlands,	Who were devils in disguise, is
Die verkappte Teufel waren.[55]	Is just a pile of devil's dreck.[54]

Heine depicts Mount Sinai as the birthplace not only of moral and political liberation but of the sensuous, too. By calling the Sabbath meal "Schalet, " a kosher type of ambrosia, he clearly sets out to combine the sensuous with the ethically refined. According to the late Heine, God did not reveal to Moses the tables of the Ten Commandments to the detriment of sensuous life. Rather, ethical refinement goes hand in hand with the joys of this life. Thus, Heine attributes to Judaism an "ability to accommodate both moral restraint and sensual pleasure."[56] In doing so, he revises a counterhistorical opposition between the Hellenic, on one hand, and the Jewish-Christian, on the other. Although he now embeds the Jewish within a more "worldly" setting than he did in his early work, he nonetheless does not conceptually differentiate it from both ascetic elements in Christianity and their pseudotheological revisions in German transcendental philosophy. As we shall see, this is precisely what Freud does in his version of "another Enlightenment" (see chapter 9).

5   POLITICAL ANTI-SEMITISM AND ITS GERMAN JEWISH RESPONSES AT THE END OF THE NINETEENTH CENTURY: HEINRICH GRAETZ AND OTTO WEININGER

Nothing more distorted, more damaging, more dishonest has ever anywhere been written than that which has been written on the religion of Israel.

— LEOPOLD ZUNZ, ON RABBINIC LITERATURE

Heine's vacillation between counterhistory and counternarrative was bound up with the sociopolitical pressures of his time. During the nineteenth century German Jews were increasingly forced to renounce their Jewishness. Heine's conversion to Protestantism was a case in point. The first part of this chapter examines the anti-Semitism with which Heinrich Graetz's counternarrative of a German Jewish identity was met in German society of this period. This chapter closes with an analysis of Otto Weininger's internalization of German idealism's prejudicial discourse about Jews and Judaism.

Between 1879 and 1880, the renowned historian Heinrich von Treitschke published a number of articles in a prestigious academic journal. In one of his papers in the *Prussian Yearbooks (Preussische Jahrbücher)* he voiced his discomfort with "a dangerous spirit of arrogance" that had allegedly "arisen in Jewish circles."[1] He referred his readers, in particular, to Heinrich Graetz's *History of the Jews:* "What a fanatical fury," he wrote, "against the 'arch enemy' Christianity, what deadly hatred of the purest and most powerful exponents of German character, from Luther to Goethe and Fichte!"[2] Treitschke continued by constructing a binary opposition between German idealism and Jewish materialism, an opposition with which we are familiar in the writings of Kant, Hegel, Feuerbach, Schopenhauer, and Wagner.

Following Wagner's anti-Semitic anticapitalism, Treitschke reinforced this contrast with a distinction between labor and capital. Work for work's sake seems to represent German idealism. Treitschke did not understand that "concrete labor itself incorporates and is materially formed by capitalist social relations."[3] Rather than recognizing that labor creates use-value, whose value in turn the value-measurement "money" or "capital" determines,

Treitschke contrasted "contemptible materialism" with the alleged "joy the German [feels] in his work."[4]

As we shall see in chapter 6, Treitschke's anti-Semitic articles of 1879 and 1880 had a crucial impact on Hermann Cohen's critical engagement with German idealist philosophy. Why, however, did Treitschke allude to Graetz's *History of the Jews* in order to have a contemporary point of reference for his opposition between German idealism and Jewish realism? Treitschke took particular exception to Graetz's criticism of "the purest and most powerful exponents of German character, from Luther to Goethe and Fichte!" In volume eleven of his *History of the Jews* (1868), Graetz indeed took issue with the most noteworthy exponents of German high culture. At the same time, he formulated a counterhistory in which he traced almost all progressive elements in modern German culture to their Jewish origins.

To be sure, Graetz, as a historian, was not very interested in a positivist account of historical events. Rather, he searched for the main idea that motivated the Jews throughout history. Does this interest in the conceptual essence behind past events indicate that he was an idealist? This characterization of his work certainly holds true. But his idealism differed in striking ways from that formulated by the major exponents of German idealism (Kant, Hegel, Fichte, and so on). Indeed, as Ismar Schorsch has pointed out, in "his adamant refusal to impose a rigid developmental scheme on the totality of Jewish history, Graetz heeded Humboldt's astute caveat against a [Kantian and Hegelian] teleological approach to the study of history."[5] Instead of following a Hegelian philosophy of history, Graetz adopted Humboldt's non-evolutionist scheme. This is all the more significant in that Wilhelm von Humboldt was quite an exceptional figure in the German philosophical scene of the early nineteenth century. For, in contrast to Kant, Hegel, and most of their followers, he did not argue that the political emancipation of the Jews depended on the dissolution of Judaism. Indeed, Treitschke's three anti-Semitic articles of 1879 and 1880 were written in order to remind German Jews of the quid pro quo that seemed to precondition Jewish civic equality: The Jews could only become full citizens of the newly founded German state on the condition that they cease being Jews. This is the main reason why Treitschke zeroed in on Graetz's *History of the Jews* as a prime example of the refusal to abandon a Jewish identity. Indeed, Graetz did more than formulate a counterhistory. To be sure, Treitschke took offense, too, at Graetz's counterhistorical account, in which German cultural achievements were traced back to Jewish sources.

More important, however, Graetz shifted the emphasis from apology to accusation, vis-à-vis German Jewish responses to the German majority culture. This can clearly be seen in his representation of Moses Mendelssohn's work. According to Graetz, with Mendelssohn modern Jewish intellectual history ceased to assume an apologetic character: "Instead of defending himself he [Mendelssohn] had come forward as an accuser, and in a manner at once gentle and forcible he laid bare the hateful ulcers of the church and state constitution."[6] Rather than calling Mendelssohn a Jewish Luther (Heine), Graetz characterized him as witty and subtle critic of the German majority culture. To this extent Graetz embedded his counterhistory in a counternarrative. He did so, first of all, by pointing to the prejudicial content within the German idealist narrative. It was this move that angered Treitschke most. Instead of submerging the main elements of Jewish heritage within German idealism, Graetz underscored the discriminatory content of idealism's supposedly all-inclusive notion of reason, which precluded such submergence. It is this accusatory move that enabled him to formulate a counternarrative. In it, with reference to Jewish history, he gave a version of idealism that offered an alternative to that formulated by German idealists. Accordingly, the idea that Graetz saw behind the unfolding of Jewish civilization is not what the German idealists understood by the term *idealist*. Related to this reconceptualization is his notion of what it means to act rationally, a notion that differs from Kant's version of the Enlightenment.

This transformation of a counterhistory into a counternarrative came most clearly to the fore at the moment when Graetz took up Hegel's and Heine's opposition between the Jewish and the Hellenic. Graetz maintained that modern civilization's cultural achievements had to be traced back to two ancient cultures: Jerusalem and Athens. How can we account for the fact that modern German culture discriminates against one and lavishes exuberant praises on the other? Graetz explained this discrepancy with reference to the presence of an ongoing and vital Jewish culture in contemporary Germany. Rather than being praised for their cultural achievements, the Jews are discriminated against precisely because they, unlike the ancient Hellenes, continue to exist.

As a result of their continued existence, the Jews are perceived to be a threat: "Jaundiced malignity and hatred are silent at the grave of the illustrious man; his merits as enumerated there are, in fact, as a rule overrated. . . . Just because of their continued existence, the merits and moral attainments of the Hebrews are not generally acknowledged."[7] Graetz then evaluated what has been devalued by the majority culture in which he lived. Instead of posing a threat, the continued existence of the Hebrews proves their vitality and thus their intellectual and spiritual importance. He criticized "deep thinkers" who "do not carefully consider how it came to pass that one nation died out notwithstanding its dominant master minds and its rich talents, while the other nation, so often near unto death, still continues to exist in the world of man, and has even succeeded in regaining its pristine youthfulness."[8] In a further counternarrative move, Graetz cast Hellenism—with which idealist German culture so often identified—in the pathological mold that has predominantly been reserved for Jewishness. He indeed maintained that the Hellenes "lost their mental health"[9] and as a result died out.

Although Graetz took issue with the anti-Semitic notion of an ill Jewish body, he did not attempt to adapt the Jewish cultural heritage to the secularized Christian agenda of German idealist philosophy. On the contrary, in a counternarrative move, he argued that German idealists gave an accurate assessment of Judaism when they depicted it in worldly terms: "So little is thought of what lies within and beyond the grave, that the Israelites have been reproached with having indulged in the enjoyments of life. And this is true."[10] Rather than giving an apologetic account of Jewishness, Graetz agreed with the pseudotheological assessment of Judaism, as formulated by Kant, Hegel, and some of their intellectual heirs. However, he reversed the conceptual matrix that formed this idealist pseudotheology. By stating that the Jews are worldly, he consented to the substance of the accusations leveled against Judaism by some German idealist thinkers. The Jews are indeed free of any "monkish asceticism,"[11] but this does not turn them into superstitious and irrational materialists. On the contrary, in Graetz's view, the worldliness of the Jews represents "a wandering revelation."[12] They are thus carriers of "the secret of life."[13] To this extent, a heteronomous orientation to the "goods of this world" (Kant) does not necessarily bespeak intellectual and spiritual corruption. It may well indicate the intellectual and social validity of Jewish history as it unfolds from ancient Israel to the present day.

Indeed, Graetz implicitly referred to Kant's denigratory assessment of Judaism as a religion without religion when he wrote that "Judaism, in the strict sense of the word, is not even a religion . . . but rather a constitution for a body politic."[14] Whereas Kant argued that Jewish messianism exemplifies a will to power over "worldly goods," Graetz argued that in Judaism a spiritual idea refines everyday political activities:

> On the other hand, these material and social purposes are permeated by metaphysical ideas, formed and interwoven with religious dogmas. . . . Knowledge of God and social welfare, religious truth and political theory form the two components of Judaism which are destined to flow through history thoroughly mixed. The dogmatic and the social or, to put it another way, the religious and the political, constitute the twin axes around which Jewish life revolves.[15]

This union between materialism and spiritualism reversed a Kantian radical divide between the realms of nature and freedom. According to Graetz, spirit has guided matter during the course of Jewish history. This mutual interaction between the dogmatic and the social became gradually severed with the destruction of ancient Israel. Although Graetz appreciated the achievements of Diaspora Judaism, he, unlike Mendelssohn, held out hope for a rejuvenated Jewish state. His historical work should in a sense establish a bridge between ancient Israel and a future Jewish state. By writing the *History of the*

Jews, Graetz "was determined to recreate the historical memory of his Jew-ish readers, to enable Jews to repossess a past from which acculturation had detached them."[16] With this re-creation, Graetz did not so much write a counterhistory as establish a counternarrative in which Judaism spiritually embodies the social contours of "another Enlightenment." With Gilles De-leuze and Felix Guattari's anti-Oedipus, so to speak, he said to Treitschke and his followers "No, I am not of your kind, I am the outsider and the deterrito-rialized."[17] To this extent, Graetz, in contrast to Heine and Geiger, estab-lished difference rather than congruency.

His revision of Jewish history had a much more radical perspective than Theodor Herzl's vision of a Jewish state. Herzl mainly constructed a counter-history, whereas Greatz advanced a counternarrative. A counterhistorical ac-count reverses the way in which a given majority culture depicts the history of minorities. Thus Herzl argued that the Jews are as capable of nationalist aspi-rations as their Gentile compatriots are. The only difference pertains to the fact that latter already have a nation-state, whereas the former still have to construct one. A counternarrative account, however, establishes difference not so much along temporal but rather along conceptual lines. Instead of im-itating modern Western nations, a future Jewish state, said Graetz, would in-troduce a different type of nationhood.

By saying that the Jewish question is neither a social, nor a religious, but a national issue,[18] Herzl ironically reinforced Jewish acculturation. The Jews did not differ from the modern Christian world in their social or religious identity. Rather, as Herzl argued, their difference resided in a lack, namely, the lack of statehood. The future Jewish state should be proof positive that the Jews are just like any other European nation. No wonder Herzl laid emphasis on a masculine military identity.[19] To be sure, Herzl did not want to "sacrifice our beloved customs."[20] However, he did not develop a rationale that would explain why they are worth preserving, in spite of the disrepute into which they had fallen throughout the centuries. This is exactly what Graetz did when, contra Kant and the mainstream of German idealism, he established an immanent ideal of the sensuous.[21] It is this interchange between the religious and the political, between spirit and matter, by which, in Graetz's view, Jew-ish history differs from the "monkish asceticism" that characterizes Christian Europe and its "enlightened" secularizations.

As mentioned at the opening of this chapter, Graetz's counternarrative move caused a stir in German intellectual circles. Indeed, Treitschke's anti-Semitic response to the *History of the Jew* contributed to making racism so-cially and intellectually acceptable in fin de siècle Germany. As Eric Voeglin put it, "the anti-Semitic movement would hardly have been capable of its de-cisive contribution to the formation of the community [of the German people] if anti-Semitism had not at that time become 'socially acceptable' thanks to the intervention of a scholar of Treitschke's caliber."[22] Indeed, writing when anti-

Semitism was becoming gradually institutionalized (1933), Voeglin attempted to pinpoint the beginning of pseudoscientific anti-Semitism in Treitschke's three articles on Jews and Jewishness: "Treitschke's public position gave this experience [of anti-Semitism] scientific legitimacy, in the eyes of wide sections of the population, particularly in academic circles. Through Treitschke this experience gained that tone of absoluteness, and legitimacy that is conferred in this time of the decline of Christian truth by 'scientific truth.'"[23]

Although it is true that, at the end of the nineteenth century, anti-Semitic stereotypes became—by reference to science and scholarship—seemingly objectified, anti-Semitism itself remained firmly embedded in a pseudotheological discourse. In this way, many apparently nonscientific texts about Jewish immutability had scientific pretensions, while many supposedly scientific works by anti-Semites pretended to capture the essence of Jewishness in Judaism. Accordingly, Houston Stewart Chamberlain, the Kantian and Wagnerian pseudoscientific anti-Semite, zeroed in on Jewish law as quasi-scientific proof for the immutable depravity of the Jewish people.[24] In his infamous book *The Foundations of the Nineteenth Century*, he in fact equated both biblical and talmudic law with a "law of blood." He first posited immutability in the "alien law,"[25] to which the Jews are "indissolubly bound,"[26] only to unmask the entire Jewish cultural heritage as the cornerstone for the modern notion of race. In a mocking manner, he praised Judaism as follows: "The Jews deserve our admiration, for they have reacted with absolute consistency according to the logic and truth of their own individuality, and never for a moment have they allowed themselves to forget the sacredness of physical laws because of foolish humanitarian day-dreams which they shared only when such a policy was to their advantage. Consider with what mastery they use the law of blood to extend their power."[27] In this way, Chamberlain held Judaism responsible for having given birth to his own version of pseudoscientific anti-Semitism! The racist distances himself from the "dirty" biology of blood and attributes it exclusively to the victims of his own blood-and-soil ideology. In this strange commixture of pseudotheology and pseudoscience, Jewish immutability first results from religious and social law. The latter, in turn, coincides with the "scientific" objectivity of blood laws. Despite its biological pretensions, this racist discourse nevertheless tries to slip into the clothes of idealist language by projecting its own materialism on the "religion of the Jews." As a result, it turns out to be not a religion but a science of blood.

At the end of the nineteenth century German anti-Semites such as Treitschke and Chamberlain framed their discourse around a divide between materialism and idealism. Countering this radical divide between spirit and matter, Graetz's image of Jewishness opened up vistas to a coexistence of the spiritual with the material, which it preserves and refines. Politics does not need to be a blind struggle for power. It can also serve to manifest the social materiality of intellectual values. As we shall see in chapter 8, Rosenzweig attempted to give a spiritual account of bodily existence that was similar to Graetz's evaluation of Judaism's messianic and political dimensions. Rather than signifying matter without spirit, blood symbolizes God's creation and must therefore not be endangered by political bloodshed. Like Graetz, Rosenzweig saw in Judaism a spiritual sanctification of material existence.

Nevertheless, Graetz's version of an immanent ideal, of the sensuous, did not find a strong public reception. This comes clearly to the fore if one compares the limited audience of his *History of the Jews* with the best-seller status of Otto Weininger's anti-Semitic and "idealist" book *Sex and Character*. I will therefore briefly discuss a German Jewish response that was neither counterhistorical nor a counternarrative. Indeed, Weininger seems to have internalized German idealism's prejudicial depiction of Judaism. He in fact builds his misogynist and racist discourse around a cluster of Kantian ideas. Significantly, his *Sex and Character* combines pseudoscientific with pseudotheological discourse in quite a striking manner. Accordingly, Weininger blends "biomedical theories with Kantian ethics to formulate a metaphysical approach to psychology, social reform, and cultural politics."[28]

Chamberlain's *The Foundations of the Nineteenth Century*, not surprisingly, shaped Weininger's thought in his most formative period.[29] These writers had at least two intellectual affiliations in common: both combined Kantianism with a pseudoreligious worship of Wagner's operas and his theoretical writings. Weininger, for one, accentuated an anti-Semitic divide between Aryan idealism and Jewish materialism when he explicitly placed the Judaic under the typological rubric of the feminine. The feminine, in turn, represents "matter" per se. According to Weininger, woman " does not wish to be treated as an active agent; she wants to remain always and throughout—that is just her womanhood—purely passive, to feel herself under another's will."[30] This dependence on another's will, however, describes one aspect of what Kant understood by heteronomy. Another crucial ingredient of the heteronomous consists in the self's ability to be directed by his or her inclinations to depend on the outside world. By means of his radical divide between the spheres of nature and freedom, Kant in fact established an idealist anthropology in which human achievements always involve the overcoming of a dependence on the material world. Then Weininger posited women as "matter." In this equation woman of course becomes a thing; she turns into an object and thus resembles the essence of heteronomy. Accordingly, matter indicates the lack of individuality: "Matter, which in itself is absolutely unindividualised and so can assume any form, of itself has no definite and lasting qualities, and has as little essence as mere perception."[31] It is this malleability that Weininger sees in both the Jew and the woman.

Thus Weininger's writing concerning Jews and women seems to embed

Kant's pseudotheology in a pseudoscientific setting. What differentiates Jew from Aryan and woman from man quasi-biologically is Kant's autonomy-heteronomy divide. A recent study locates in Kant an intellectual source for Weininger's misogyny.[32] But Kant had already combined the misogynistic with the anti-Semitic. As we saw in chapter 1, Kant primarily stigmatized the Jewish as an embodiment of heteronomy. Indeed, Weininger followed this Kantian equation when he argued that Jews are even more heteronomous than women. He first feminized Judaism by writing that it is "saturated with femininity."[33] Indeed, a lack of autonomy defines the mind-set of both women and Jews: "Jews, then, do not live as free, self-governing individuals, choosing between virtue and vice in Aryan fashion."[34] To this extent, only the Aryan man seems to be a rational creature, in the Kantian sense of the term.

Although Weininger associated both the feminine and the Jewish with heteronomy, he demonized the latter more than the former. To be sure, in his view it "is the Jew and the woman who are the apostles of pairing to bring guilt on humanity."[35] Both are, therefore, embodiments of the sensuous, which, in Weininger's Kantian context, inevitably results in the incurrence of guilt. Noted that in the German original, Weininger used the colloquial term *kuppeln* (to match-make), rather than the high-minded *apostle,* employed in the standard English translation. Weininger nonetheless interpreted woman as, at least partly, a victim of the desires she arouses in man. As a result, man deals with her in a manner that violates Kant's ethical demand, to wit, one should never entertain another person as a means to an end. As Chandak Sengoopta has recently put it, "in Weininger's Kantian universe, it was always wrong to use individuals as means, no matter how noble the end: 'The sexual impulse negates the body, and the erotic impulse the mind of the female.'"[36] In contrast to his apparent empathy with women as victims of the desire they evoke in men's psyches, Weininger never referred to anti-Semitism, which clearly victimizes Jews for economic and other shortcomings, in society at large.

Indeed, he cited the pseudotheological image of an immutable tie between Jehovah and his people. We have seen how Feuerbach and Wagner employed this image in order to demonize the Jews as a threat to the Gentile world. In Weininger's psychotic view, women are "matter" to be formed primarily by men, whereas Jews are shaped primarily by the omnipotent Jehovah. Whereas Kant and Hegel interpreted Jewish obedience to Jehovah's laws as illusory desire for material happiness, Wagner and Feuerbach interpreted this heteronomous relationship as desire for world power. We are thus not far from the anti-Semitic scenario constructed in the fictitious *Protocols of the Elders of Zion,* which appeared around the time when *Sex and Character* was first published in 1903. Weininger wrote of the Jew's "submission to the powerful will of an exterior influence, with the reward of earthly well-being and the conquest of the world."[37] Here he clearly combined the Kantian and Hegelian denigratory assessment of Jewish religiosity as intrinsically materialist (seeking "earthly well-being") with the Wagnerian fear of Judaism as a demonic world power ("conquest of the world"). Materialism, and the associated threat of omnipotence, resulted from an immutable tie to Jehovah's will: "His relations with Jehovah, the abstract Deity, whom he slavishly fears, whose name he never dares to pronounce, characterise the Jew."[38] Enslavement to Jehovah seems to hold out the promise of "earthly happiness."

Why, however, should this tie be immutable? It seems to depend, after all, on a conscious decision to abandon free will in exchange for happiness and power. Did not Weininger characterize Jewishness as "a tendency of the mind?"[39] Rather than being immutable, the notion "tendency" seems to leave room for change. Even though Weininger gave pseudotheological anti-Semitism a (pseudo)scientific spin when he attempted to establish a congruency between the biology of the woman and the psychology of the Jew, he associated the Jewish with immutability when he cited the anti-Semitic image of the Jews as an immutable tie to Jehovah. For it is Jehovah's posited omnipotence that precludes any change of direction on the part of "his people."

Indeed, it was this pseudotheological notion of immutability that drove Weininger to suicide. After having converted to Protestantism, he despaired about the perceived immutability of his Jewishness and, as a result, killed himself in the house in which Beethoven had died.[40] The fact that Weininger committed suicide, and the way in which he dramatized this event, has indicated to many critics that he subscribed to a racist definition of Jewishness that posits an eternal Jewish character.[41] What has so far not been analyzed is the pseudotheological point of reference from which such racism emerges. I hope I have shown that, rather than grounding his notion of race in a pseudoscientific discourse about immutability, Weininger established a sense of an eternal Jewish character by tying the Jewish people to an omnipotent and inevitable deity that held them eternally in thrall with promises of earthly happiness and world domination. In doing so, he simply revamped the Jehovah fantasy with which we are already familiar from the writings of the German idealists.

In contrast to Graetz, who developed a counternarrative, and in contrast to Heine and Geiger, who deconstructed German idealism's pseudotheology with counterhistories, Weininger internalized a pseudotheological narrative advanced with increasingly violent implications by Kant, Hegel, Schopenhauer, Feuerbach, and Wagner. As has been pointed out by Barbara Hyams and Nancy A. Horrowitz, in "numerous anti-Semitic tracts and treatises, Weininger's thought was quoted out of context by Nazi ideologues, like their *völkisch* precursors, as one of many 'confessions' by Jews that they belonged to an inferior race."[42] The context, ignored by those who abused *Sex and Character* as proof of the validity of anti-Semitism, had largely to do with the fact that Weininger turned the hatred he found in his social and intellectual environment against himself. His writing concerning the immutable tie that binds the Jews to an omnipotent and uncanny Jehovah constituted an internalization of an abusive image that he found in some works of German idealism and in their romantic revisions. He thus internalized what he had read in Kant and Wagner and what, no doubt, by that time had already become (via Chamberlain and others) a popular notion.

This chapter has served as an introduction to the following chapters by explaining Graetz's historical writings as examples of counternarrative. As we will see, Cohen, Rosenzweig, Freud, and Benjamin developed similar counternarratives in their response to the prejudicial aspect of the German idealist account of what constitutes reason and thereby humanity. The discussion of Weininger's Jewish self-hatred, on the other hand, has shown how pervasive the pseudotheological notion of Jewish immutability had become in German culture at the end of the nineteenth century. The philosophical discourse of German idealism did indeed have an impact on social and intellectual history. For once, it informed academic culture, which, in turn, shaped various aspects of educational training in German-speaking countries. As we saw in chapter 3, Wagner's *Bayreuther Blätter* did their part in making pseudotheological stereotypes socially acceptable. Moreover, some academics, such as Carl Schmitt, reemployed the discriminatory account of Judaism that they found in Kant and Hegel for political ends. Thus Schmitt, in the context of his friend-enemy opposition, quoted Hegel's statement about the Jews as the most reprobate people and therefore the most worthy of rejection.[43] Taking up Wagner's proposal for the identification between rulers and the ruled,[44] Schmitt argued that the Jews are outside of the allegedly homogenous structure of *Volk* and thus must be excluded, if not killed. The stereotypical image of an immutable tie between Jehovah and his people thus seems to have informed the National Socialist opposition between the Jews and the *Volksgemeinschaft* (community of the people). The Jews, proclaimed anti-Semites at the end of the nineteenth and the beginning of the twentieth century, eternally belonged to the omnipotent and abstract entity "Jehovah." As a result, they were the enemy of the *Volk*. In the following chapters I will discuss how Cohen, Rosenzweig, Freud, and Benjamin questioned the presuppositions of this pseudotheological fantasy.

6 BETWEEN MENDELSSOHN AND KANT: HERMANN COHEN'S DUAL ACCOUNT OF REASON

The Lost Manuscript

In his introduction to Hermann Cohen's Jewish writings, Franz Rosenzweig presents an anecdote about a lost manuscript. He calls this little-known story a most "intimate personal affair" and narrates it not in the text but in a footnote, as if to hide it from the public by placing it on the margins of his essay. The anecdote offers clues as to how the anti-Semitic content of Kant's moral philosophy deeply hurt the neo-Kantian philosopher. Rosenzweig argues that the element of "Christian prejudice" *(Christliche Voreingenommenheit)* in German transcendental philosophy hit Cohen at his most "vulnerable point" *(empfindlichsten Punkt)*. He eventually voiced his suffering in a "short paper on whose posthumous publication he placed the highest value." Rosenzweig in fact emphasizes that Cohen did not want to see this "most intimate" document published during his lifetime. Thus we hear him say to Rosenzweig's mother in September 1917: "This shall once be published out of my unpublished works." The sheer presence of the paper had a somewhat healing effect: he is said to have spoken about both "its destined posthumous publication" and "the calming effect of it lying there" *(von seiner Beruhigtheit, daß das daläge)* in front of him.[1]

Rosenzweig abruptly ends this anecdote by stating that "unfortunately, the strange document" *(das merkwürdige Dokument)* seems to have been lost."[2] I have dwelled on this neglected story for several reasons. Most important, it sheds light on Cohen's critical engagement with Kantian moral philosophy, but its placement at the margins of a discussion concerning his Jewish writings also indicates the rather difficult issues involved in this critical engagement. Rosenzweig might well have marginalized this rather personal anecdote, which has so many pertinent public dimensions, out of piety for his intellectual mentor. As we shall see in chapter 7, Rosenzweig himself voiced his difficulties with rather dubious aspects of German idealism, much more outspokenly and publicly than Cohen. In *The Star of Redemption*'s opening pages, he called his mentor the first "idealist" to break with idealism.[3]

How may we account for Cohen's need to marginalize his sense of being hurt by the prejudicial dimension of Kant's transcendental philosophy? The historical context in which Cohen composed his philosophical texts helps clarify this point. As we saw in chapter 4, at a time when German Jews did not have any political rights, Mendelssohn avoided a confrontation with "Christian prejudice" on the "public battleground" *(öffentlichen Kampfplatz)*.[4] Jewish civic equality was granted de jure in a law established by the North German Federation on July 3, 1869, which states that "all remaining restrictions in civil and political rights based on the differences of religion are hereby abolished."[5] Nonetheless, "the practical implementation of civic equality remained a matter of dispute."[6] As a result, a gap opened between legal theory and political as well as social practice that widened owing to the increase in anti-Semitism after the stock market crash of 1872.

An intensification of Jewish acculturation coincided with the rise of anti-Semitism at the end of the nineteenth century. Now, the major strands of German Judaism (Reform and Neoorthodoxy) somewhat resembled German Protestantism.[7] That in the eyes of "Christian prejudice" the Jew remained an immutable other, incapable of both change and integration into German society at large, came clearly to the fore in the Berlin *Antisemitismusstreit* (see chapter 5). Ismar Schorsch has described the peculiar situation of German Jews during this period as follows: "To fight anti-Semitism at the end of the century inevitably required a public affirmation of Jewish identity. But such a display of Jewishness was precisely what the extended battle for equal rights had conditioned the Jews to fear and loathe."[8] Given that German transcendental philosophers preached a "euthanasia of Judaism" (Kant), such an affirmation of Jewish identity went hand in hand with a critique of disturbing aspects of Enlightenment thought, thus often provoking work on "another Enlightenment." Schorsch largely concentrates on Jewish organizations—such as the German-Israeli Association, the Association Against Anti-Semitism, and the Central Association of German Citizens of the Jewish Faith[9]—and thereby gives a compelling portrayal of sociohistorical circumstances that has important implications for an analysis of texts by various German Jewish writers at the end of the nineteenth and the beginning of the twentieth century.

Within this context, Cohen's philosophical texts played a crucial role. In them he draws attention to the deleterious effects of "philosophical anti-Semitism," not only in abstract but also in sociopolitical terms. Thus "Cohen warned that this academically supported charge of ethical inferiority allowed the racial anti-Semites an air of self-righteousness, lent their polemic a modicum of veracity, and hallowed their hatred as a healthy national impulse."[10] As we have seen, Kant, Hegel, Feuerbach, Schopenhauer, and Wagner cast such a notion of Jewish ethical inferiority into the mold of immutability, with direct reference to Judaism as "a religion without religion" whose very essence consists in the fantasized scenario of a permanent union between "Jehovah, the principle of power," and his people.

Scholarly examinations of anti-Semitism during this period have largely stressed the pseudoscientific context of this racist discourse. This movement from the supposedly more benign "religious bias" of the eighteenth century to the outspokenly essentialist discourse of 1860 has remained a "dark riddle." We might learn to see the continuities between the pseudotheological discourse and its pseudoscientific variant by attending to the responses to modern anti-Semitism in the work of German Jewish intellectuals. In this context, Cohen's and Rosenzweig's concern for the pseudotheological components within racist anti-Semitism sheds light on these so far unthematized continuities. As we will see in chapter 7, Rosenzweig emphasized this theme. In contrast, Cohen toned down the force of his criticism of some aspects of Kantian moral philosophy, thus confirming the impression, occasioned by the anecdote narrated above, of the marginalized and private location of such a critical response in the larger corpus of his writings.

In what follows I discuss Cohen's evaluation of Jewish law and his concomitant rejection of the "myth of guilt," which he associated with Kant's moral philosophy. The outspoken criticism of German idealism with which Rosenzweig's *Star of Redemption* opens has an as-yet unexamined precursor in Cohen's *Religion of Reason,* which gives a dual account of the rational that is at once Kantian,[11] emphasizing reason's autonomy with respect to the empirical and the sensuous, and Mendelssohnian, in that he does not depict Jewish law as Kant's freedom from the material world but rather perceives it as opening up a way toward mediation between the spiritual and the bodily.

Thus we have two conflicting versions of the Enlightenment within Cohen's conception of reason;[12] only one (the Kantian, or rather neo-Kantian) has been attended to in scholarly investigations.[13] In his late works Cohen indeed related earthly life to the eternal, but what has not been sufficiently discussed, and what warrants attention, is that he developed his famous concept of a correlation between the empirical and the spiritual while advancing a critique of Kant's notion of autonomy as freedom from any reliance on experience within empirical reality. I first analyze Cohen's interpretation of Jewish law, which revitalizes Mendelssohn's understanding of Enlightenment rationality as a heteronomous relation to both the empirical and the spiritual worlds. Then I examine how this understanding of rabbinic Judaism shaped his notion of correlation and how, by reference to a Mendelssohnian Enlightenment, he demythologized the Kantian myth of radical evil.

Cohen and the "Myth of Guilt"

The very title *Religion of Reason Out of the Sources of Judaism* has an as-yet unnoticed ironic relation to Kant's rational theology. As discussed in chapter 1, according to Kant, the Jewish exemplified the irrational, the superstitious, and therefore the heteronomous. Critics have of course noticed that the title of Cohen's book refers back to Kant's *Religion Within the Boundaries of Mere Reason.*[14] But no one has examined the ways in which Cohen set out to give an account of Judaism that questions Kant's prejudicial equation of Jewishness and superstition. In his posthumously published last book Cohen took issue with Kant's demeaning depiction of the Jewish. Significantly, he posited an alleged personal attack by Kant on Mendelssohn's character and work, for which I could not find any textual evidence,[15] and treated this confrontation as metonymic for the Kantian assault on the imagined ethical inferiority of Jewish law. In doing so, Cohen drew attention to the harm done to individual Jews by a philosophical discourse that generalizes about the "irrationality" of Judaism.

As we saw in chapter 1, Kant established the stereotype of the immutable tie between Jehovah and his people with direct reference to Jewish law, which allegedly made the Jews "hostile to all other peoples."[16] Although Cohen criticized Mendelssohn for "limiting" Judaism "to a religion of law,"[17] he defended him and his philosophy against the Kantian attack as follows: "Kant was therefore wrong with regard to Mendelssohn's point of view when he reproached him for 'lacking friendliness for man.' This view is only possible if one considers it self-evident and beyond doubt that the Jewish laws can be experienced only as a heavy yoke."[18] Cohen did not give a reference to this apparent quotation from Kant. In this context, however, it does not really matter whether Cohen "invented" it. Instead, I would like to draw attention to his defense of both Mendelssohn and what the German Jewish Enlightenment philosopher apparently stood for, namely, the ethical and rational validity of Judaism. Even though Cohen criticized the Mendelssohnian reduction of the Judaic to Jewish law, he defended the broad outline of Mendelssohn's *Haskala* vis-à-vis the attacks leveled against it by Kant's Enlightenment philosophy.

The appraisal of Jewish law in *Religion of Reason* in fact develops, and deepens, Mendelssohn's Jewish philosophy (as discussed in chapter 4). Crucially, Cohen implicitly critiqued German idealism's fantasy as to the immutable tie between Jehovah and the Jewish people when he gave an account of Jewish law's rationality: "Isolation is not the unique end of the law, but rather the idealization of all earthly activity by the divine. Worship is not limited to the synagogue; the law fulfills and permeates the whole of life with it. The Jew is known for his outward appearance, but insufficiently for the continuing effect of the law on his inner life and for the hereditary foundations of the law."[19] "Outward appearance" refers to physiognomic stereotyping in the literature of pseudoscientific anti-Semitism but, more important, Cohen positions this reference within a discussion of a Kantian pseudotheological discourse, which reduces the religion of the Jews to the immutable essence of power.

Whereas German idealist writers perceived in Jewish law an instrumental device that guaranteed possession of worldly goods, Cohen, following Mendelssohn, differentiated it from "outward appearance" so as to give a theological appraisal that attempted to correct a pseudotheological reduction of Judaism to the outward sphere of materialist power. Rather than resulting in a nonrational dependence on the goods of this world, Jewish law correlates the bodily with the spiritual, enabling a mediation between the intellectual and spiritual, on one hand, and the performative, on the other: "For this is the meaning of the law: to establish and to maintain the connection between knowledge and action, and therefore also between knowledge as religion and action as moral deed."[20] Here Cohen clearly deepened and developed two major points advanced in Mendelssohn's version of a Jewish Enlightenment. Although the term *knowledge (Erkenntnis)* has Kantian overtones, it ultimately refers back to the Mendelssohnian concept of *Lehre* (teaching, doctrine), precisely because it eventually (in the second part of the sentence) coincides with religion. In contrast to Kant's rational theology and moral philosophy, here religion, rather than an autonomous self-referential rationality, preconditions moral action. More important, reason's dependence on particular laws concerning particular empirical objects has huge implications for an understanding of the Mendelssohnian perspective on the rational that Cohen adopted in his discussion of Jewish law. As we saw in chapter 1, Kant's notion of the irrational as the heteronomous forecloses any meaningful relation between human subjectivity and an external world that has not been reshaped by the will of autonomous reason. Kant attacked Jewish law for allegedly relying on the factual, given realm of material existence: he labeled Judaism "superstitious," and he defined superstition along the lines of Mendelssohn's perspective on Jewish law, namely, as a way of mediating between the human and the external world. In following Mendelssohn's appraisal of Jewish law, Cohen also deviated from a Kantian view of reason that defined heteronomy as an affectionate reliance on the materially given.

Cohen's critique of Kantian autonomy went back to the year 1880, when he "first took a public stance in defense of Judaism."[21] As discussed in the preceding chapter, the respected "liberal" historian Heinrich von Treitschke, in articles dating from 1879 and 1880, demanded the complete dissolution of Jewishness into German "national" culture. In particular, he attacked Heinrich Graetz's counterhistorical and counternarrative account of a rational idea that unfolds in Jewish history. In this context, it is worth mentioning that Graetz was one of Cohen's mentors at Breslau's Jüdisch Theologisches Seminar.[22] By 1906, Cohen had in fact already developed a theory of moral motivations that countered the line of argument by means of which Kant attempted to explain autonomous law's ethico-political necessity. As Michael Zank has recently pointed out, a Kantian "rejection of libido as lawgiver is mitigated, . . . in that Cohen wished to preserve and justify sensuality to the degree that it follows and boosts reason as the moving principle of the will."[23] This is exactly what Cohen did when, in his *Ethics of the Pure Will* (1907), he warned that the "upswing [*Aufschwung*] of the will must not forgo [*verlustig gehen*] the swing [*Schwung*] which it receives from the emotions and which the emotions alone can impart."[24] He thus puns on the verb *verlustig gehen*, which literally means "to lose one's inclinations" (that is, to lose one's *Lust*) and thereby underlines, in a witty way, the importance he attributed to the emotive side of the motivations that help instigate moral actions.

Nonetheless, at other points in his work, Cohen clearly devalorized the emotional facet of human intersubjectivity. Although it is true that one aspect of Cohen's late work clearly accounts for reason as the anti-sensuous and nonempirical, his understanding of rationality has dual ramifications that so far have not been accounted for in the critical literature. In *Religion of Reason*'s first part (mainly in the discussion of monotheism) Cohen clearly "expels" *(abgewiesen)* sensuality from the sphere of religion,[25] and yet the end of the book keeps the promises announced in its title: it gives an account of Judaism's rationality with direct reference to the "worldly," which does not need to be overcome by autonomous reason.

How did Cohen account for the rational, as well as the religious, validity of Judaism, thus inverting Kant's explanation of the irrational and the superstitious? As we saw in chapter 1, Kant conflated the Jewish with the worldly. Significantly, Cohen's appreciation of Judaism's rationality went hand in hand with his trust in what he considered the underlying benevolence of this world. Nathan Rotenstreich has ingeniously analyzed the differences between Kant's notion of radical evil and Cohen's understanding of the innate benignity of the worldly: "Evil is not present in the world because God created the world. . . . There seems to be a difference between the notion: Religion within the *limits* of Reason alone, and the notion of the Religion *of* Reason. The first is only within the scope of reason, the second brings together religion and reason. . . . There is no evil in terms of created reason."[26] Cohen's radical optimism resulted from describing this world in terms of its creation by God. Kant's theory of radical evil, on the other hand, relied on the Christian doctrine of original sin. Indeed, in *Religion Within the Boundaries of Mere Reason*, he made it clear that "the Fall," as well as the concomitant division of the universe into heaven and hell, only appertains to the Christian portion of the Bible.[27] This division between good and evil redraws the opposition between autonomy and heteronomy. The Fall "has the force of something virtually 'innate'"[28] to human nature as long as we choose to fol-low our inclinations toward "the goods of this world." Kant employed the Pauline image of the old and the new Adam in order to emphasize reason's ca-pacity in regard to the creation of an utterly changed humanity that has over-come its worldly—and therefore evil—foundations. Thus, if we choose to remain in the state of nature, we confine our existence to the condition of per-petual guilt.

Now, Cohen maintained that the irrational or mythical "has one of its deepest roots in the concept of guilt."[29] We will see how Benjamin—who ex-plicitly referred to Cohen and Rosenzweig in his book about German baroque tragedy—as well as Freud marked Judaism off from a pagan or Christian conflation of guilt with the state of nature that both saw as opera-tive in Kant's moral philosophy. Note that Cohen took issue with "a mistake of pessimism," as well as with "the common view of the radical evil in men which Kant, to be sure, idealized both correctly and profoundly."[30] Despite its polite and qualifying words ("correctly and profoundly"), this passage as-sociates Kantian moral philosophy with the irrational myth of guilt against which *Religion of Reason* expounds Judaism's rationality. Whereas Cohen argued for God's indemnifying capacities ("God makes innocent"),[31] Kant defined radical evil in close relation to a divide between God, qua the rational, and humanity, qua the natural, that can only be bridged by means of reason's independence from any external, that is to say, worldly and therefore corrupt orientations.

According to Kant, the divide between evil and good issues from our free-dom of choice: "the will's capacity or incapacity arising from its natural propensity to adopt or not to adopt the moral law in its maxims can be called *the good or the evil heart*."[32] Thus the will's failure to cling to the categorical imperative, disregarding any particular circumstance in the empirical world, constitutes a radically immoral act. The English translation leaves out a cru-cial word that Kant attributed to this incapacity of the mind to follow an ab-stract and universal law: "arbitrariness" *(Willkür)* denotes the influence of empirical and therefore contingent (arbitrary) motivations. The aribtrariness of the external world thus moves the human heart in the direction of wicked-ness.

Cohen refuted this Kantian account of an evil will that makes for an evil heart, while arguing against any claim that would use the book of Genesis as biblical backup for the concept of original sin: "This idea, which would solve our question [concerning the origin of evil] by attributing the origin of evil to the predisposition to evil of the human heart, of the human will, cannot be supported by the passages in Genesis. Rather, man has the holy spirit in his heart."[33] This passage refers to two key phrases from Kant's discussion re-garding the roots of radical evil: the human will and the human heart. Now, as we have seen, Kant made neither the will nor the heart ultimately responsible for corrupt deeds. Rather, their "evil" resides in being swayed by "arbitrariness," that is, by the contingency of the external world. Cohen, however, disputed the claim that the human mind can willfully be directed to evil by worldly influences, since both the world and humanity are products of God and are thus correlated to the "holy spirit."

Indeed, *Religion of Reason* closes with an assessment of Judaism's correlation between this world and eternity, thus undermining the Kantian conflation of an inclination to depend on "the goods of this world" and radical evil. Cohen examines this correlation with a view to "Jewish linguistic consciousness" *(jüdische Sprachbewußtsein):* "It is significant for the Hebrew linguistic consciousness that the Hebrew word for world, *olam,* at the same time means eternity: 'He hath set the world [*olam*] in their heart' (Eccl. 3:11). 'The world' also means eternity, so that one could translate this sentence to mean that God set eternity into man's heart."[34] This account of both religion and reason sharply contrasts with Kant's notion of autonomy as freedom from an orientation toward the goods of this world, which the Fall supposedly corrupted. Rather than removing humanity from the world, in Cohen's account, God implants the world as an image of the eternal into the human heart. This strong correlation between the worldly and the eternal does not associate an orientation toward the goods of this world ("heteronomy") with moral corruption.

Rather, the philosophical assumption of a potentially evil heart initiates the perpetration of evil deeds. Those who feel guilty might indeed enact their feeling of guilt, like John Valentine in Alfred Hitchcock's *Spellbound,* who sets out to kill simply because he (wrongly) assumes that he has killed in the past. This is exactly what Cohen meant when he wrote: *"guilt cannot be an offence,* it cannot be a hindrance to the liberation from sin."[35] The English translation is rather misleading, for the German original is roughly as follows: *"guilt must not [darf nicht] get something going [zum Anstoß werden];* it must not become an obstacle to the liberation from it [*nicht zum Hindernis der Befreiung von ihr werden*]." But this is what, in Cohen's view, the myth of guilt does: it assumes an evil will and the assumption indeed becomes a reality; it becomes an *Anstoß,* that is to say, an offense to moral consciousness as well as an initiator of evil actions.

Instead of presupposing a potentially corrupt heart, Cohen argued for the ability to learn from mistakes that the moral actor perpetrated in the external world. Guilt opens the door for a turning back (*t'shuvah,* "turning around")[36] from the iniquitous, rather than serving as provocation for a repetition compulsion, in which one mistake—be it in a fantasized or in the real past—presents a justification for its reenactment in the present and the future. Refuting the myth of an intrinsically evil character, Cohen again employed the crucial term *Anstoß* in the sense of both an initiator and a stumbling block so as to critique an idealization of guilt: "Guilt should not be a 'stumbling block.' Guilt can in no way establish the evil character of man. Rather it is the gateway to his perfection, to that higher elevation where his innocence can be recovered."[37] Cohen's linguistic playfulness, inevitably lost in translation, brings out the complexities involved in debunking the myth of humanity's radical evil, "which Kant, to be sure, idealized both correctly and profoundly." Guilt constitutes an offense *(Anstoß)* to an ethical sensibility. However, as offense, it can easily be idealized in terms of human essence and thus become a stumbling block *(Anstoß)* to moral improvement. In prohibiting a turning-back from evil, with reference to a supposedly innate evil will, the idealization of radical evil gives rise to the initiation *(Anstoß)* of evil deeds.

Kant revolutionized moral philosophy by introducing a radically noncontingent and universally valid categorical imperative so as to eradicate the corrupt and the immoral from the face of the earth. Thus, autonomy as freedom from the contingent and the empirical liberates this world from its imperfection, but this transposition of heaven onto earth inevitably proceeds according to both transcendental (immanent) and transcendent (otherworldly) rules. As we have seen, Kant blamed Jewishness for the impossibility of the body's (nature's) transformation into a utopian ethical commonwealth (the realm of "freedom").

In this chapter I have examined Cohen's polite inversion of idealism's prejudicial aspects. By correlating the empirical with the spiritual, Cohen warned against an idealist conflation of heaven and earth, for this conflation runs the risk of both excluding the given external world and of holding a minority responsible for the ultimate noncoincidence between entities that cannot be fully harmonized. The concept of correlation, after all, presupposes a separation between the elements that are correlated. As we shall see in the following two chapters, Rosenzweig gave an appraisal of Jewishness in precisely the language with which German idealism has depicted the Judaic as a "stumbling block" to the establishment of heaven on earth. The reappraisal of Mendelssohn's *Haskala,* over and against its Kantian denigration, set the path for this bold affirmation of an identity that had been blamed for the nonidentity between freedom and nature.

FRANZ ROSENZWEIG, OR THE BODY'S INDEPENDENCE FROM THE BODY POLITIC

Nationalism and Theology

In related but different ways, Cohen, Rosenzweig, Freud, and Benjamin reflected on the hegemony of idealist philosophy in German intellectual culture. This discourse helped politicize the anti-Semitism that saturated the public sphere in Germany by the end of the nineteenth century. Now "the defense of the national cause was a duty of political idealism."[1] Responding to this context, Rosenzweig's *The Star of Redemption* opens with an outspoken critique of German idealism's rejection of the body's independence from the body politic. Although he first referred to philosophy in general, and has often been said not to have distinguished between ancient Greek and modern German thought, in the introduction to *The Star* he did, indeed, mark Hegel and Kant as a break within Western metaphysics. On the battlefields of World War I, Rosenzweig emphasized, rather than trying to "escape any kind of fetters" *(irgendwelchen Fesseln entfliehen)*[2]—as philosophy sets out to convince us— "man . . . wants to remain, he wants to—live."[3] To be sure, he did not see any causal connection that would tie a philosophical dualism between immanence and transcendence—or, between belief and knowledge—to the carnage perpetrated in World War I. On the contrary, blood had been shed in order to increase a nation's economic and political influence. Behind this nationalist aggrandizement, however, Rosenzweig saw a pseudotheological conflation of the immanent with the transcendent. Instead of being aware of the gulf that lies between these two entities, nationalist politicians wanted to deify the immanent notions of nation and *Volk*.

Nationalism and German idealism both set out to realize the promises that traditional metaphysics and theology had circumscribed to the realm of belief. According to Rosenzweig, Western philosophy prior to German idealism allowed for a component that cannot be reduced to the same, since it is itself "other." It is the "unknown." It is belief. What distinguishes German idealism, as Rosenzweig understood it, from past philosophy is the bold move with which knowledge usurps the place of infinity. Within German idealism, the transcendent—instead of constituting a question of belief—is fully known, since it has formed a total unity with the immanent. It is this conflation of what has in past ages been a matter of belief with a total and absolute epistemology that provoked Rosenzweig to dedicate the first part of *The Star* to an insistence on separation between the epistemological (factuality or knowledge) and the speculative (belief). German transcendental philosophy had silenced the voice of the unknowable other by both turning matters of belief into matters of fact and (at the same time) undermining the concept of revelation: "One silenced the voice which claimed possession, in a revelation, of the source of divine knowledge originating beyond reason. Centuries of philosophical labors were devoted to this disputation between knowledge and belief; they reach their goal at the precise moment when the knowledge of the All reaches a conclusion in itself."[4] Rosenzweig perceived in Hegel's thought the "innermost interconnection" *(innerlichster Zusammenhang)*[5] between knowledge and belief in which philosophy fulfills "what was promised in revelation" *(Erfüllerin des in der Philosophie Verheißenen).*[6] A few pages after this discussion of an all-encompassing knowledge that implements the promises of religious beliefs immanently in the sphere of world history, Rosenzweig interpreted the Kantian *Weltanschauung* of German public culture in the context of what Levinas would analyze as totality: "And even in Kant's case the concept of the All again carried off the victory over the individual through his formulation of the law of morality as the universally valid fact."[7] In the German original Rosenzweig wrote not "even" but "especially" *(gerade bei Kant),* thus emphasizing the importance of Kant's reformulation of metaphysics and moral philosophy. He in fact traced Hegel's all-encompassing notion of knowledge back to Kantian moral and political thought. Thus, "Kant himself serves as godfather to Hegel's concept of universal history, not only with his political philosophy and his philosophy of history [*staats-und geschichtsphilosophischen Ansätzen*], but already with his ethical fundamentals [*ethischen Grundbegriffen*]."[8]

Indeed, Rosenzweig developed his notion of meta-ethics as an inversion of Kant's all-encompassing categorical imperative, with a view to allowing contingency, as an independent entity, into the sphere of ethics. As we saw in chapter 1, the categorical imperative works without any consideration for the specific context in which a moral actor finds himself or herself. Thus, the law has to be followed for law's sake, as commanded by a rationality that has freed itself from the imperfection of immanence (that is, contingency or arbitrariness). Inverting the autonomy of the categorical imperative, meta-ethics places law at the service of empirical and contingent humanity so that "the law [*das Gesetz*] is given to man, not man to the law."[9] Meta-ethics thus "refers to the independence of (created) man,"[10] but this independence does not bespeak human autonomy in the Kantian sense. Rosenzweig's "meta" instead denotes the independence of the body (the empirical) from the body politic (freedom from the empirical by means of ethics and politics).

This critique of an idealist transformation of the body into the body politic came clearly to fore when Rosenzweig took issue with the Kantian notion of autonomy. Autonomous law demands that the individual abandon any meaningful relation to the external world. It points to an entity without specific content. Indeed, "the requirement of autonomy requires man to will only in general, only altogether."[11] According to Rosenzweig, it is, however, "impossible to will 'something' and nevertheless only to will 'in general.'"[12] Kantian autonomy therefore does not apply to context-specific ways of acting. Instead, it demands the universal application of a supposedly universally valid categorical imperative. As the very term *imperative* indicates, it works by means of compulsion. As we shall see in chapter 9, Freud associated Kant's "modern" philosophy with the compulsion inherent in "primitive" taboo behavior. In a related manner, Rosenzweig turned the tables on Kant by arguing that the categorical imperative institutes a modern Western version of Islam. He defined the Islamic using the same terms with which Kant described Jewishness. In an important essay, Paul Mendes-Flohr has analyzed "Rosenzweig's patent transfer of the charge of heteronomy to Islam."[13] But it has not been noticed that this projection of heteronomy onto Islam constitutes the first step toward a critique of Kant's notion of autonomy. Rosenzweig in fact developed a counternarrative, in which he deconstructed the conceptual opposition between the heteronomous and the autonomous. He did so by associating Kantian autonomy with the very heteronomy that he projected onto the Islamic:

> Thus the word act in Islam means the practice of obedience. . . . This straightforward, obedient piety is based on a free self-denial ever laboriously regained. And it finds an exact counterpart, strangely enough, in the secular piety of more recent times which freely confirms to universal law. The ethics of Kant and his followers, for instance, as well as the general consciousness, sought to evolve such a piety.[14]

That which Kant characterized as freedom, the "free self-denial ever laboriously regained" *(freien, mühsam immer neu gewonnenen Selbstverleugnung)*, Rosenzweig theorized as the enslaving principle of Kantian autonomy. Here he analyzed the pseudotheological structure behind Kant's moral philosophy. He in fact argued that such an ethics instantiates "the secular piety [*Welt-*

frömmigkeit] of more recent times," in which the worldly is seen to be able to abolish its contingency by means of strict obedience to all-embracing and therefore noncontingent general laws.

To this extent, an ethical (Kant's moral philosophy) or political (Hegel's philosophy of history) attempt to turn the contingent into the material for its own overcoming, in a world that has lost its worldliness, does not constitute the end of theology. Rosenzweig made this point clear in his discussion of idealist production, which (as we will see) he differentiated from God's creation. He spoke of the "monumental error of idealism," which "consisted in thinking that the All was really wholly contained in its 'generation' ['*Erzeugung*'] of the All."[15] Kant's freedom consists in this construction of an immanent world, which the autonomous human mind builds along the lines of a theological conception of the "otherworldly"—purged of any bodily and therefore contingent imperfection.

Yet idealist production requires the empirical as material with which to construct an otherworldly, that is to say, a noncontingent heaven on earth. In this context, Rosenzweig employed Marxist analysis of capitalist economics in order to describe the mystification at the heart of idealism's rationality. Idealism obfuscates the means of its production, that is to say, it hides the chaos of the particular that preconditions its idealist constructions: "But idealism does not cherish this allusion to an underlying chaos of the distinctive [*dunkles Chaos des Besonderen*], and it quickly seeks to get away from it."[16] Rosenzweig referred to the material foundation of the divine, as delineated in Schelling's *Ages of the World*.[17] Schelling's idealism differed from that of German transencendental philosophy in that he argued for the chaos and materiality that constitute not only God's creation but also God's very character. Rosenzweig also associated the particular *(Besondere)*, which resists an idealist transformation of the body into the body politic, with Judaism. This gets lost in the English translation, in which we read of "an underlying chaos of the distinctive." By contrast, he wrote of the *dark* chaos of the particular. In doing so, he recalled "the dark drive," which he characterized as "my Judaism"[18] and of which he became aware in the crisis year of 1920, when, with reference to this darkness, he rejected the position of a university lecturer (offered to him by his academic mentor, Friedrich Meinecke).

Whereas Rosenzweig's Jewish thought remained cognizant of its particularity, German idealism belied its own particular and material foundations while attempting to erase what Schelling charmingly called "the modesty of matter"[19] by the production of a world that is "universal" owing to its indifference to "worldly," that is, material and particular determinations. Rosenzweig pointed out that such production nevertheless works with matter. Matter provides nourishment for the apparatus of "otherworldly" production, thus feeding reason's autonomous machinery with energy. Rosenzweig interpreted this immanent production of transcendence not in terms of a movement away from the theological but as an anti-creaturely theology, as a rational theology that wants to do away with its contingent, "bodily" foundation: "For us, Idealism had proven to be in competition, not with theology in general, but only with the theology of creation. For [*sic*] creation we had sought the way to revelation.[20] Note that the German original reads, "from [*von*] creation we had sought the way to revelation." Thus, the separation between world and God does not result in a radical divide between immanence and transcendence. Such a divide would indeed require the overcoming of the immanent by immanent means (reason's autonomy, which frees the human from any dependence on matter) or, otherwise, a miraculous destruction of immanence by transcendence. Rosenzweig, however, affirmed the independence of God, world, and man, only to prepare the ground for their correlation, in which, thanks to the distance between these three entities, love of one for the other becomes possible. Thus, he combined the elements of what vibrated in Cohen's thought as an unbridgeable tension. The sensuousness of the worldly indeed constitutes a radical contrast to the purity of the divine, but this separation between creation and the creator does not mean that the worldly can only be redeemed by its self-production as the otherworldly. As we have seen, Cohen clung to a Kantian notion of reason as freedom from contingency. He nevertheless argued that this contingent world is intrinsically good and does not need to be overcome. The temporal world is good because it is at the same time eternal, that is to say, created by God. Developing and deepening Cohen's Mendelssohnian reading of Kant, Rosenzweig correlated that which remains separated and thus affirms an equality of infinity between God, man, and world.

Strikingly, German idealism's production of the worldly as otherworldly results in depriving matter of its otherness. That is to say, it takes away the transcendence that dwells in the immanent and that comes to the fore in moments of revelation, which occur when one individual helps preserve the life of another. Thus, creation reveals redemption: "Both revelation and redemption are creation in a certain manner that cannot be analyzed as yet."[21] In the course of *The Star* Rosenzweig indeed "links creation and redemption through revelation, the latter understood as *love*."[22] Love, however, originates in an awareness of the distinctive, irreducible otherness of an individual, despite the general attributes of contingency and mortality.

By equating the general with the particular (Rosenzweig's formula $A=B$), idealism reduces the individual to the generality of death, from which he or she can only escape by willingly forsaking his or her empirical existence for the sake of a greater entity (Kant's ethical commonwealth or Hegel's spirit). This is what Rosenzweig meant when he wrote that Hegel's philosophy "had locked . . . every Beyond from its view."[23] He clarified this point by arguing that the worldly has become the other of reason's autonomy: "Thus the world is a beyond as against what is intrinsically logical, as against unity."[24] As we saw in chapter 2, according to Hegelian logic, reason realized the illusion of immediate being by speculatively positing the endpoint of existence, namely death, within the presence of empirical life. Rosenzweig had this dialectical reduction of being to nothingness in mind when he wrote that the worldly has become the transcendent.

Levinas and Rosenzweig

To this extent, philosophy "has to rid the world of what is singular, and this un-doing of the Aught is also the reason why it has to be idealistic."[25] What Rosenzweig criticized here in German idealism Levinas depicted as violence qua totality, and he contrasted it with ethics qua infinity. Levinas in fact opposed the idealist (and Heideggerian) notion of freedom to that of justice: "If freedom denotes the mode of remaining the same in the midst of the other, knowledge, where an existent is given by interposition of impersonal Being, contains the ultimate sense of freedom. It would be opposed to justice."[26] *Totality and Infinity* in fact radicalizes the philosophical, qua ethical, critique of German idealism as first and most clearly spelled out in *The Star of Redemption,* a work to which Levinas referred only once to emphasize that it "is too often present in this book to be cited."[27] Radicalizing Rosenzweig, Levinas redefined philosophical terms such as *metaphysics* and *freedom* against Kant's notion of autonomy.[28] He represented freedom as heteronomy, as openness to an infinite variety of particulars: "The presence of the Other, a privileged heteronomy, does not clash with freedom but invests it."[29] As we saw in chapter 1, Kant had precisely argued that freedom and heteronomy contradict each other. He maintained that a free subject establishes his independence from both nature and religious traditions by following the autonomous laws of self-sufficient reason.

Before returning to Rosenzweig's "new thinking" (see chapter 8), I will further examine Levinas's implicit continuation of a Rosenzweigian critique of German idealism's totalitarian agenda. This examination will help clarify what appears to be *The Star*'s affirmation of the radical distinction between the worldly and the otherworldly that paradoxically goes hand in hand with a theology of the mundane. In the important but often neglected essay "Signature," Levinas in fact spelled out the relevance of a Kantian autonomy-heteronomy opposition for his analysis of both violence and totality.[30] He defined "moral consciousness" as "an acces to external being," maintaining that "external being is, *par excellence,* the Other."[31] Against a Kantian philosophy that "reduces the Other [*l'Autre*] to the same and the multiple to the totality, making of autonomy its supreme principle," Levinas, implicitly expounding Rosenzweig's "new thinking," proposed that "philosophy as love of truth aspires to the Other [*l'Autre*]" and thereby "is heteronomy itself," which, in turn, "is metaphysical."

Rather than being opposed to the external, empirical world, the metaphysical resides in the ethical care for, and not the epistemological penetration through to the essence of, bodily existence. Levinas's critique of the German idealist notion of autonomy thus helps clarify the apparently self-exclusive tension between immanent and transcendent tendencies in Rosenzweig's "new thinking." According to Levinas, a metaphysics that correlates transcendence (or, for that matter, "freedom") and heteronomy perceives of mundane, material life in terms of an opening toward the spiritual. The other, or the flesh-and- blood neighbor with whom we interact in everyday life, embodies revelation as long as we do not reduce him or her to the sameness of an abstract law in which he or she would function as a nonparticular, general entity: "The absolute other, whose alterity is overcome in the philosophy of immanence on the allegedly common plane of history, maintains his transcendence in the midst of history."[32] What Levinas described as a "philosophy of immanence" seems to delineate his and Rosenzweig's understanding of German idealism.

As we have seen, in the opening pages of *The Star* Rosenzweig represented idealism's distinctive identity via an examination of its attempt to erase from the face of the earth the particular, or "the other." In his view, this constitutes a theoretical wish for the reconfiguration of the empirical as pure spirit. Rosenzweig took issue with the ethical consequences of such philosophical displacement, for, on a sociopolitical plane, the theoretical manifestation of immanence that has fully turned into transcendence results in the expulsion of those who are perceived to remain immutably bound to the limitations of what Hegel called immediate being. From a theological perspective, these philosophical abolitions of distance anticipate redemption, for they turn the world into the otherworldly, the outcome being that the immanent has now—at least within the parameters of idealist discourse—fully become the transcendent by its own (namely, rational) means. When Rosenzweig and Levinas characterized "history" as idealism's collaborator, they clearly referred to Hegel's dialectics. The latter theorized war—in which the members of a specific community become acquainted with their "master," death—as realization of the idealist insight into the "nothingness" of empirical life.

Counterposing this totalitarian reduction of the individual, the particular, in short, the other to the sameness of mortality, Levinas developed his philosophy of the face by a means in which he illustrated the Mosaic commandment "Thou shall not kill." Thus the human face embodies two aspects of heteronomy: that of the neighbor as I interact with him or her in the external world and that of the divine whose correlated image I perceive in the face through which, as through a burning bush, God speaks to me. Thus Levinas's philosophy of the other both affirms the separateness between immanence and transcendence and theorizes the body as the site of revelation, as a broken embodiment of the spiritual. This coexistence of separation and correlation between immanence and transcendence in the Levinasian face helps one understand what Eric L. Santner has recently decribed as Rosenzweig's paradox.[33] Revelation in Rosenzweig (and later in Levinas's "face") does not remove us from the world in which it is taking place; rather, it brings us closer to an understanding of the spiritual validity that enfolds our mundane activities. Why, however, does Rosenzweig insist on separation? The discussion above concerning Levinas's critique of totality helps us understand Rosenzweig's concern with the separate existence of man, God, and world, because the Levinasian face embodies both the worldly and the otherworldy without reducing the one to the other (that would precisely be totality).

8 THE POLITICS OF BLOOD: ROSENZWEIG AND HEGEL

The Deification of Humanity and the Killing of Human Bodies

What impact did Rosenzweig's idiosyncratic analysis of the loss of worldly transcendence have on his understanding of Judaism? In order to address this issue I will first engage in a reading of the essays "Atheistic Theology" and "Apologetic Thinking" before examining his turning the tables on Hegel's metaphysics of eating in the last part of *The Star of Redemption*. In "Atheistic Theology" (1914) Rosenzweig examined the pseudotheological pattern that informs "modern" anti-Semitism. He did so by analyzing the total erosion of "otherness" that, as discussed above, goes hand in hand with German idealism's attempt at translating the worldly (the body) into the otherworldly (the body politic). As we shall see, Rosenzweig (here following the German idealists) identified this otherness of the worldly with Jewishness. Note that in "Atheistic Theology" he examined the close relation between a philosophical conception of human autonomy and nationalist politics:

> Instead of trying—in the eternity of philosophical thought or in the temporality of the historical process—to show the human under the might of the divine, one tries, on the contrary, to understand the divine as the self-projection of the human into the heaven of myth. Here the people [*Volk*] is the human actuality, which as such already recommends itself as a content of faith to a positivistically meticulous generation[1]

Rosenzweig argued that Feuerbach's critique of religion as "self-projection" of the human onto a divine image radicalized the Kantian demand for human autonomy. As in *The Star,* idealism marks a historical and theological break. Whereas pre-idealist thought represents humanity as subservient to the power of a deity, after the Feuerbachian radicalization of Kant's transcendental philosophy man himself has a right to the potential that he timidly projects onto a supernatural force. Yet the empowerment of the human has quite inhuman consequences, for it results in the pseudotheological deification of a nationalist body politic. Paradoxically, the transposition of heaven onto earth turns the worldly into the transcendent, or other (or that which Rosenzweig called *Jenseits*) within a world that has now become—according to this new cultural perception—the otherworldly. Thus, the immanent entity "nation" *(das Volk)* now fills the space of "belief-content" *(Glaubensinhalt)* that had previously been occupied by transcendent concepts.

How does the notion *Volk* fit into either Kant's or Feuerbach's philosophy? It clearly does not belong to either of them. What about Richard Wagner? In the passage above, Rosenzweig did not refer to specific writers; he only uses key terms such as *Selbsprojection,* which are citations from specific theoretical texts. But he employed these citations as markers that point to the work of individual thinkers. Did he posit a German transcendental trajectory from Kant, via Hegel and Feuerbach, to Wagner? In a letter of 4 August 1909 to Hans Ehrenberg he did precisely this, calling Wagner a "gateway" *(Einfalltor):* "From him [Wagner] the path leads on the one hand via Feuerbach to Hegel and on the other to Hegel too, via the Young-German movement."[2] In this letter Rosenzweig spoke of his plan to write a dissertation (what would materialize as his book *Hegel and the State*) about the path backward from Wagner to German transcendental philosophy. This retrospective investigation would uncover the foundation of "*the* empire as such, even if only in its 'cultural' aspect."[3] Far from belittling the role of culture for an understanding of German history, Rosenzweig emphasized the thin line that links German national culture to German politics: "Little distance lies between 'culture' and the 'gun.'" *(Von der 'Kultur' zur 'Kanone' ist ein kleiner Schritt).*[4] As we shall see, he indeed analyzed the pseudotheological paradigm that has shaped German national culture.

By forming a total unity with the transcendent, the immanent term *nation* has occupied the theological position of otherness, that is to say, of transcendence. In "Atheistic Theology" he examined how the philosophical concept of autonomy results, on a political plane, in the "rationalist deification of the people [*Volk*]."[5] Thus, German nationalism set out to make the otherworldly immanent by means of nationalistic politics. We have seen how Wagner—radicalizing Hegel—justified this reconciliation of the state with both religion and art by referring to the transcendence of empirical life as demanded by the patriotic call to "selfless sacrifices" for the "greater good" of the nation. Rosenzweig emphasized that this pseudotheology differs not only from Jewish but also traditional Christian thought: "Instead of asserting God's becoming human, one asserted His being human; instead of His descent to the mountain of the giving of the law, the autonomy of the moral law."[6] Whereas traditional Christian thought focuses on the possible return of the human to the state of being created in God's image, modern nationalism makes use of a pseudotheology that proclaims the divinity of man. Rosenzweig aligned this deification of humanity with the Kantian autonomy of the moral law, which he contrasted with the revelation of Mosaic legislation.

In what way can a theory that announces the deification of humanity demand the death of human bodies? This question sheds light on the contradictions inherent in a kind of humanism that could be instrumentalized by nationalist thought (such as Wagner's). As we have seen, German transcendental philosophy posited human self-sufficiency only with regard to the nonbodily aspect of humanity and thus radically rejected the spiritual validity of the body. This is exactly what Marx criticized in his "Theses on Feuerbach" when he set out to appreciate human bodily practice over and against idealist contemplation of the sensuous as something that has to be overcome: "He [Feuerbach] regards the theoretical attitude as the only genuinely human attitude, while practice is conceived and fixed only in its dirty-judaical manifestation."[7] Here Marx alluded to the idealist equation of the body with the Judaic. As a result of this rejection of sensuousness, German idealism deifies humanity only with a view to the autonomous and therefore immanent transcendence of bodily needs. As we saw in chapter 1, there are contradictions as far as the issue of autonomy is concerned: the individual's rational capability needs to be embedded in a civil society that prescribes the forgoing of sensuous interests. Thus, Marx replaces "'civil' society" with "*human* society, or socialized humanity,"[8] in which the bodily needs of individuals matter as much as their intellectual aspirations.

How did Marx's critique of Feuerbach illuminate Rosenzweig's discourse about the inhumanity of the humanism in German idealism? As we have seen, in "Atheistic Theology" Rosenzweig cited the Feuerbachian unmasking of the divine as self-projection of the human. In the preceding passage he examined the pseudotheological foundations of racism, which only *seem* to develop from "pseudonaturalism." If the deification of humanity amounts to that of the nation, then the making transcendent of the national also invests race with divine attributes. Indeed, according to Rosenzweig's analysis, humanity—liberated from its "dirty" body—becomes divine in the nation and the divine being of this nonbodily body politic has, in turn, its foundation in what German nationalists consider to be the divine purity of race. He did not dispute the connections between this threefold idolization—in which the human falls into place with nation and race—and idealism, but he nevertheless drew attention to the emphasis on the "pseudonaturalist" term *race*, which clearly deviates from German transcendental philosophy:

A representation of people [*Volk*] developed, not without contact with that older conception of peoplehood [*Volkstumsbegriff*] of German Idealism, yet nevertheless essentially new, which granted it the rank of an eternal existence. He who is able to see through the pseudonaturalist wrappings of the race idea, to which this idea owes its broad popularity, recognizes here the striving to transform the concept of peoplehood in such a way that the people maintain the right to exist simply from their existence, independently of their factual achievements.[9]

By looking through the pseudonaturalist veils of the notion of race, Rosenzweig thus analyzed the pseudotheology that substantiates and grounds pseudoscientific racism. Racism draws its absolutist claims to truth from a strange conflation of the immanent and the transcendent, even though racists do not, of course, theoretically reflect on this issue. With disregard to the realm of sensuous practice, racism deifies a specific group of people with exclusive reference to its being as such. Rosenzweig discussed this *Dasein* (being) of the people a few paragraphs further on as the *Menschsein* of God. He did so in the passage quoted above, in which he differentiated the gradual incarnation of Christ in the human body *(Menschwerdung)* from the deification of a nonbodily humanity that results in the idolization of the people as an invincible body politic.

By positing humanity in terms of nonbodily spirit, German idealism did not allow for the contingencies or imperfections of bodily existence. Rosenzweig distinguished this kind of humanism from the racism of the late nineteenth century, but he emphasized that such disregard for the needs of empirical life lays open the possibility for a nationalist as well as racist conception of the body politic. He pointed out that racism disguises a pseudotheology behind its apparent "naturalism," for racist discourse depicts both nation and "national blood" with the language of absolute self-sufficiency that has traditionally been employed to characterize the divine. This is what Rosenzweig meant when he wrote that the sheer being of the people justifies its fantasized existence: race and nation are idols that demand in their quasi-divinity the lifeblood of "unworthy" empirical bodies.

Presentations of an invincible "Aryan" body strike us as naturalistic. Rosenzweig argued that this apparent naturalism makes for the popularity of racist ideology but obfuscates the latter's pseudotheological foundations. Against the background of Rosenzweig's analysis, racist and nationalist glorifications of muscular strength serve to emphasize an ideal body that has overcome its frailty and contingency and can thus serve a body politic that sets out to do away with otherness. This explains the obsession with the Jewish body in racist discourse, for it stigmatizes Jewishness—via a bizarre depiction of physical features—as illness, which is another word for the frailty and the contingency of empirical existence.

How did Rosenzweig's examination of the pseudotheology behind racism's apparent pseudonaturalism affect the development of his own Jewish theology? In the essay "Apologetic Thinking" he underlined the social and political consequences of representing otherness in a derogatory manner by asking his reader: "Can the other, if he is as I here depict him, still—live?"[10] The depiction of rabbinic Juadaism as legalism without spirit denies the life of Jews: "These legalistic machines, lacking humor and soul, whom the Christian so gladly represents under the [name] 'Pharisees,' would be incapable of living."[11] In the same essay Rosenzweig emphasized that this derogatory depiction of Judaism by Christian thinkers also has an impact on Jewish thought. Thus modern Jewish philosophy has an apologetic dimension: "Apologetic thinking remains dependent on the cause, the adversary. And in this sense Jewish thinking remains apologetic thinking"[12] Rosenzweig attempted to break with apologetic thinking by pointing out its basic congruency with the non-Jewish majority culture. In his essay on "The New Learning," he argued that Jewish thought needs to find a path to the heart of Jewish life, instead of proving a relation between the Jewish *(Jüdischem)* and the non-Jewish *(Außerjüdischem)*.[13]

This is exactly what Rosenzweig did in *The Star of Redemption*: he affirmed the difference between the Jewish and the non-Jewish worlds.[14] As we shall see in the conclusion of this chapter, in this affirmation he followed a Hegelian metaphysics of eating while turning the tables on Hegel's speculative account of "spirit." Thus, Rosenzweig's nonapologetic thought responded to the prejudicial account of Judaism given in Kant's and Hegel's transcendental philosophy. This response did not internalize the charges that both German idealists leveled against rabbinic Judaism. (Such internalization can, for example, be witnessed in Freud's dismissal of priests and ceremonies as being alien to the sentiment of the Jewish people. See chapter 9.)

Rosenzweig's and Hegel's Metaphysics of Eating

Following Mendelssohn and Cohen, Rosenzweig depicted Judaism in terms of an interchange between learning and action, between human subjectivity and its engaging relationship with the external world.[15] Whereas Mendelssohn and to some extent Cohen did not take issue with an idealist dismissal of material practice and heteronomy, however, Rosensenzweig—here following Marx[16]—criticized the German idealist attempt to transpose heaven onto earth to the detriment of "earthly" life. The reconception of the worldly as the otherworldly by means of a transformation of the body into an idealist body politic does not put an end to theology; rather, it turns the rejected material basis of life into the transcendent other of reason's autonomy.

When he thus saw in the Jewish the embodiment of the other, Rosenzweig followed the line drawn by German transcendental philosophy. But whereas Kant and Hegel built their respective systems on the ground of the exclusion of this flesh-and-blood otherness, Rosenzweig made it the cornerstone of his affirmation of modern Jewish thought. Why, then, did he characterize the Jewish people as a community of blood? This characterization has proved to be quite controversial, and critics have not tired of defending Rosenzweig against the charge of racism. In the most recent defense, Leora Batnitzky maintained, "'the blood community' is a philosophical construct that is meant to undo the priority of philosophical constructs."[17] This raises the question, To which line of thought did Rosenzweig's community of blood refer? Did he mainly have philosophy as such in mind, or did he, rather, wish to undermine the philosophical and theological espousal of political violence?

As discussed in chapter 7, *The Star* opens with an outspoken critique of German idealism's rejection of the body's independence from the body politic. How does this relate to Rosenzweig's peculiar conflation of the Jewish people with the life substance blood at the end of *The Star*? Critics have so far not paid sufficient attention to the element with which he contrasted blood. He clearly elaborated on a contrast concerning the Jewish and the Gentile worlds, allocating blood to one and earth to the other: "We were the only ones who trusted in blood and abandoned the land; and so we preserved the priceless sap of life which pledged us that it would be eternal. Among the peoples of the world [*Erde*], we are the only ones who separated what lived within us from all community with what is dead."[18] Here Rosenzweig made it clear that his notion of blood reacts only against philosophical concepts that set out to justify the shedding of blood for the political possession of land. He associated the earth with death and blood with life, and it is this clinging to life that distinguishes the Jews from a post-idealist Gentile world in which such behavior has been demoted as "un-heroic," "non-idealist," and—as Hegel would call it—"non-dialectical."

What constitutes the relation between Hegel's metaphysics of eating and Rosenzweig's philosophical opposition between an identity that sees itself grounded in blood and one that demands the conquest of land? We have seen how Hegel ontologized war and sacrifice by focusing on the process of eating (see chapter 2). Consumption of food delineates the dialectics of everyday life, since the one who eats realizes the similarities between his or her own bodily constitution and the empirical object of nutrition that he or she is in the process of consuming. Thus, to eat means to sacrifice and to sacrifice means to eat.

Now, Rosenzweig did not discuss the topic of eating in his *Hegel and the State*,[19] but he did analyze Hegel's philosophical appraisal as regards the sacrifice of the individual for the "greater good of the state."[20] He detected an uncanny conflation of the state with the notion of destiny, as a result of which the individual has no theological and philosophical justification to avoid the sacrifice of his or her life as demanded by this political unity that speaks with the inevitable voice of the pagan deity "fate."[21] Thus, in his book on Hegel, Rosenzweig analyzed speculative thought as a philosophical deification of politics: the "thinker in the state [*Denker im Staat*]" promotes the opposite of "human rights [*Menschenrechte*]" and thereby refrains from making "justice" the ethical yardstick of his philosophical system.[22]

Following the guidelines of human rights, justice would insist on respect for the life of the individual over and against political demands for an increase in possession of land, as put forth by state authorities. As we have seen, Hegel focused on the prohibition against eating blood as proof of the lack of both speculative and state-like thinking in rabbinic Judaism. He contrasted the respect for the blood of life with the secularized Christian notion of the modern state. The members of this state are true dialecticians in that they have realized—by way of speculation—the nothingness of their own blood, which can therefore willingly be shed for the becoming of the state.

Against this idealist notion of freedom as the liberation from bodily existence Rosenzweig defined freedom as saying no to nothingness,[23] but this no does not denote the rational invalidity of immediate being, as Hegel would have had it. On the contrary, the "nothing" refers to the destruction of the external world, which Rosenzweig's theology of creation perceived to be the work of a divine creator who "in the beginning" acted freely by saying no to a world emptied of empirical matter. If the reference to freedom in *The Star* concerns the free act of creation, Rosenzweig had human freedom in mind when he wrote in "'The Germ Cell' of the Star of Redemption (Letter to Rudolf Ehrenberg of 18 November 1917)" about liberty in contrast to its idealist conception as autonomy: "My 'freedom,' and to be sure not my freedom as the philosophers lie about it, in that they draw off from it the red blood of arbitrariness and let it run into the vessel of 'sensuousness,' of 'drive,' of 'motives,' and admit as freedom only the bloodless residue of obedience to the law."[24] Here Rosenzweig reconfigured the Hegelian topics "blood," "immediate being," and "freedom." Thus, freedom consists in saying no to death by affirming the spiritual validity of one's blood, that is to say, of one's bodily life.

In this way, the idealist enslavement to the goods of this world describes Rosenzweig's notion of freedom. A reversal has taken place in which the one who inverts a philosophical paradigm at the same time mimics its ideational structure. Rosenzweig agreed with the idealist depiction of Jewishness as sensuousness, as blood, but at the same time he did not deprive the stuff that constitutes life of spiritual as well as intellectual validity. Instead, Hegel's "spirit" turns out to be without spirit, for the speculative penetration to the essence of "immediate being" opens the way to a compulsive denial of life that not so much sustains the individual but works for the aggrandizement of a political unity—the state. By grounding Jewish identity in blood as the "juice of life" and by opposing this identity to the political will for the conquest of land, Rosenzweig undermined German idealism's attempt to transform the body into the body politic. The state sets out to glorify its power by shedding blood in order to gain possession of land. This triumph of one state over other states by means of domination of their space would realize Hegel's absolute spirit, which turns *Weltgeschichte* (world history) into the *Weltgericht* (judgment on the world).

Critics have not noticed that Rosenzweig reversed Hegel's metaphysics of eating when he opposed Jewish identity, as defined in terms of blood, with a non-Jewish world that sacrifices the juice of life for the establishment of power structures. If Hegel maintained that the prohibition on the consumption of blood evidences a nonspiritual as well as a nonintellectual and illusionary clinging to immediate being, then Rosenzweig turned the tables on Hegel when he argued that the chosen people are chosen precisely because they do not have a state and therefore refrain from sacrificing life for an increase in political power.

Rosenzweig's writing concerning the blood community of the Jewish people might well be indebted to Schelling, who, according to a recent study, stood out among German idealists by not taking part in a derogatory discourse about Jews and Judaism.[25] Whereas Hegel denied the Jews any participation in the sphere of spirit with direct reference to the dietary laws that forbid a violation of immediate being, Schelling argued that the Jews are chosen (and are thereby an example for the rest of humanity) on account of their nonparticipation in the violent struggles between different nations and different political states.

Rosenzweig no doubt found ample support in Schelling for his critique of Hegel as a dialectician of the state. His conception of a Jewish identity that consists mainly in living in blood with a view of living in life, however, constitutes an original response to a metaphysics of eating according to which one comes closer to spirit by consuming the juice of life. In Hegel's view, this consumption makes the eater aware of the nothingness, or in other words, the illusion, of immediate being, that of his or her own body included. I would therefore offer a new reading of Rosenzweig's notions of blood and earth. From this perspective, the former resembles the body and the latter symbolizes the body politic, which demands the shedding of the juice of life for gaining possession of land.

Accordingly, Rosenzweig's Jewish critique of history has a "a bearing on the ultimate course of world-history."[26] Strikingly, he argued that the Jews remain outside the realm of both history and politics for precisely the reason that they live in their blood. Thus he conceived of the historical along the lines of Hegelian speculative thought, with the crucial difference that he refused to endow the politics of nations and states with either a spiritual or an intellectual aura. In a fascinating agreement with Hegel, who called war the true realization of idealism and who referred to a metaphysics of eating in order to exclude Jewishness from both idealism and the realm of political struggle, Rosenzweig argued that the Jew is the only pacifist in a Christian world: "In the whole Christian world, the Jew is practically the only human being who cannot take war seriously, and this makes him the only genuine pacifist. For that reason, and because he experiences perfect community in his spiritual year, he remains remote from the chronology of the rest of the world."[27] In so defining Jewish identity, Rosenzweig concurred with Hegel's analysis of Judaism while at the same time depriving speculative thought of its spiritual costume. Behind the nothingness of immediate being we do not encounter a becoming. To think that way is to fall prey to an idealist illusion. Thus dwelling outside the sphere of worldly time (that is, history), the Jews help preserve worldly life by living in the blood of life rather than living for the deadness of the earth.

Paradoxically, Rosenzweig's otherworldly community establishes the spiritual and intellectual validity of the worldly. This paradox is related to the paradox of idealism: on the opening pages of *The Star* we read that with Kant and Hegel, the immanent has become the transcendent. German transcendental philosophy does not tolerate the needs of the body, which it conflates with the essence of Judaism. Responding to the idealist paradigm in a nonapologetic mode, Rosenzweig argued that the people of God *(Gottesvolk)* represent the eternal within transitory time: "So far as God's people is concerned, eternity has already come—even in the midst of time! For the nations of the world there is only the current era. But the state symbolizes the attempt to give nations eternity within the confines of time, an attempt which must of necessity be repeated again and again."[28] The state attempts to endow its people with eternity by trying to turn world history into judgment on the world, whereas the Jews, having no state, live the eternal within time. Rosenzweig here discussed Hegel (whom, as we have seen, he called the "thinker of the state") without mentioning his name. The state holds out the promise of immanent eternity by means of a violent transformation of the worldly into the otherworldly, as achieved by the immanent changing of the body (blood) into the body politic (conquered and accumulated land). In Rosenzweig's analysis, this idealization of war represents secularized Christian thought, which has now turned into totalitarian politics.

Jewish particularity helps promote the redemption of the world by reminding the universal of its incompleteness and thus keeps it from turning totalitarian. German transcendental philosophy, however, set out to separate "Christian essence" from its Jewish foundations and in doing so attempted to free itself from this remainder of incompleteness. Thus the Christian state sees Jewishness as a "competitor" *(Nebenbuhler)*[29] in its attempt to make the earth eternal by warlike means. Rosenzweig's critique of the idealist conflation of politics and Christian essence pointed to the pseudotheological underpinnings of nationalism. In contrast to the pagan, the modern Christian state does not recognize mortality, and as a result Christ's sacrifice undergoes an immanent transformation into the individual's sacrifice for the state, in which, by way of Hegelian dialectics, the death of being (the body, that is, the blood of life) turns into becoming (the body politic, that is, the state, which attempts to conquer the earth).

With what kind of theology did Rosenzweig counter the pseudotheology of nationalism and anti-Semitism? His nonapologetic Jewish philosophy goes hand in hand with a theory of Jewish law: "For in the law everything of this world that is comprised in it, all created existence, is already given life and soul directly as content of the world to come."[30] The law mediates between God and the world and thereby prohibits any violation of life. Thus Rosenzweig contrasted the violent production of the otherworldly out of the material of the worldly, with the respect for immediate being found in rabbinic Judaism. Rabbinic law endows the body with spiritual validity: "The Jew sanctified his flesh and blood under the yoke of the law, and thereby lives constantly in the reality of the heavily kingdom; the Christian's constant profane flesh and blood sets itself in opposition to redemption, and he learns that he himself is not permitted to anticipate redemption emotionally."[31] The "yoke of the law" does not describe enslavement to the goods of this world, as Kant argued; rather, it prepares the ground for a bodily existence that has regained its spiritual validity. According to Rosenzweig, the law sanctifies *(heiligen)* the body. Thus, a life lived according to the law opens up a perspective onto the revelation that dwells in the work of creation.

This coincidence between revelation and creation describes the work of redemption, which unfolds in human works of love. By keeping the law, the Jew, in Rosenzweig's view, enacts love, for he or she respects the life of immediate being. This is precisely what Hegel attacked in his metaphysics of eating: he saw in Jewish law a restriction on humanity's autonomy, which should re-create—or, in Rosenzweig's terminology—"produce" a perfect otherworldly body politic from the imperfection of a bodily and therefore contingent world. Rosenzweig agreed with Hegel's description of Judaism but did not concur with his philosophical conclusions. The Jew, who lives according to the law, lives in the blood, for she or he sees the empirical world as correlated with God's creation. This correlation demands works of love. Thus, Jewish law does not counteract charity, as has often been proclaimed in the theology of post-Reformation Christianity; instead, law enacts love. God's commandments to love are prohibitions against the violation of life: "The commandments of God, as far as they belong to that 'second tablet' which specifies the love of neighbor, are throughout phrased in the form 'Thou shalt not.' They cannot assume the garb of laws except as prohibitions, as delineation of the boundaries of that which can on no account be reconciled with love of neighbor."[32] Hegel's metaphysics of eating took issue with precisely these prohibitions against the violation of "immediate being." According to Hegel, they are irrational, since they contradict a notion of rationality, which German transcendental philosophy circumscribes as human autonomy. Rosenzweig, on the other hand, affirmed the raison d' être of the law's taboo-like apparel, which consists in safeguarding the survival of empirical life. As we have seen, Levinas defined the love of that which lies in immediate proximity *(Liebe zum Nächsten)* as heteronomy, thus employing a term that Kant and Hegel used in order to prove the irrationality of Judaism. Rosenzweig described this concern for the well-being of the external world in terms of love. Law, which helps set limits to violence, constitutes the rationality of *caritas*, as Rosenzweig understood it. The concept of living in blood undermines the apparent rationality of Hegel's speculative dialectics. In formulating this concept, Rosenzweig called into question the purported autonomy of a body politic that consumes bodies in order to turn world history into judgment on the world.

9   FREUD'S OTHER ENLIGHTENMENT: TURNING THE TABLES ON KANT

I strongly believe that there is something fundamentally wrong with the tacit dichotomy—the binary opposition—that is frequently presupposed in these controversies: the dichotomy between being a Jew (and taking one's Jewish heritage seriously) and being an Aufklärer (committed to the Enlightenment ideals of universal science and rational critique). Freud was both, and he was proud of being both—a Jew and an Aufklärer.
    —RICHARD J. BERNSTEIN, FREUD AND THE LEGACY OF MOSES

The Illusions of Human Rationality and Christian Innocence

Whereas Franz Rosenzweig developed a philosophy of the law, Sigmund Freud, following Kant, discarded Judaism's ceremonial and ritualistic aspects. This chapter mainly analyzes how Freud interpreted the Judaic in terms of his revision of Enlightenment thought. The Freud that emerges from this examination is more kindly disposed toward religion than is generally supposed. Recent studies have stressed his work's spiritual dimension.[1] A scientific Freud, who criticizes religion as a psychological illusion, can clearly be found in his *Future of an Illusion*. There is, however, another Freud, as is evident from his other writings. For example, Regina M. Schwartz has recently argued that we "only read *Moses and Monotheism* as a lapse from his scientific rationalism into a dark realm of superstitious religious myth if we privilege one text over the other, *The Future of an Illusion* (1927) over *Moses and Monotheism* (1939)."[2] As Peter Gay has pointed out, Freud in fact "disparaged *The Future of an Illusion* as 'childish' and 'feeble analytically, inadequate as self-confession.'"[3] Indeed the scandal of Freud's *Interpretation of Dreams* (1899) consisted precisely in this self-confessional mode of analysis, which many critics dismissed as "unscientific."[4]

    Could Freud have had a notion of scientific truth that closely related to his Jewish identity? The argumentative structure of this study does not permit a full investigation into this complex issue, but it should be noted that Freud interpreted certain aspects of both Christian theology and Kant's moral philosophy in the light of an avoidance of reality. While accepting the close relation between Judaism and Christianity, he also recognized the issues that divide these two religions. He saw the most glaring of such differences in

Christian anti-Semitism. According to Freud, anti-Semitism results from a state of illusion and thus coincides with the illusory element that he saw in Christianity. In this state "an inner psychical reality holds its sway over the reality of the outer world."[5] The illusory paves the way to "insanity."[6] Insanity, in turn, finds its outlet either in the frequently occurring forms of neurotic phobias or in the psychotic withdrawal from reality in toto. As we shall see, Freud called this fantasy world of the mentally ill a "state within the state." He thus turned the tables on anti-Semites who accuse the Jews of exploiting the commonwealth (see chapter 1).

Matters are more complicated by the fact that Freud posited as humanity's primal scene a traumatic event, which causes such a withdrawal from the external world. The killing of the primeval father (as narrated in *Totem and Taboo*) determines human psychology as such. As his writings on psychoanalytical practice amply demonstrate, Freud sought with his new science to cure such neurotic—or worse, psychotic—withdrawal from the external into an internal world. Traumatic events such as the killing of the primeval father precipitate that insane flight into the illusory.

Paradoxically, this deceptive withdrawal from reality arises from amnesia, from the denial that traumatic events have actually taken place. Thus Freud saw the task of the psychoanalytic "cure" in the "removal of amnesia": "Once all memory gaps have been filled, once light has been shed on all gaps in psychic life, a continuation and even a renewal of illness has been made impossible."[7] Significantly, Freud discerned in Judaism this conscious remembrance of past traumas, which precisely distinguishes psychoanalysis from anatomical forms of medical practice. As early as 1891 "he is already closer to the more clinical-minded French than to the more anatomical-minded Germans."[8] This tentative move away from the German school of physiological and quantitative analysis (whose teaching he never completely abandoned)[9] also implies a critical attitude toward the "naturalizing" Kantianism of his scientific mentors.[10] By focusing on the invisible forces of unconscious fears and desires, psychoanalysis questions the ethical and epistemological assertions of Kantian philosophy. Reason is no longer viewed as determining both the internal and external worlds. Indeed the illusion of pre-Freudian thought consisted precisely in supposing consciousness's independence (its autonomy) from irrational drives. As Freud stressed in his writings concerning psychoanalytical practice, "our unconscious is not the same as that of the philosophers, and moreover most philosophers are not interested in the unconscious psyche."[11] How, then, does the unconscious do its work? It attempts to erase the conscious remembrance of traumatic events while preserving and even intensifying the psychic impact of traumata as unacknowledged memory traces.

Now, Freud theorized psychoanalytic practice in close relation to that which he understood as Judaism. He did so by setting the psychoanalyst the task of making the patient conscious of exactly what happened in his or her past. This is not an easy mission to fulfill, since the culturally accepted illusions of both human rationality and Christian innocence[12] seem to preclude reflection on an irrational and violent past. Freud called feelings of guilt and the closely related desire to be punished "the worst enemy of our therapeutic endeavors."[13] Rather than locating exactly when and where the traumatic event happened, the patient avoids such confrontation with reality. This resistance to psychoanalysis grows out of a cultural setting in which the articulation of sexual and aggressive desires is prohibited by the illusory standard of a human consciousness, which should have full control over irrational desires and wishes.[14]

To this extent, Freud saw in Judaism another cultural paradigm that encourages the conscious remembrance of traumatic events. Only in *Moses and Monotheism* did Freud fully embed psychoanalytic theory and practice in his understanding of Judaism. Here he maintained that by killing Moses the Jews repeated the primal scene (as narrated in *Totem and Taboo*). This repetition activates the conscious work of memory and initiates the psychoanalytic passage away from an unconscious feeling of guilt to the remembrance of concrete deeds that proved to be traumatic. Freud thus reversed the anti-Semitic stereotype of the "savage Jew" (the "Jewish criminal"),[15] which functions as a strong contrast to the image of the rational, self-controlled Gentile.

This chapter analyzes how Freud developed a concept of Enlightenment that, albeit formulated in similar terms, differs from that conceived in the idealist philosophy of Kant. These differences are to a large extent bound up with Freud's ambivalence toward Christianity. Owing to the free-thinking environment of his childhood home Freud was exposed to Catholicism at an early age by his Czech nanny. So it is not surprising that in a letter of 9 May 1929 he wrote to Pastor Oskar Pfister about his "special sympathy for St. Paul as a genuinely Jewish thinker."[16] In a similar way he seems to have sympathized with Jesus and the early Christians. He took issue, however, with the Christian refusal to remember the "murderous deed"[17] from which human civilization evolved. In place of such conscious remembrance of a traumatic past, Christians cling to "fantasy in form of a redemptive message *(Gospel)*."[18] This illusion gives rise to resistance that makes a psychoanalytic confrontation with the sexual and aggressive dimension of the psyche more difficult than it would "naturally" be.

In short, according to Freud, anti-Semitic thinkers presuppose the self-sufficiency of human consciousness and project human shortcomings onto the Jews. In this way, they imagine the Jews to be castrated as punishment for sexual and other "mundane" excesses. As Freud argued in the case history of "Little Hans" (1909), "the castration complex is the deepest unconscious root of anti-Semitism, because even during his upbringing a boy hears that something has been cut off from the Jew's penis."[19] The boy takes this to be "a part of the penis."[20] This castration complex "gives him the justification to despise Jews."[21] With reference to Otto Weininger's *Sex and Character*, Freud compared anti-Semitism to misogyny. Misogynists and anti-Semites claim that women and Jews have their penis cut off as punishment for "mundane" indulgences. This accusation seems to justify both forms of hatred: "The feeling of superiority over 'woman' [*das Weib*] too does not have a stronger unconscious root [than in the anti-Semitic castration complex]. Weininger, this highly talented and sexually disturbed young philosopher, . . . has . . . treated Jews and 'woman' with the same hostility and has hurled the same abuses against both."[22] Freud detected such refusal to confront humanity's internal strangeness in the work of many Gentile writers (and self-hating Jewish ones, such as Weininger). After all, Jung's "retreat from inconvenient truths about the sexual drives inhabiting the human animal"[23] was the prime reason for his break with Freud. Freud also criticized his good friend Pastor Pfister for his "resistance to sexuality."[24] This resistance hampers the work of psychoanalysis.

According to Freud, resistance seems to be culturally conditioned by Gentile illusions. Although it was founded by "genuinely Jewish thinkers" such as Paul and Jesus, "the inner development of the new religion soon came to a standstill, perhaps because it lacked the profundity, which in Judaism's case resulted from the murder of its founder."[25] Judaism's profundity thus coincides with its acceptance of humanity's internal strangeness (that is, the irrationality of human aggression and sexuality). Whereas the Jews acknowledge their role in the killing of Moses, Christians put the blame for the murder of their savior Jesus Christ on the Jews. In this way Christianity projects violence and other forms of irrational behavior on the other, the Jew. Freud in fact aligned Christianity with "the apparently rationalistic religions of the East."[26] The latter "are in essence ancestor cults" and therefore stop "short at an early stage of the reconstruction of the past."[27] In critiquing the Christian "fantasy of expiation," Freud also questioned the secularized version of this illusion: he exposed the tendencies toward pathological hubris in the orthodox Kantian notion of rational autonomy—in both ethics and epistemology.

How else could one describe Freud's writing about Oedipus than as a plea to remember one's own aggressive and sexual drives? Recently Freud has been taken to task for this conscious identification with Oedipal violence. Critics have often confused this self-critical identification with an alleged support of an Oedipal culture.[28] Those who thus take pleasure in "bashing" Freud seem to act out their irritation in response to a subtle critique of reason's supposed autonomy, as most cogently laid out in Kant's transcendental philosophy.[29]

Indeed, Freud emphasized the revolutionary significance of the psychoanalytic problem: psychoanalytical theory and practice trace the enigma of unconscious motivation and describe it as an offense against humanity's self-confident perception of its position within the world. In his 1917 *Introductory Lectures to Psychoanalysis* he emphasized that "psychological research provides proof for the ego[30] that it is not Lord in its own house but remains dependent on pathetic information derived from something which takes place unconsciously in the life of its soul."[31] This indefinite "something" *(von dem, was)* makes nonsense of any claim to an unambiguous self-knowledge. It therefore strongly undermines the Kantian position concerning transcending the empirical world because of the autonomy of the rational mind.[32] According to Kant, reason shapes the material of external life in an a priori manner (see chapter 1) and, as a result, is capable of freedom from natural conditions. In Freud's *Introductory Lectures* of 1933 Kant appears as the godfather of philosophers[33] who argue that "time and place are necessary forms of psychic activities" *(Raum und Zeit notwendige Formen unserer seelischen Akte seien)*.[34]

Far from being able to create stable spatial structures and temporal rhythms, the human mind easily turns mindless when it removes the ego from the flow of time and thus also from the flow of life. This process occurs when there is an excess of bio-psychic energy that prevents any meaningful organization of experience. Past events, which are traumatic insofar as the ego cannot make sense of them,[35] generate this excessive energy, which resists metabolization.[36] Being unable to bring them to consciousness, the ego perceives these traumata to be "timeless." They thus seem to display a representation of the "essential" nature of the world from which the ego sees itself as an outcast. It is the task of psychoanalysis to "rob" these unconscious productions of their energy charge *(ihrer Energiebesetzung beraubt)* by working through their position within a past. To this extent the psychoanalyst helps make the patient conscious of the position of these traumatic events within the flow of everyday life. The psychoanalytic cure thus demystifies that which the ego experiences as the fate-like necessity of guilt and suffering: "They [traumatic elements] can only be recognized as past and thus be devalued and robbed of their energy charge when they have come to consciousness through analytical work."[37] This relativizing of traumatic elements, which keeps the ego from its place in the world, forms the foundation of psychoanalytical treatment.[38]

Psychoanalysis does not undermine human megalomania *(Größensucht)*[39] with the end of diminishing human self-esteem. Rather, Freud set out to criticize the Kantian position, according to which human freedom resides in freedom from any heteronomous relation to the world. This chapter thus examines how the Freudian psychoanalytical enterprise works both against a devaluation of empirical life and for a reintegration into the flow of life of patients, who have forfeited their place within the empirical world by having been thrown off their axis.[40]

This is the first detailed discussion of Freud's reaction to the anti-Semitic strains within Kant's transcendental philosophy.[41] As we saw in chapter 1, Kant singled out rabbinic Judaism as the opposite of the moral refinement of the modern.[42] He did so by arguing that the Jews are oriented toward the "goods of this world" *(Güter dieser Welt)*,[43] whereas transcendental philosophy not only overcomes this "realm of nature" *(nicht ein Reich der Natur)* but also contrasts it with the "realm of freedom" *(sondern der Freiheit)*.[44] Freud, on the other hand, developed a psychoanalytical therapy that helps reduce symptoms and suffering caused by a radical estrangement between the psyche of the patient and external reality. In this way psychoanalytical theory and practice question the transcendental presuppositions of Kant's Enlightenment.

Freud associated an appreciation of worldly existence with the "essence of Judaism that is both full of meaning and full of the joys of life."[45] Although Freud's reading of Kant sheds light on his Jewish identity, it nevertheless remains unclear how it influenced the supposed complicity of psychoanalysis with an Oedipal culture. As has frequently been said, Freud seems to argue that "the keynote of the psychological situation of Jewish believers is renunciation but not of all oedipal attitudes nor of a paternal construction of reality. The masculine resolution of the Oedipus complex that Freud portrays in *Moses and Monotheism* is one in which paternal restrictions have become internal."[46] But what characterizes Freud's "paternal" or "Oedipal" internalization? As Judith van Herik acknowledges, the renunciation demanded of the ego concerns a phantasmagoric world that precludes any valid contact with the external: "Again, pleasure, wish and infantile narcissism are chastened by maturation which moves toward acknowledgement of harsh reality and orientation to the external."[47] However, the external as the material, as matter, has a strong association with the maternal, not the paternal, at least in the chauvinist discourse in which Freud allegedly participated (see the discussion of Otto Weininger in chapter 6). Indeed, Kant accused the Jews of such an orientation toward the material. As Eric L. Santner has shown, it was this Kantian paradigm of a radical divide between the material or empirical, on one hand, and the transcendental or nonempirical, on the other, that helped drive the Kantian Weininger to self-hatred. Having internalized Kant's writing about Jews and their alleged inability to transcend a heteronomous relation to the external world, Weininger saw his Jewishness as an immutable barrier to both masculinity and a transcendental philosophy. To this extent masculinity seems to be characterized by the overcoming of matter. According to Santner, "for Weininger, femininity and Jewishness are in essence the names for the metaphysical guilt man brings upon himself by commingling the purity of his theoretical, moral, and aesthetic callings with the base needs and desires of material, embodied existence."[48]

I first discuss Freud's Kantian reading of Judaism (but in doing so I intend to draw attention to his revision of Enlightenment thought). I then set out to show how a detailed interpretation of Freud's response to Kantian moral philosophy helps us understand the agenda of "another enlightenment" implicit in the foundation of psychoanalysis. In the third part of this chapter a discussion of *Moses and Monotheism* establishes a link between Freud's construction of two Moses figures and his Enlightenment revision of Kantian thought. In this revision Freud enthroned psychoanalysis as the true heir to both Judaism and a rationalist tradition that has overcome its German transcendental opposition to the external, to matter. In what follows, I show how Freud distanced himself from both the masculine and the German transcendental by interpreting the morally progressive as the regressive, by perceiving in Kant the archaic specter of Oedipus.

Politics as Family Romance

So far critics have ignored the fact that Freud read Kant's categorical imperative as a modern version of the archaic Oedipus complex. He did so in an ironic manner. That is to say, Freud was fully aware that he was making a primitive of the modern Enlightenment philosopher. Freud in fact turned the tables on a "progressive" thinker who stigmatized the Jews as regressive. Against this background it seems quite unlikely that Freud's identification with the anticolonial agenda of Hannibal extended to an approval of Oedipus' mindless self-punishment for deeds perpetrated unknowingly. Critics, however, often see Freud as confirming Oedipus' actions. According to Daniel Boyarin, for instance, "Freud is unconsciously fantasizing that he is not circumcised Schelomo, son of Jakob, but the uncircumcised and virile Greek Oedipus, son of Laius, just as earlier he had consciously fantasized that he was Hannibal, son of the heroic Hamilcar, and not son of his 'unheroic' Jewish father."[49] Freud's fantasy about Hannibal, as narrated in the *Interpretation of Dreams,* indeed had to do with an espousal of a military identity, but this did not necessarily amount to identification with Oedipal violence: whereas Oedipus kills his father unbeknown to himself, Hannibal consciously sets out to destroy a colonizing empire.

Freud identified with Hannibal in order to undermine the very structure that drove him into such "heroic" behavior and he was aware of the pathology of such martial fantasies. This is borne out by the fact that he called them "deeply neurotic."[50] Indeed, the very heroism that he found lacking in his father turns out to be ridiculous, nothing but "hero worship," as he wrote to Wilhelm Fliess.[51] So Freud had a rather ambiguous relation to his dream about conquering Rome. This indicates that he may well have been disturbed by a nagging question in regard to the possible coincidence between the revolutionary and that against which the revolution is waged. If psychoanalysis undermines a megalomaniac confidence in the transcendence of empirical, female-gendered matter (which is supposedly gained by the autonomy of a mind that is male-gendered), then it could be asked whether Freud's project might end up with the same or similar overweening pretensions. The colonial subject, Hannibal, might become another Caesar once he has subjected an imperial power. On the other hand, he might change the political and cultural outlook of Rome.

If the colonial situation of Carthage urges Hannibal to defeat the authority that oppresses him and his people, then Freud's neurosis seems to be the outcome of a similar colonial position. His position is that of a German Jewish intellectual who has been denied spiritual and philosophical capabilities by the very majority culture in which and for which he works. The superego (Rome) that drives Hannibal to conquering and perhaps destroying the power that alienates his and his people's self-esteem bears a similarity to the prejudicial pressures that the philosophy of German transcendentalism put on the German Jewish intellectual Freud and many of his contemporaries, such as Weininger.[52] If Hannibal attempts to turn Rome into Carthage, then Freud set out to invert a Kantian moral philosophy that stigmatizes the Jews as superstitious and depraved.[53]

Boyarin's criticism of an aggressive male voice in Freud still holds, even though this chapter attempts to draw attention to the multidimensionality of the appropriation of Kant's transcendental philosophy by psychoanalysis. As we will see, Freud attributed a Kantian quest for truth and justice to the nature of the Jewish people. However, as Boyarin has pointed out: "Traditional Judaism has very little to do with Kantianism. The desperation to make this not be so becomes nearly an obsession in the writings of Freud's Jewish contemporaries."[54] Although a Kantian notion of truth and justice as indifference to any determination by empirical objects might well be at odds with rabbinic Judaism, Freud's reformulation of these Enlightenment terms might well be different from what Kant and the German philosophers following him understood by them.[55]

This may help explain Freud's substantial critique of the categorical imperative, which reaches to the heart of Kant's moral philosophy. A quite ironic version of this critique introduces the reader to *Totem and Taboo* (1912–13). Indeed, there Kant serves as a link between the "regressive" and the "progressive" so that his categorical imperative constitutes the survival of primitive elements within the modern: "Taboo continues to remain within our midst; even though it has been interpreted negatively and has been directed toward different contents, it is according to its psychological nature nothing else but Kant's categorical imperative, which sets out to work compulsively and which refuses any conscious motivation. . . . The social and technical progress of humanity did not harm taboo behavior as much as it did the totem."[56]

If Kant depicted rabbinic Judaism in terms of a perpetuation of the primitive within the modern, as he indeed did when he called the Jews Palestinians in the heart of Europe, then Freud truly turned the tables on the Enlightenment philosopher when he perceived in the categorical imperative a primitive remnant of taboo.

There is, however, a wider issue connected to Freud's ironic depiction of Kant as a primitive, one that may help explain the enigmas of authority in psychoanalytic theory. Freud singled out the psychological kernel of taboo by aligning it with unmotivated commandments, that is, with meaningless but categorical demands. Kant interpreted Jewish law somewhat as he did taboo. He in fact described it in terms of an orientation toward the goods of this world.[57] Kant thus stigmatized Jewish law as the embodiment of heteronomy. He politicized this philosophical vilification when he accused the Jews of not respecting the property and ownership distinctions of a modern, bourgeois society. Kant went so far as to call the Jews a "nation of cheaters"[58] who do not respect civil society's separation between "what is mine and what is yours."[59]

Here we witness how Freud avoided articulating a Kantian philosophy. Rather, in his view the Enlightenment philosopher is not the self-proclaimed thinker of modern society but a remnant of the primitive within modernity. Freud's response was a careful, albeit ironic, interpretation of Kant's work that took the sting out of the philosopher's "progressive" agenda. He correctly ascertained that Kant not only devalued but denied any motivations that derive from the consciousness of the subjects, since such motivations are clearly not derived from the "pure" and "universal" law. This position led Kant to condemn any heteronomously oriented laws—such as those he perceived in rabbinic Judaism—that respond to the distinctive qualities of objects in the external world. Law must be a self-sufficient motivation without any reference to conscious wishes and needs (such as "love of honor," "self-love," "charity" and "compassion")[60] that he explicitly excludes from his moral philosophy, and he justifies this exclusion with a view to the contingency and arbitrariness *(Willkür)* of the empirical world.

In the course of *Totem and Taboo* Freud in fact discussed primitive taboo behavior as an enactment of Kant's moral and political philosophy. He wrote that "taboo-prohibitions lack any justification; their origin is unknown; they are incomprehensible to us but seem to be self-evident for those who are under their domination."[61] If we interpret the reference to Kant and the modern as the continuation of the primitive, then the distinction between "them" and "us" gains in nuance. As we have seen, the Enlightenment philosopher forbid any conscious motivations in his moral philosophy; rather, law should be obeyed for law's sake. In the same way, he argued against any critical investigation into the origins and the significance of the supreme power of the state: "The origin of supreme violence must not be inquired into by the people who are dominated by it."[62] The fact that the philosopher prohibited the use of reason (what he calls *vernünfteln*)[63] to criticize authority structures exemplifies Freud's crucial insight that "reason is being used to cover over unreason."[64] Kant seems to have been preoccupied with the enigma of authority, which generates through its meaningless and therefore violent commandments a traumatic surplus energy in the ego, and yet he did not analyze this process but simply affirmed it.

At this point Freud's "other Enlightenment" sheds light on the violence inherent in reason. Freud in fact demolished any break between the irrational as an alien force and a healthy, self-sufficient mind. Psychoanalysis thus analyzes reason's irrationality.[65] Indeed, the "rational order" of a society whose supreme violence must not be subjected to reasoned scrutiny prohibits any meaningful relation between the law and those who are to follow it. This order generates the unconscious by flooding the ego with traumatic demands, the source and meaning of which remain secret, exactly like Kant's "supreme violence." Thus, on a political level, Kant's categorical imperative resembles the supreme power that upholds a law that has no significance for those who must obey it. Both are meant to work directly on the unconscious "without any conscious motivation."[66] According to Santner, "the unconscious is best understood to be structured not so much like language as like a citational system or 'machine' in which the original signifier—the revealed word—to which the authority of all the others is referred is already a citation, already marked by *ibidity*."[67] Santner uses the term *ibidity* to refer to the compulsive and restless aspect of the superego voice, whose origin is unknown, and the meaning of whose utterances remains secret, so that it drives those who are dominated and unconsciously captivated by it into a never-ending enjoinment to its rule. Santner's *ibidity* has a revelatory dimension: it establishes a link between the id and the compulsive commandments of the superego. These commandments are excessive precisely because they lack meaning, and because of their meaningless force they keep the ego in a compulsive state. As a result, the ego does not find any rest in conscious self-reflection. Instead it falls prey to an unconscious sense of guilt the grounds for which it does not know.

Freud discussed the immorality that arises from the psychological core of the categorical imperative (namely, *Tabu*) in the second chapter of *Totem and Taboo*. There he argued that a not-to-be-defined authority enforces taboo in the ego's unconscious, thus forbidding any fulfillment of its wishes and inclinations ("externally imposed—by an authority—directed against humanity's strongest desires").[68] The inhibition of humanity's most dominant desires manifests perversion, not sublimation. More specifically, the prohibited wishes are channeled in estranging, perverse directions: "The people who obey taboo have an ambivalent attitude toward that which is tabooed. The magical power, which is attributed to taboo, derives from its ability to lead individuals into temptation, since the prohibited desire becomes displaced onto something else."[69] We have seen how Kant's law acts precisely like the taboo mechanism described here. It does so by operating in a self-referential mode and by allowing only itself as a motivation. Significantly, other motivations, including desires, inclinations, wishes, and ambitions, are prohibited. Thus, the confluence between the categorical imperative within modernity and primitive taboo does indeed have a pertinent point of reference in Kant's philosophical *oeuvre*.

In the *Ego and the Id* (1923) Freud radicalized his position toward Kant's moral philosophy as outlined in *Totem and Taboo* when he wrote, "the ego submits to the categorical imperative of the super-ego."[70] A few pages before this passage he explained, in elusive terms, the compulsive force of the super-ego as the enactment of Kant's moral philosophy:

> The superego will preserve the character of the father. The stronger the Oedipus complex was, that is to say the more rapidly it was repressed (under the impact of authority, religious doctrine, school and reading), the more severely will the super-ego rule over the ego in the form of a conscience, or perhaps as unconscious feeling of guilt. I will make a conjecture about from where it derives this force—the compulsive character that expresses itself in the categorical imperative—which enables such domination.[71]

Interestingly, Freud conjectured that the compulsive force within the super-ego has its manifestation in the categorical imperative. In this way the categorical imperative marks the violent force of the superego's demands. The repression of the conflict with a father authority, that is, the repression of the archaic Oedipus complex, results all the more cogently in the internalization of its modern revision, as formulated in Kant's moral philosophy.

If the Oedipus complex describes the workings of authority and violence within a private sphere, as a family romance, then the categorical imperative functions as a political strategy adopted by the power structures within a male-dominated family unit in order to become extended to a broader societal sphere. The institutions of the modern state, which attempt to shape individuals by educational means, try to repress Oedipal conflicts. By refusing to subject aggressive and sexual impulses to conscious examination, the paternal superego can exert its power more strongly in the public sphere. Thus, unconscious feelings of guilt make the ego willingly succumb to moral teachings, which are so hypermoral that, like the id, they preclude any nurturing relation between mind and external world. Oedipus literally puts an end to meaningful exchanges with his surroundings by blinding himself, and yet this violent act derives from his conscience. After all, the act of self-blinding results from a mindless desire for self-punishment. It is mindless because he does not know why he did what he did. This is precisely what Freud meant by conscience, which is an "unconscious feeling of guilt": Like the amorality of the id, the hypermorality of the superego drives the ego into mindless actions that destroy its chances of survival in the empirical world.

In the context of his discussion of the superego as a political manifestation of the categorical imperative, Freud further elaborated on the Kantian divide between autonomy and heteronomy. An excess of demands exiles the ego from reality, and at the same time an excess of ideals compels it to self-hatred and destructive behavior in the world. Thus the superego wages war within the psyche of the ego: "While the ego is essentially the representative of the external world, of reality, the superego opposes it as advocate of the internal world, of the id. Conflicts between the ego and the ideal will in the end (we are now prepared for that) mirror the conflict between the real and the psychic, between external and internal world."[72] Here Freud explicitly established a link between the amorality of the id and the hypermorality of the superego. As we shall see, it is a link on which he expanded in *The Economic Problem of Masochism* (1924).

How does the harsh categorical hypermorality of the superego coincide with the amorality of the id, of the drives? Freud, as we have seen, undermined the Kantian notion of autonomy by shedding light on the inseparability of reason and irrationality. As a result, the moral authority that is supposed to be completely autonomous from any emotional impulses is in fact driven by drives, by inward powers that produce fantasies. Like the mechanical internal forces that render the relation between the internal and the external world pathological, the ideal of philosophical idealism undermines the ego's relation to empirical reality. The categorical imperative forces the ego to forego a meaningful relation with matter. Thus it severs both the epistemological and the ethical links that relate the moral actor to empirical reality. This conflict reflects the alienation of the neurotic's psyche from the external world. Freud thus defined neurosis as that which pushes the ego out of real life.

This gap between the real and the psychic is where the excessive demands of a transcendental, that is, antiempirical, Kantian moral philosophy and the perversions of a libido without a "real" empirical object meet and reinforce each other. As Freud explained in *The Unconscious* (1915), "neurosis involves the renunciation of the real object and the libido that has been divested of a real object falls back onto a fantasized one and from there retreats to a repressed one (Introversion)."[73] In other words, a radical devaluation of anything that establishes an orientation to the empirical world first provokes a libidinal displacement from reality to an imaginary substitute (an *Ersatzvorstellung*), which then results in the alienation of the ego from his or her emotional life and thus introduces the repression of the libidinal.

This movement describes the causes of neurosis, as Freud understood them: "The protecting wall around the imaginary substitute has to be moved further outside with each increased stirring of the drive. This whole construction, which is established in analogous manner in other neuroses, bears the name of a *phobia*. Avoidances, renunciations and prohibitions are the expression of the escape from the conscious occupation of the displaced imagination."[74] After the superego has forced the libido to orient itself away from the empirical world, it becomes displaced onto imaginary substitutes, which in turn are projected onto objects of the empirical world. The drives that are no longer directed to empirical, living beings now develop an uncanny force of their own, one that bedevils the external world as such.

Can we distinguish between drives and the libido, and if so, how? Let us begin by clarifying the term *libido*. As Jonathan Lear has pointed out, Freud "was willing to abandon the fundamental opposition between the sexual drive and the I-drive, but only to substitute another for it."[75] Initially, Freud conceived of a libido that attacks the psychic peace of the ego. In his later work, however, the "sexual drive was 'transformed' into Eros, the love or life drive, and the new Something Else is the death drive, a force in every living cell for decomposition and return to an inorganic state."[76] Thus the concept of libido embraces two conflicting drives, one that is oriented toward objects in the empirical world and one that has been displaced—by means of the superego—onto imaginary substitutes. Kant's moral philosophy, which advocated a transcendence of desires in the external world, helped establish a hypermoral culture in which the superego voice of the categorical imperative causes pathologies.

Freud's response to Kant might well explain the transcendental bent in psychoanalysis. As Françoise Meltzer has pointed out, Freud almost never took things as they are empirically constituted, but instead read in them both displacements of anxieties and forms of infinitely displaced desires.[77] According to this view, the transcendental shapes the pathological. In contrast, Kant saw a complete indifference to any determinations by the external world as constituting moral achievement. Indeed, Freud argued in *The Economic Problem of Masochism* that the categorical imperative as "direct heir of the Oedipus complex"[78] makes out of the external world a representation of the superego, for the latter is as much "the representative of the id as it is of the external world."[79] Whereas Kant claimed that the autonomous mind creates a sense of time and space, Freud argued that it displaces the empirical with imaginary substitutes, which are themselves products of a hypermoral force that prohibits a libidinal bonding between the ego and the external world.

In *Beyond the Pleasure Principle* Freud "subjects Kant's proposition, according to which time and space are necessary forms of our thinking, to a new discussion that is informed by certain psychoanalytical insights."[80] He seemed to cast this Kantian transcendental proposition into a pathological discourse. With an ironic twist, he revealed the autonomy of reason to be nothing more than the self-rule of "inward agitations . . . that are treated as if they did not work from the inside but from the outside."[81] Kant's creation of time and space through an autonomous mind came down to projection: "This [taking inward imaginary substitutes for a libidinal orientation toward the external world for the external world] is the origin of *projection,* for which is reserved such an important role in the causation of pathologies."[82] Thus Freud treated the pathological with the ironic respect that is normally reserved for the important Enlightenment philosopher whose importance seems to be one of clinical interest only. If the hypermorality of Kant's moral philosophy precipitates a radical estrangement from reality, then its libidinal force can be described in terms of Lear's reading of Freud's death drive. "Love," however, "is not just a feeling or a discharge of energy, but an emotional orientation to the world."[83] The therapy of psychoanalysis resides in reorienting the damaged ego to the world. This, then, is Freud's "other Enlightenment." In the next section I discuss how such a revised conceptualization of the Enlightenment connects to his understanding of Judaism.

From Taboo to Totem

In the wake of Yosef Hayim Yerushalmi's famous essay *Freud's Moses: Judaism Terminable and Interminable, Moses and Monotheism* has become the central text for discussions of Freud's Jewish identity. Much has since been made of the response by the late Freud to anti-Semitism at the time in which he was working on this book (1934–38). It was a time in which racist hatred was encouraged and sponsored not only by the "mob" but also by the intellectual and political elite of Nazi Germany and fascist Austria.

This discussion has recently undergone a complex and radical turn in Jan Assmann's fascinating and idiosyncratic study *Moses the Egyptian.* Whereas Yerushalmi emphasized the Jewish identity publicly belittled by Freud himself, Assmann wondered why the founder of psychoanalysis made Moses into an Egyptian. According to Assmann, Freud did so in order to undermine the basis of counterreligious movements, which is instantiated in the opposition between Egypt in error and Israel in truth. This opposition thus adumbrates European anti-Semitic discourse in which the Jews as representatives of the "primitive" past are contrasted with with the Christians, the promoters of progress.

Now, Assmann gave his argument a provocative spin when he claimed that monotheism is ultimately to blame for anti-Semitism.[84] According to Assmann, Freud was in fact attacking the alleged intolerance of monotheistic distinctions between true and false (or new and old) beliefs while composing his idiosyncratic essay: "Not the Jew but monotheism had attracted this undying hatred. . . . Freud concentrates all the counter-religious force of biblical monotheism in Akhenaten's revolution from above. This was the origin of it all. . . . It is this hatred brought about by Akhenaten's revolution that informs the Judeophobic texts of antiquity."[85] By turning monotheistic "revelation" into cosmotheistic "translation," Assmann's Freud stood in an Enlightenment tradition whose deconstructive method calls into question all forms of distinction. In doing so it replaced binary oppositions with a notion of universality.[86]

The argumentative structure of this study does not permit a discussion of *Moses the Egyptian* that would do justice to its complexity,[87] but it should be noted that Freud did portray Mosaic monotheism in the ethical and universalist tone that Assmann seemed to attribute almost exclusively to cosmotheism. Freud emphasized that the religion of Aton develops "the conception of a universal God"[88] and that this type of theology gives rise to the divinity of Maat, the "goddess of truth, order and justice."[89] Yet Assmann may indeed have highlighted an important issue in Freud's *Moses and Monotheism*, namely, that of a critique of monotheistic commandments that are rather intransigent and exclusive. This element of critique, however, may not necessarily confirm an espousal of cosmotheism and the Enlightenment. Instead, it could point to a revision of eighteenth-century enlightened thought. Freud voiced his rather critical stance toward these "progressive" movements when he wrote that by 1938 "progress has entered a pact with barbarity."[90] Moreover, Yahweh, as Harold Bloom has pointed out in an important essay, "is not an authority, which after all is a Roman conception, and not a Jewish one."[91] Yahweh as "a creator, a revealer, and a redeemer, whose attributes yield us the blessings of more life,"[92] may well be reconcilable with Freud's critique of authoritarianism.

In the following I focus on Freud's reading of a harsh superegoistic aspect of monotheism in Egypt. Freud did not, however, do away with monotheism as such. Rather, he differentiated between two strands of Judaism, just as he distinguished two Moses figures. We shall see that one strand, which is represented by the priests and is at odds with the sentiment of the Jewish people, bears a resemblance to Kant's depiction of the Jews as ritualistic and ceremonial. Freud associated this compulsive element with taboo and thus with Kantian moral philosophy—the categorical imperative. The second strand coincides with the totem. In totemism, however, a community of brothers renounces all forms of violence. They are thus no longer provoked to hatred by the taboos that an almighty father figure imposes on contact with women, who are his possession. *Moses and Monotheism* in fact traces the process from taboo to totem, from the Oedipal to the overcoming of the Oedipus complex, from the paternal to the fraternal. It is perhaps surprising that this process has not been traced in the critical literature until now, even though Freud himself saw *Moses and Monotheism* as an elaboration on *Totem and Taboo*.[93]

Strikingly, Freud characterized the biblical Moses as an ambiguous figure: he liberates the Jews and gives them their law[94] and yet he also forces a new religion on them.[95] The verb *to force (zwingen)* has rather violent connotations, which are emblematic of this Moses figure, and they stand in stark contrast to Freud's description of Michelangelo's statue. In his essay on Michelangelo Freud also characterized the biblical lawgiver and liberator of the Jewish people as "violent-tempered" and "subject to bursts of passions."[96] But he saw in the Renaissance sculpture a figure who, by means of moderation, overcomes the harsh features of a superegoistic father figure: Michelangelo's Moses "renounces his affection for anger in order to fulfill his ethical task."[97] Significantly, the renunciation of instinct in *Moses and Monotheism* points to this renouncing *(verzichten)* of violent anger in which the harsh elements of the superego seem to be suspended.

How can we account for such a discrepancy between two characters that bear the same name? We witness such contradictions in *Moses and Monotheism* where one name is given to two foundations of religion and another to two of its founding members. This naming strategy is complicated by the fact that the more ethically refined Egyptian Moses seems to bear a resemblance to the later Median Moses, who is linked to the "volcano god" Jahve, "an uncanny, bloodthirsty demon who works at night and who shies away from daylight."[98] Freud tried to separate the contradictory characteristics of the biblical figure—at once "despotic, violent-tempered and even acting violently" and "also the mildest and most patient of men"[99]—by assigning them to two different personalities (one Egyptian and the other Median). Nevertheless, he rather tentatively placed all violent and authoritarian features in Moses, follower of Jahve—rather than of Aten—when he wrote that "they may belong to the other [Moses], the Median."[100] Such caution may indeed be called for, if we recall that Moses the Egyptian shares with the first worshiper of the one and universal God Aten a despotic character: "Moses, like Ikhnaton, met the same nemesis that awaits all enlightened despots."[101] Indeed, the Jews kill Moses the Egyptian. In doing so they demonstrate that they value freedom from any form of despotic regime—whether enlightened or not—more highly than do the "tame Egyptians": "However, while the tame Egyptians waited until the nemesis had removed the sacred figure of the Pharaoh, the savage Semites took hold of the nemesis' role and rid themselves of their tyrant."[102] Here we find the grounds for a critique of monotheism that Assmann has ingeniously uncovered in Freud's work about Moses. Yet this coexistence of the violent and the benign does not indemnify the ethical validity of the one and universal God Aton. Rather, it asks for a transformation of monotheistic worship, and such transformation is indeed initiated, thanks to the "savagery" of the Jews and not to the "tameness" of the Egyptians.

The binary opposition between the savage Jew and the tame Gentile of course reproduces anti-Semitic discourse only to undermine it. It is in fact their very wildness that enables the Jews to *liberate* themselves from their

Egyptian liberator, who turns out to be an Egyptian tyrant, an Oedipal son of Ikhnaton. The act of patricide, as Sander L. Gilman has pointed out, shaped Freud's understanding of the Jewish experience: "The struggle of the male with the male defines Jewish history in terms of the Jew's masculinity. Not the murderer, but the victim is at fault."[103] This violent struggle among males mirrors the primal scene, as depicted in *Totem and Taboo*. But it also prepares the ground for a specifically Jewish identity in which the primal scene, remaining constitutive for the rest of humanity, makes room for an overcoming of violence. Gilman focuses on a nonviolent cultural foundation that informs Freud's argument, according to which the "Jews had at least attempted to overcome the power of the libido through their 'rejection of sexual or aggressive instinctual demand.'"[104] Yet violence preconditions the renunciation of violence: savagery enables a valid form of nonviolence, if past violence is properly remembered and not repressed. By not killing Ikhnaton, the "progress of spirituality/intellectuality," which Freud attributed to monotheism, moves past the Egyptians as if it never happened.

The trauma of patricide (killing the Egyptian superego, the father figure Moses) stays with the Jews over a long period of time until it comes to consciousness with the rise to power of a second father figure, namely, the Median Moses, who is visibly violent and despotic, just like the God Jahve, for whom he works. This Median Moses introduces the rule of priests, who preside over ceremonies and rituals. Their rule thus bears a striking resemblance to the "cumbersome ceremonies and customs"[105] that characterize the superstitious mind-set that Kant attributed to rabbinic Judaism. And here we witness a fascinating instance of Freud turning the tables on Kant's reading of Jewishness.

Kant depicted Christ as a revolutionary who inaugurates "an overthrow of that which represses all moral attitudes, namely both a belief in [Jewish] ceremonies and the public esteem of [Jewish] priests."[106] Freud advanced an ironic inversion of this revolution. In his account the Jews liberate themselves from a tyrannical rule by killing the Median priests, just as they liberated themselves when they killed the Egyptian Moses. According to Freud, a traumatic event[107] such as the killing of the first Moses preconditioned the consequent shaping of Judaism. His is a prophetic kind of Judaism. It thus represents the opposite of a community that is enslaved to the compulsive rule of priests.[108]

Significantly, only the traumatic murder of the enlightened despot Moses makes the Jews value political and intellectual liberty. This value constitutes the "progress of spirituality/intellectuality." Indeed, it marks the uniqueness of Judaism. Rather than imposing religious truths, as Ikhnaton and Moses the Egyptian did, the prophets proclaim a search for truth and justice. Finding their core identity in this prophetic search, the Jews are the true enlighteners, practicing enlightenment beyond the superego, beyond despotic rule.

Moving from Moses the Egyptian to the shaping of a prophetic Judaism, Freud traced the process from taboo to totem, which he already outlined in *Totem and Taboo*. There the sons are provoked to murder by the taboo-imposing authority of the father, who is able to declare every woman untouchable by anyone but himself. Both Ikhnaton and Moses the Egyptian are described as "holy,"[109] and holiness in turn is invested with the power to establish prohibitions "without rational justification."[110] After killing Moses the enlightened despot, the Jews attempt to renounce the Oedipal conflicts that caused the trauma of murder. They thus change from sons into brothers. As brothers they venerate the father, now their totem, whom they killed. With this act, they cease being sons, that is, they renounce the instincts that drove them to sexual jealousy and consequently to the perpetration of violence.

In this way the renunciation of instincts is not, as is commonly assumed, a Kantian autonomous and masculine (hero-like) renunciation of the pleasures of life. Rather, it ensures peaceful survival: "In order to live peacefully the victorious brothers renounced possession of the women for which reason they had killed their father."[111] Connected with this renunciation is the prohibition of images, which Freud perceived as the cornerstone of the progress in spirituality and intellectuality introduced by Judaism, but not for the reasons for which Kant attributed the same prohibition *(Bildverbot)* to "the Jewish people in their moral epoch."[112] Whereas Kant saw in the *Bildverbot* a transcendence of the material world so that "the moral law in itself works as a sufficient and original determinant in us and does not even permit us to give it any determining point of reference outside itself,"[113] the Freudian renunciation of instinct amounts to a refusal to be driven into encounters with danger in the external world. The ego that refuses the satisfaction of demands imposed by the drives *(Triebanspruch)* avoids "a situation of danger" *(Vermeidung einer Gefahrsituation)*.[114] To this extent "the ego refrains from satisfying the drives in view of obstacles in the external world, namely, then, when it realizes that the action concerned would provoke a serious danger to the ego."[115] A Kantian indifference to the external world turns out to be psychotic, whereas the Freudian reality principle *(Realitätsprinzip)*[116] guides one along the path to a rational way of action. The "domination of an inner psychic reality over the reality of the external world opens the door to psychosis"[117] and results in "an inhibition of life" *(Lebenshemmung)* and an "inability to live" *(Lebensunfähigkeit)*.[118]

Thus Freud unveiled the etiology of psychosis (and to a lesser extent neurosis, too) in Kant's moral philosophy. As he turned the tables on Kant, so he turned the tables on political and pseudoscientific anti-Semites by arguing that this psychotic situation of being isolated from the external world constitutes a "state within the state" (and not, as anti-Semitism claims, "the Jew").[119] Whereas Kantian transcendentalism and its political and pseudoscientific revisions end up as pathological fantasies, a Jewish way of life rests on the foundation of a "particular confidence in life" *(eine besondere Zuversicht im Leben).*[120] Freud saw this kind of healthy optimism as the pleasure beyond the pleasure principle. It is a pleasure that has renounced the necessity of sacrificing or endangering life in order to derive an excess of joy.

He acknowledged that "it is not obvious and immediately understandable why a progress in spirituality/intellectuality—that is, a reduction of sensuality—should raise the self-confidence of an individual or of a people."[121] After all, "obedience to the reality principle does not at all provide pleasure."[122] However, interaction with the external world, which does not undermine the position of the self within this world, generates a joyful kind of energy that is not excessive and can therefore be metabolized by the ego without traumatic consequences. According to Freud, the Jews' "blissful state of being chosen" *(beseligenden Auserwähltheit)* contrasts with the pathological Christian idea of having to be freed from the world through God's redemption *(befreiende Erlösung).*[123] By undermining the Kantian radical divide between morality and the external world, Freud sets out to question a secularized and politicized version of this pathological theology.

In *Moses and Monotheism* Freud thus related psychoanalytic theory and practice to what he saw as Judaism's conception of rationality. This kind of Enlightenment differs from Kant's idealist definition of reason. While working on his "new science," Freud in fact turned the tables on Kant by shedding light on reason's irrationality. This irrationality consists in what Kant understood by reason's "purity." Kant's reason is pure inasmuch as it is "independent of experience."[124] In Freud's revision of Enlightenment thought the Jews become the beacons of truth and justice precisely because they have not closed their minds to the experience of the mindless. It is this element of conscious remembrance that relates Freud's understanding of Judaism to psychoanalytic theory and practice.

10 WALTER BENJAMIN'S TRANSCENDENTAL MESSIANISM, OR THE IMMANENT TRANSFORMATION OF THE PROFANE

Freud analyzed the psychological and social consequences of a Kantian divide between the individual and the external world. Benjamin focused on a related problematic, albeit in a distinctive idiom and by reaching different conclusions.

Did the Kantian worldview of German public culture play a role in Benjamin's idiosyncratic conception of the messianic? The first part of this chapter analyzes how Benjamin's writings concerning capitalism, popular culture (Mickey Mouse), and baroque aesthetics constitute a materialist revision of German idealism's attempt to transform the body into the body politic. If the experience of World War I intensified Rosenzweig's critical stance toward Kantian and Hegelian thought, Benjamin discovered that the "rhetoric of German idealism . . . lent itself all too easily to the sophistry of the 'ideas of 1914.'"[1] A comparison between the two writers vis-à-vis their responses to the battlefields of the Great War would bring out contrasts in their respective engagements with German idealism in particular and with modernity in general. Whereas Rosenzweig argued for the independence of the body, which, embodying life and thereby (in his interpretive framework) Jewishness, rightly refused to be transformed into the body politic, Benjamin was convinced that a pre-Kantian metaphysics of experience could not be regained. Rather, hope precisely resides in the hopeless. That is to say, any attempt at transforming the empirical into the noncontingent by immanentist means results in the annihilation of what exists and thereby makes room for redemption.

Benjamin, as we will see, saw such loss of belief in a transcendent force that could redeem the empirical in a nonviolent manner "at the end of time" in both the economic practices that developed in the age of Reformation (capitalism as religion) and in Kant's post-Reformation philosophy. In Benjamin's reading, German idealism's rational theology and moral philosophy in fact coincide with the immanentist religion of capitalism. This rather idiosyncratic co-analysis of intellectual and economic history has, indeed, textual points of reference. To mention only one of them: in his *Religion Within the Boundaries of Mere Reason* Kant posited in the God turned man (Jesus Christ) an image of immanent redemption, in which the body may overcome its material basis by means of complete control of reason and thus in an autonomous manner. Reason's absolute control over the body all too easily results in regimens of discipline. The disciplined body has learned to forgo its needs. It can do without inclinations (for food, shelter, emotional intuitions, and so on). Benjamin interpreted the concept of *Erfahrung* as the experience of these inclinations. This "experience [*Erfahrung*] has fallen in value, amid a generation which from 1914 to 1918 had to experience some of the most monstrous events in the history of the world."[2] After the war (in 1918), he still thought that such experience could be retrieved by bridging the gap between the realms of nature and freedom, that is, the two entities that Kant tried to turn into exclusive contradictions. In "On the Coming Philosophy" Benjamin thus argued that with the restoration "of a concept of experience which would provide a logical place for metaphysics, the distinction between the realms of nature and freedom would be abolished."[3] Soon he would abandon any hope for such a return to a metaphysics that Kant's transcendental philosophy has done away with. This chapter will focus on such essays as "Critique of Violence" and "Capitalism as Religion" in which, with a despairing gesture, Benjamin saw in the reinforcement of such a divide its messianic overcoming.

In "On the Coming Philosophy" he had already discussed Kant as the godfather of such destruction of metaphysical experience. Kant "undertook his work on the basis of an experience virtually reduced to a nadir, to a minimum of significance."[4] In this 1918 essay Benjamin associated the post-Reformationist philosopher with the reformationist aesthetics of the baroque. He did so by linking Kant's "validity without significance"—wherein the absence of a meaningful relation between the individual and the external world results in the melancholy that characterizes baroque tragedy—to the *Trauer* as thematized in the *Trauerspiel* (baroque tragedy). Accordingly, "one can say that the very greatness of his [Kant's] work, his unique radicalism, presupposed an experience which had almost no intrinsic value and which could have attained its (we may say) sad significance only through its certainty."[5] Benjamin elaborated on this point in his book *The Origin of the German Baroque Tragic Drama*.

Indeed, one should read this book in conjunction with his "Capitalism as Religion" and his "Critique of Violence." Such analysis would indeed do justice to Benjamin's critical methodology, which lifts *"the mask of 'pure art'"* and shows "that there is no neutral ground for art."[6] He saw in baroque tragedy "the comprehensive secularization of the historical in the state of creation."[7] The disgust with nature, with the body, with the profane brings about the desire to read the world allegorically. Baroque allegory, in Benjamin's understanding, immanently transcends the immanent to the point of annihilating it. As we shall see, this is exactly what he perceived to be operative in the nonsignifying economical transactions that characterize the religion of capitalism. Related to capitalist economics as (at least in Benjamin's view) it emerged within the Christianity of the Reformation, the reformationist aesthetics of the baroque destroys profane bodies. Only in their annihilation do they come close to a signification that would be transferred to them in their redeemed, resurrected state. This commandment of the destruction of the profane rules the workings of allegory, just as it motivates the abrupt coming of a redeemed society: "The human body could be no exception to the commandment which ordered the destruction of the organic so that the true meaning, as it was written and ordained, might be picked up from its fragments."[8] This allegorical destruction of the body gains in force as capitalist society progresses.

Benjamin read the pop culture symbols of such society in precisely this way. He explained the huge popularity of the Disney cartoon by seeing in it the mirror image of the very public that is enchanted by it. The aesthetics of Mickey Mouse films hides their material truth-value, while embodying it: "So the explanation for the huge popularity of these films is not mechanization, their form; nor is it misunderstanding. It is simply the fact that the public recognizes its own life in them."[9] What characterizes this mirror image of a modern capitalist society? It retraces in the sphere of pop art the work that baroque allegories do on the body. It chips away body parts. It fragments the body into ruinous parts. And here the aesthetics of fragmentation, which Benjamin analyzed in baroque allegory, are clearly immersed into the economic, theological, and cultural sphere from which they emerge and which they embody: "Property relations in Mickey Mouse cartoons: here we see for the first time that it is possible to have one's own arm, even one's body, stolen."[10] Mickey Mouse, who loses various limbs, thus depicts the violence that capitalist economics exerts on the flesh-and-blood bodies of those who fall victim to it. It does so however, not in a critical manner. On the contrary, it celebrates this loss of experience.

After Kant's Copernican turn, *physis* (the body or nature) lost its intrinsic relation to a meta-, to a transcending realm. As we shall see, Benjamin saw this loss economically, as well as theologically, enacted in capitalism. Note that such absence of signification engulfs the whole of nature (human nature included) in a maelstrom of guilt. In other words, the body without signification might not be worth preserving, since it has become nonsensical. Benjamin came back to this theme of sadness *(Trauer)* and guilt *(Schuld)* again and again in his writings on Kant (and capitalism and law) and in his aesthetical works. In his essay "Goethe's Elective Affinities" he made it clear that the loss of supernatural reference points submerges human nature into an all-encompassing abyss of guilt: "With the disappearance of supernatural life in man, his natural life turns into guilt, even without his committing an act contrary to ethics. For now it is in league with mere life, which manifests itself in man as guilt."[11] Kant's destruction of traditional metaphysics thus theoretically justified a monetary disregard for the specific constitution of specific objects whose value it autonomously determines. After all, they are intrinsically valueless and are thus in a state of guilt. In the capitalist world of Mickey Mouse films this conflation of mere life with guilt has gone so far that body parts with which one experiences the world have been torn to fragments: "These films disavow experience more radically than ever before. In such a world, it is not worthwhile to have experiences."[12] Human nature, and therewith experience in the external world, has become deprived of any validity. In the following, I analyze how Benjamin's critique of modern law and capitalist economics enveloped a critique of Kantian transcendental philosophy. Whereas Rosenzweig and Freud advanced clear counternarratives to the Kantian narrative of the Enlightenment, Benjamin did not see historical validity for such philosophical countermovements. He thus developed his idiosyncratic messianism along Kantian lines. At the same time, he did so with a consciousness of despair. This comes nowhere clearer to view than when he contrasted Kant's secularization of Christian values with, in his view, the absent world of rabbinic law and messianic justice.

Law and Justice

Benjamin's contrast between law *(Recht)* and justice *(Gerechtigkeit)* meant a confrontation between the secularized Christian capitalist (and therefore deceiving) mythical law and a Jewish messianic notion of justice. Indeed, the law discussed in the "Critique of Violence" (1921) is the secular law of the state founded on the immanentist justification of Kant's autonomous reason. Benjamin aligned this secular law with prehistory in the same way he did in his 1934 essay on Kafka, "Potemkin." In "Potemkin," however, Benjamin contrasted the prehistoric "pagan" law, which declares life guilty, with Mosaic law, which aims at the protection of life. As we shall see, Kafka emerged as the Jewish critic of a modernity marked by Kant, in both its Christian and capitalist forms. Kafka, however, did not affirm Jewish law; rather, he described in his parables the radical distance between contemporary society and the doctrines of Halachah. Accordingly, Benjamin characterized Kafka's narratives as Haggadah (story) without Halachah (teaching, guidance). Benjamin's reading of Kafka evidenced his distrust in a way that could lead back from a Kantian Christian and capitalist society to one that is founded on the guidance of Jewish law. Jewish law, which is not discussed in the "Critique of Violence," appears in the 1934 essays as a contrast to the corruption of the society Kafka depicted, a contrast, however, that has been lost to the extent that Kafka himself seemed to be ignorant of it. In the following, I examine how Benjamin disregarded rabbinic Judaism and how he opted for a transcendental messianism. He clearly perceiveed Kantian Christianity as having thoroughly corrupted biblical scripture. As we saw in chapter 1, the post-Reformation philosopher indeed set out to redefine religion in a radically anti-Judaic way.

In his "Capitalism as Religion" (1921) Benjamin singled out modern Christianity as the only religion that is grounded in an absolute equation of life with guilt, which does not allow for any form of atonement. Rather than working for a change of heart, Christianity that has become capitalism tries to declare the whole of life guilty so that redemption can only be attained in complete despair, which heralds the utter destruction of profane life: "Capitalism is entirely without precedent, in that it is a religion which offers not the reform of existence but its complete destruction. It is the expansion of despair, until despair becomes a religious state of the world in the hope that this will lead to salvation. God's transcendence is at an end. But he is not dead; he has been incorporated into human existence."[13] The strong messianic tones (*Zertrümmerung*, that is, complete annihilation) in this depiction of capitalist Christianity indicate Benjamin's paradoxical identification with his object of critique.[14] As we shall see, this critical appreciation of the religion of capitalism (Christianity) parallels Benjamin's affirmation of Kant's transcendental method, while subverting its immanentist Christian agenda promoting a nonrabbinic, transcendental messianism. Benjamin defined Christianity as a religion without transcendence in which the divine becomes involved with the human. Indeed, the divine, as exemplified by the figure of Christ, turns into the anthropoid. In Benjamin the incarnation of the divine into immanence means that the former participates in the guilt appertaining to the latter: the immanentism of Christianity, as capitalism, universalizes guilt to the point where it even implicates God in the existence of a fallen world. It was Kant who developed the Christology to which Benjamin was implicitly referring in the quotation above. Like Benjamin, Kant contrasted Mosaic law and rabbinic Judaism with the God turned immanent whose divinity does not consist in his life but in his acceptance of death, which should be an example for all Christians. Mosaic law and rabbinic Judaism, by contrast, are concerned with the spiritual guidance of empirical life, according to the teaching of divinely revealed law. Whereas Judaism is oriented toward the "goods of this world,"[15] in becoming immanent and therefore guilty (as all of a fallen humanity) Christ can only return to his divine origin by means of the radical rejection of all empirical life, even if it is not necessarily impure. In Kant, Jesus

Christ appeared as a revolutionary who overturns Judaism, and this is precisely because his worldly life illustrates the radical unworthiness of all bodily existence.

Like Benjamin, Kant emphasized the involvement of the divine with the human only to argue that the divine's turning immanent underlines the necessity of despair in, and rejection of, life that precludes obedience to the commandments of an immanent morality (Kant's *Sittlichkeit*). Kant made it, in fact, quite clear that he defined morality in relation to the laws of autonomous reason in radical separation from the religious statutes offered in divine revelation (as in Mosaic or rabbinical law).[16] Benjamin took over Kant's language of martyrdom (see the discussion of the Kantian term *absterben*—to die away—in chapter 1) but replaced autonomous reason with the messianic. It is this element of apocalypse *(Zertrümmerung)* that also fascinated Benjamin in the religion of capitalism.

This transcendental devaluation of life as guilt conditioned Benjamin's rejection of law in its Kantian sense. Indeed, "Capitalism as Religion" equates Christianity not only with capitalism (money) but also with law: "Capitalism and law. The heathen character of law. . . . Methodologically, one should begin by investigating the links between myth and money throughout the course of history, to the point where money had drawn so many elements from Christianity that it could establish its own myth."[17]
This conflation of money and law in the context of Christian metaphysics of course recalls *The Metaphysics of Morals*, in which Kant exemplified his secularized Christian concept of law in the workings of money. Thus Benjamin's equation of Christianity and money has a philological point of reference in Kant, for it is Kant who depicted money as a convincing illustration of the metaphysical as the nonempirical, the purely formal.

Kant, as a post-Reformation Enlightenment philosopher, had in fact a significant bearing on Benjamin's understanding of modern Christianity as capitalist. In "Capitalism as Religion" Benjamin pinpointed the Reformation as the time at which a capitalistic way of life manifested itself as Christian: "The Christianity of the Reformation did not favor the growth of capitalism; instead it transformed itself into capitalism."[18] Informed by a Lutheran reformation tradition, Kant formulated Christianity as capitalism in a philosophical manner. We have already seen the vital role money played in Kant's *metaphysische Rechtslehre*. We have also seen how Kant developed his Christology in close relation to his transcendental philosophy. Kant's understanding of Christianity and law as rationalist and antisensuous helped shape German political and intellectual culture. The pervasive Kantianism within Germany's public sphere, in turn, contributed to the mode in which Walter Benjamin perceived modernity. Benjamin interpreted Kant's devaluation of life as mere life (as matter without a spiritual point of reference) as pagan and modern Christian. This association has to do with Benjamin's understanding of Judaism. Benjamin defineed pagan religions by their equation of life with guilt: "So many pagan religions. So many notions in which nature is posited as guilty. Guilty is somewhat always life; and the punishment for this guilt is death. One form of natural guilt is sexuality. . . . Another is that of money. . . . Jewish: not life, but only the acting individual can become guilty."[19] Benjamin drew on a dialectic between sensuous life and death as an atonement for it that, as we saw in chapter 1, was established by Kant's Christology. Benjamin contrasted this post-Reformationist Christianity with Judaism, in which one can only become guilty as a result of actions. The knowledge of a variety of particular laws enables a possible avoidance of becoming guilty because of sinful actions. Benjamin interpreted Mosaic law as the conditioning of such avoidance of guilt in empirical life. Mosaic laws guide empirical bodies away from sin:

> [T]hey [the Mosaic laws] belong to the legislation governing the realm of the body in the broadest sense (presumably) and occupy a very special place: they determine the location and method of *direct* divine intervention. And just where this location has its frontier, where it retreats, we find the zone of politics, of the profane, of a bodily realm that is without law in a religious sense.[20]

This quotation demonstrates that Benjamin appreciated a Mosaic and rabbinic understanding of law that contrasted sharply with the immanent capitalist notion of Kantian *Recht* as discussed in the "Critique of Violence." Mosaic law establishes a bridge between body and spirit. It thus provides experience with spiritual reference points. These markers prevent it from endangering its life by committing sinful, that is, violent acts. The body that follows Mosaic laws thus strikingly differs from that of Mickey Mouse, who indeed loses limbs because of mindless behavior. Mickey Mouse thus embodies mere life. The body that follows Mosaic laws, on the other hand, sanctifies the physical by spiritually valid action. Accordingly, this Jewish coordination of the spirit and nature contradicts the Kantian radical divide between the free and the natural.

It is this juxtaposition of the physical and the moral that preconditioned Kant's binary opposition between law and charity. Benjamin took issue with the Kantian antagonism between the moral and the physical as well as with the post-Reformation Christian dichotomy between law and charity as theoretically formulated by Kant. In "On Kantian Ethics" (1918) Benjamin criticized "the doctrine of 'rational beings'" which makes "the number of ethical subjects" independent "from that of human bodies."[21] He also argued for an evaluation of the term *inclination (Neigung),* which Kant denigrated: "The notion of 'inclination,' which Kant takes to be ethically indifferent or anti-ethical, is, through a change of meaning, to be transformed into one of the highest notions of morality, in which it is perhaps destined to occupy the place which was once taken by the concept of love."[22] As we shall see, Benjamin, however, clearly believed that a capitalist Christianity had universally and effectively declared the physical to be guilty so that a return to rabbinic Judaism, in which particular spiritual guidelines could safeguard human actions from contact with sin, is precluded. As I discuss below, Benjamin indeed evaluated inclination—not as love, however, but as anarchic violence that confounds all Kantian immanent law and thus enables the messianic destruction of the existing social order. It is a social order that Benjamin saw depicted in Kafka's novels, one which has lost knowledge of Jewish law.

Benjamin's Rejection of Kantian Law and His Affirmation of a Transcendentalist Messianism

The starting point of Benjamin's critique of law is violence, that is to say, that which in "profane" empirical life threatens the well-being of empirical life. Kant paid attention to violence not as a threat to material bodies but rather as a subversion of the rational order of things: his law attempted to preclude the revolutionary violence of those who rebel against a bourgeois state founded on the rationalization of money and property. It therefore acted against a violent return to the original, "natural" state in which the earth was everyone's possession. Benjamin did precisely what Kant interdicted: he reasoned against the violence of positive law. But he only abolished Kant's immanent law, which issued from autonomous reason and was upheld by the political ruler, in order to replace it with a transcendental violence, a "divine violence" *(göttliche Gewalt)*, which ushers in a messianic age by means of the utter destruction of the profane. In this way, Benjamin still clung to a Kantian divide between nature and freedom, although he undermined the post-Reformation philosopher's immanentist and capitalist agenda.

Indeed, Benjamin did not discuss the rabbinic notion of "oral law," which tries to prevent any static and violent impositions on empirical life, wishing instead to be employed so as to minimize loss of life as well as violence. Rather, Benjamin exclusively discussed the positive law of state authority grounded in a static notion of rationality as delineated by Kant: "Lawmaking is powermaking, assumption of power and to that extent an immediate manifestation of violence."[23] The violence of law is, however, connected to the keeping secret of a spiritual doctrine by means of which men and women could avoid transgression. Using the guardians of law, the ruling powers enforce the violent suppression of a way of life in which guilt and sin could be avoided:

or from the point of view of violence, which alone can guarantee law, there is no equality, but at most equally great violence. . . . Laws and circumscribed frontiers remain, at least in primeval times, unwritten laws. A man can unwittingly infringe upon them and thus incur retribution. For each intervention of law that is provoked by an offense against the unwritten and unknown law is called "retribution" (in contradistinction to "punishment").[24]

As in "Capitalism as Religion," Benjamin aligned the modern bourgeois society with pagan and archaic *Urzeiten*. Similarly, in the 1934 essay on Kafka, "Das bucklige Männlein," Benjamin emphasized the triumph of the archaic within the modern: "Kafka did not consider the age in which he lived as an advance over the beginnings of time. His novels are set in a swamp world. In his works, the creature appears at the stage which Bachofen has termed the hataeric stage."[25] If in archaic times laws as spiritual guidelines were kept secret from the populace, then this also holds true for modern Kantian *Recht*. As we saw in chapter 1, Kant forbade any exploration into the origins of both state power and state law: the subjects of the state must not question the validity of the violence that enforces positive law. Rather, they have to be aware of the debt they owe to the *Recht*. In "Potemkin" Benjamin discussed the enforced secrecy imposed by the powers of *Recht* on laws for spiritual guidance: "Laws and definite norms remain unwritten in the prehistoric world."[26] In the context of an examination of Kafka's *Der Prozeß*, Benjamin contrasted the secret laws of both the modern state and archaic ruling classes with particular descriptive spiritual guidelines *(umschriebene Normen)*. In "Potemkin" he defined these norms as Mosaic laws. In distinction to archaic unwritten laws, in the modern bourgeois capitalist state "the written law is contained in lawbooks, but these are secret; by basing itself on them, the prehistoric world exerts its rule all the more ruthlessly."[27] Paradoxically, modernity reinforces pre-modernity. The keeping secret of the written law intensifies the legal voluntarism that Benjamin identified with pre-modern times. In this way, on account of both the Kantian prescription of the nonexplorability of violence and law and its consignment to the ruling classes that uphold the modern state, modern *Recht* affirms the unwritten laws.

The unwritten laws lead the populace inevitably into guilt, for they have no guidance in avoidance of guilt and the ensuing atonement for it. In another 1934 essay about Kafka, "A Childhood Photograph," Benjamin discussed Kafka's narrations as mirrors of the archaic as well as of the modern. They open up a world corrupted by those who hold power and in doing so abolish the accessibility of law as spiritual guidance for empirical action.[28] They are parables without a spiritual point of reference. For this reason Kafka was "a writer of parables but he did not found a religion:"[29] the signs in his parables are empty of any spiritual or redemptive signification; they exclusively refer to the corrupt politics of an immanent capitalist religious system. Even those who—like the "Mann from Lande" in "Vor dem Gesetz"—try to study the law are denied access by the pillars of such a system, by the "Türvorsteher": "The law which is studied but no longer practiced is the gate to justice. The gate to justice is study. Yet Kafka doesn't dare attach to this study the promises which tradition has attached to the study of the Torah. His assistants are sextons who have lost their house of prayer; his students are pupils who have lost the Holy Writ [*Schrift*]."[30] Benjamin described here the loss of both Haggadah (the practiced, acted-on law as illustrated by Talmudic narrations) and the ignorance of Halachah (the spiritual guidance that Talmudic law offers). In a society in which the spiritual guidance offered by law is ignored, a dedication to the study of this unpracticed law might work for justice *(Gerechtigkeit)*. Yet even the contemplative life of study, rather than praxis, has lost its validity in a society that has become so corrupted that even the texts of the Scriptures have not escaped corruption.

Accordingly, Benjamin saw no validity in rabbinic tradition on account of the erasure and corruption of such tradition by the capitalist religion of post-Reformation Christianity. Yet he perceived in this very process of corruption and fear a sign of hope: "What corruption is in the law, anxiety is in their thinking. It messes a situation up, yet is the only hopeful thing about it."[31] Utter corruption of the spiritual guidance by means of which empirical life could avoid guilt with just actions according to the Halachah, also leads to the utter destruction of a corrupted empirical life and to its resurrection in a messianic age. Thus, in "Critique of Violence" Benjamin concurred with Kant's critique of the "Pharisean watchword," but he agreed with it only to undermine its anti-Judaic connotations:

> The proposition that existence stands higher than a just existence is false and ignominious, if existence is to mean nothing other than mere life. . . . It contains a mighty truth, however, if "existence," or better "life" . . . means the irreducible, total condition that is "man," if the proposition is intended to mean that the nonexistence of man is something more terrible than the (admittedly subordinate) not-yet-attained condition of the just man. . . . Man cannot at any price be said to coincide with the mere life in him, any more than it can be said to coincide with any other of his conditions and qualities, including even the uniqueness of his bodily person.[32]

"Mere life" means empirical life without any spiritual guidance (from Halachah as doctrine, teaching). Benjamin defined the religion of capitalism as an immanent cult that does not provide any guidance for empirical life: "capitalism is a purely cult religion . . . capitalism has no specific body of dogma, no theology."[33] Here Benjamin turned the tables on Kant, who in his *Religion*

Within the Boundaries of Mere Reason argued that Christianity is "the most apt means of introducing a pure moral religion in place of an old cult."[34] Kant characterized Judaism precisely as such an old cult. Benjamin, by contrast, maintained that liberal economics, theorized by Kant as the foundation of his new "metaphysics of law," amounts to nothing but the immanentist cult of capitalism.

In a world determined by the doctrineless religion of capitalism, created life has become corrupted into life that is incapable of any halachic direction, for like Kafka's Haggadahs (here used in the sense of simple stories), it has become completely ignorant of spiritual guidance. Faced with such modernity, Benjamin concurs with the Kantian transcendental destruction of mere life as the empirical without any creaturely relation to the divine, but not with the annihilation of life as God's creation. Benjamin adopted Kant's transcendental method. He used it, however, for his messianism, thus undermining the Kantian ideal of autonomous reason. In "On the Coming Philosophy," Benjamin in fact delineated the possibility of a transcendental experience that is religious rather than mathematical "to create on the basis of the Kantian system a concept of knowledge to which a concept of experience corresponds, of which knowledge is the teachings. Such a philosophy in its universal element would either itself be designated as theology or would be superordinated to theology to the extent that it contains historically philosophical elements."[35] This theological notion of experience finds its fulfilment in a transcendental messianism that Benjamin most strikingly affirmed at the end of "Critique of Violence." As we have seen, he rejected law as violence in its Kantian capitalist sense before focusing on theological experience, which consists in a transcendental messianism.

This rejection of Kantian law conceals a melancholic farewell to rabbinical Jewish law as voiced in the 1934 essays on Kafka. As such, these essays could be read as the missing link in "Critique of Violence." In these essays, Benjamin discussed what he repressed in his rejection of Kantian *Recht*: Mosaic and rabbinic law. In "Critique of Violence" Benjamin contrasted Kantian *Recht* with Jewish *Gerechtigkeit*. In this context, he only mentioned Mosaic law's interdiction against murder. In doing so, he tried to reconcile his transcendental messianism with the Hebrew Bible. He differentiated between the violence of Kantian immanent law, which upholds the post-Reformation religion of capitalism, and the divine violence of transcendental messianism. The latter is "violence . . . with regard to goods, right, life, and suchlike, never absolutely with regard to the soul of the living."[36] Yet Benjamin endorsed immanent violence, for it could enact divine violence. In this he qualified the Mosaic injunction against murder, arguing that only God can act as a judge as regards the justification of killing mere life that is not just *(gerecht)*. As Benjamin maintained in "Capitalism as Religion," however, the world as shaped by post-Reformation Christianity has indeed lost any form of theology that could enact just life, rather than mere life, and, as such, it necessitates a Kantian antiempirical transcendentalism that is messianic. The hopelessness that Kafka's Haggadahs depict, on account of their loss of Halachah at the same time, manifests hope in the destruction of such unjust life by the violent and loving redemption of a messianic revolution. This very destruction is Kantian, that is, transcendental in method, while it destroys that which Kant helped bring about by revolutionizing (or, rather, corrupting) nonpagan, Jewish elements in the Bible.

Benjamin's radical subversion of Kant's philosophy of law as justification for state power became apparent at the end of "Critique of Violence." It was here that Benjamin justified any form of violence that is anarchic, that is, disconnected from any positive law: "Once again all the eternal forms are open to pure divine violence, which myth bastardized with law. Divine violence may manifest itself in a true war exactly as it does in the crowd's divine judgment on a criminal. But all mythic, lawmaking violence, which may be called 'executive,' is pernicious. Pernicious, too, is the law-preserving, 'administrative' violence that serves it.[37] Violence as a form of messianic justice, rather than of immanent law, that supports the Kantian religion of capitalism, manifests itself in anarchic destruction, which does away with the establishment and the keeping of laws that could set limits to the revolutionary destruction preceding a messianic resurrection of mere life into just life. Benjamin's intense messianism must not be confused with an expectant messianism; it is intense to the point at which it welcomes imminent and immanent revolutionary violence as a *"göttliche Gewalt."* This kind of messianism is as immanent and political as the religion of capitalism, as defined by Benjamin. Indeed, Benjamin made it clear that in contemporary society a relation to God can only be established by means of political violence:

> In its present state, the social is a manifestation of spectral and
> demonic powers, often, admittedly, in their greatest tension to God,
> their efforts to transcend themselves. The divine manifests itself in
> them only in revolutionary force. . . . In this world, divine power is
> higher than divine powerlessness; in the world to come, divine
> powerlessness is higher than divine power.[38]

Here Benjamin continued Kant's transcendental method in establishing a dichotomy between the realms of worldly nature and of something else. In Benjamin's case, however, the latter is not the Kantian (secularized Christian) notion of the otherworldly realm of freedom that gradually turns immanent, but the new world of a messianic or communist age. As in Kant's transcendentalism, the empirical overcomes its arbitrariness by immanent means.

Benjamin's new society, then, depends on the violent self-transcendence of worldly capitalism as a result of its destruction. From this perspective his fascination with Kant's transcendentalist, antiempirical method and with the universalization of the feeling of despair generated by the religion of capitalism makes sense. As in Marxist philosophy, in Benjamin's revolutionary messianism capitalism is a necessary step toward a redeemed society. Benjamin was well aware of Marx's dialectical view of history. In his essay on Bert Brecht he thus emphasized that "Marx . . . set himself the task of showing of how the revolution could arise from its complete opposite, capitalism."[39] Accordingly, Benjamin even welcomed the *Zertrümmerung* (complete annihilation) ultimately brought about thanks to the immanent religion of capitalism. The feeling of despair generated by capitalism evokes anarchic violence and in doing so ushers in a communist society. In this way the destruction of corrupted "mere life" should resurrect life and with it the body *(leibliche Person)* in a fully redeemed, messianic age.

Nonetheless, Benjamin employed the word *Gewalt,* thus not concealing the violent aspects of such anarchic revolution. In "Critique of Violence," however, he repressed a sense of despair at the loss of a valid Jewish tradition, thanks to whose combination of spiritual and empirical laws the messianic consists in progressive reform rather than in sudden and all-embracing violence. The "little hunchback" to whom he referred in 1934 is conspicuous by his absence in the "Critique of Violence" of 1921: "This little man is at home in distorted life; he will disappear with the coming of the Messiah, who (a great rabbi once said) will not wish to change the world by force but will merely make a slight adjustment in it."[40] Here Benjamin melancholically alluded to a rabbinical past. The words of the rabbi are literally in the past tense *(gesagt hat).* Indeed, Benjamin depicted Kafka's narrations as brooding over this past, of which the present has no proper knowledge. Even this brooding as *Studium* does not bear fruit, for the texts themselves are corrupted. The Messiah, however, still commands present-tense description *(kommt),* and it was this presence of hope within the hopeless that enabled Benjamin to read the signs of a Kantian religion of capitalism in the light of their destruction in the cause of social redemption.

Conclusion: Elias Canetti, Franz Baermann Steiner, and Weimar's Aftermath

My conclusion has been that the fact of anti-Semitism is essential for the understanding of Christian Europe; it is a main thread in that fabric. . . . Would you not say that European civilization that does no more hold other cultures in tutelage or suppression ceases to be the Europe we know? And if they do to Asiatic countries what they have done to yours, how must they treat an Oriental people which lives among them and is at their mercy?

— Franz Baermann Steiner, "Letter to Mr. Gandhi"

Despair, as we encountered it in Walter Benjamin's work (see chapter 10), may indeed have been the most honest and sadly most realistic (by hindsight) reaction to the historical and philosophical developments traced in this book. Accordingly, this study was partly composed as a response to scholars who argue that pseudoscientific anti-Semitism is more benign than traditional Christian Jew-hatred. Albert S. Lindemann wrote as follows: "On the other hand, as far as most German anti-Semites were concerned, the reasons for their hostility were not only obvious but based on sound, even 'scientific' reasoning; their positions were not derived from Christian bigotry but legitimate indignation over real issues."[1] Rather than basing their opinions on "legitimate reasoning," German anti-Semites such as Treitschke, Chamberlain, and Schmitt saw "real issues" through pseudotheological glasses. Without acknowledging it, they in fact translated the anti-Jewish content of Christian doctrine into the presumably legitimate and objective discourse of science and politics.

After World War I this legitimization of anti-Semitism intensified to the degree that it became normative and thus part of normality. The first part of this study analyzed how Richard Wagner radicalized and politicized a notion of immutability with which Kant and Hegel set out to define what they saw as the incompatibility between Judaism and either a modern ethical commonwealth (Kant) or a modern state (Hegel). The second part attended to the social, ethical, and political consequences of such integration of the mindless (anti-Semitism) into the workings of the mind (philosophy). In chapter 6 we saw how the respected and, in the German sense, "liberal" professor of history Heinrich von Treitschke popularized and, more important, legitimized anti-Semitic acts and ideas. The realm of the mind seemed to be immutably closed to the corporeality with which Jews were equated and of which they were the symbol (consider the spectacular setting of Otto Weininger's suicide). This seemed to have been a foregone conclusion determining the way the educated classes perceived reality.

This mode of perception became even more dominant after World War I. The majority of professors, schoolteachers, and lawyers made anti-Semitism part of their professional calling. This is not to say that the working classes were not anti-Semitic. It is only to foreground the significant role the educated classes played in promoting the immense growth of anti-Semitism in Germany, especially after the war. The discussion in part I sheds light on the historical and philosophical seeds of this perversion, which the Enlightenment concept of Bildung (education) underwent in the nineteenth and twentieth centuries. In this way, "Bildung, which emerged as an inclusive, cosmopolitan ethos, became not only socially privileged but also increasingly nationalized and exclusive."[2] The "most zealous students of the *Protocols [of the Elders of Zion]*" were those whose duty it was to educate the new generation. The majority of the readers of this anti-Semitic best-seller "were to be found not among the industrial workers, whether skilled or unskilled, but in the professional classes."[3] The nineteenth and the twentieth centuries witnessed in Germany the rise of the academic type of anti-Semite.

Academic anti-Semitism touted the binary opposition between idealism and materialism, whose philosophical trajectory has been traced in this study. Many of these professionals "apparently believed quite honestly that the defense of the national cause was a duty of political idealism."[4] Against whom did they need to defend the nation? The Jewish conspiracy theory as most glaringly depicted in *The Protocols of the Elders of Zion* mainly focused on the danger of materialism (represented, of course, by the Jews). Anti-Semitism, self-understood as "a bitter struggle between spirituality, embodied in the German 'race,' and materialism, embodied in the Jewish 'race,'"[5] refashioned the German idealist divide between the empirical and the spiritual qua political slogan.

The first part of this book thus traced the ways in which the stereotype of the materialist Jew grew out of the inarticulate level of German idealist philosophy and became fully articulated in the politicized revision of such thought in Wagner's theoretical and dramatic writings. The second part examined some German Jewish responses to this paradigm from Moses Mendelssohn to Walter Benjamin. This study has been written from a post-Holocaust perspective. I will therefore briefly examine the ways in which two thinkers analyzed the immediate causes of Nazism. I first focus on Elias Canetti's novel *Auto-da-Fé*. Then, a short outline of Franz Baermann Steiner's response to the Shoah will underscore the importance of seeing the Nazi genocide not as a self-contained, quasi-metaphysical occurrence but rather as an event embedded within a "before" and an "after." This does not mean that the narrative traced in this study perversely celebrates the progress of anti-Semitism. That would indeed be a Hegelian philosophy of history within the confines of evil.

To trace a development is not necessarily to promote this development as moral progress. On the contrary, the Nazi genocide starkly illustrates that historical progression does not necessarily mean human improvement. In contrast to Daniel Goldhagen, Franz Baermann Steiner did not see Nazi Germany as being cut off from the modern Western world but as deeply embedded within it. According to Goldhagen, the Nazi genocide had nothing whatsoever to do with modern Western civilization. Nazism seems to have been completely separated from any historical "before" (be it Christianity, the Enlightenment, or romanticism): "It [the Holocaust] constituted a set of actions, and an imaginative orientation that was completely at odds with the intellectual foundations of modern western civilization, the Enlightenment, as well as the Christian and secular ethical and behavioral norms that had governed modern western societies."[6] Steiner precisely undermined this self-assurance. The Holocaust showed how the rationality of the West can be used for irrational ends. In an aphorism composed shortly after World War II, Steiner pointed to the potential unreason of reason. He characterized Nazism in terms of system and organization: "On the other hand the troop of the upright in Western Europe was especially disturbed by the fact that the German reign of terror dealt in such a cold mechanical way with its victims: after all such things must not take place in an orderly manner!"[7] It is this perspective that unsettles any easy reassurance that we would see in the dawn of a new millennium a sign that the backwardness of the past will not intrude on the glorious prospects of a new beginning.

In what follows I first briefly attend to a satirical analysis of the developments traced in the present study (from the eighteenth century to the demise of the Weimar Republic). Elias Canetti sent his satire *Auto-da-Fé* to a Vienna publishing house in 1935, when the Weimar Republic had already been demolished not only by "the mob" but also by its professional pillars (professors, schoolteachers, and lawyers). I conclude with a brief discussion of the importance of Canetti's closest intellectual friend: the Prague-born German Jewish poet and Oxford anthropologist Franz Baermann Steiner.

In the first draft of *Auto-da-Fé*, the main protagonist bore the name of Immanuel Kant. Significantly, the title of the first draft was *Kant Catches Fire (Kant Fängt Feuer)*. The ultimate German title *(Die Blendung)* still retains this critical attitude toward the Enlightenment: the word *Blendung* has etymological connections with the word *blind*.[8] This act of blinding has a further connotation, because the noun *Blendung* and the verb *blenden* are often used in connection with the blinding force of pure light. To this extent, *Blendung* can describe the process of being blinded by the sun, and indeed Jakob and Wilhelm Grimm define *blenden* as "blinding by the sun" *(das blenden der sonne).*[9] Similarly, the title of Canetti's novel evokes the dazzling power of the sun.

Light often functions as a metaphor for the Enlightenment. Both titles of Canetti's novel thus associate enlightened reason with excess: either with the excessive light of fire or the excessive force of a special kind of radiance that causes blindness. In this way, both titles announce a concern with the dead-lock, the utter helplessness of an enlightenment that is unable to reflect critically on its own enterprise because it cannot come to terms with the not fully articulated form of unreason that informs its understanding of reason.

Canetti's novel in fact describes *Bildung* (education) as *Blendung*. Its main protagonist, Kien (the Weimar version of Kant), is a parody of the hegemony of idealism, which defined German culture in the nineteenth and twentieth centuries. This hegemony resulted in a particularly Weimar German legitimization of the ideological. In this context, *ideology* "means a world view that holds that ideas and ideals are primary, for the mind rules sovereign over the world of matter, including systems of government and economics."[10] This disregard for empirical reality clearly reinforced a Kantian divide between reason and matter. This idealism did not necessarily involve anti-Semitism and totalitarianism. On the contrary, a leading neo-Kantian such as Hermann Cohen reconceptualized Kant's ethical heritage in order to reform traditional socialism. Cohen's critical Kantianism set out to improve the legal system by making it compatible with the categorical imperative. In doing so, Cohen attempted to embed Kant's ethical philosophy in the social setting of constitutional theory and practice. Even though Cohen revised Kant's idealism by questioning its dismissal of matter, his liberalization of Kantian ethics nonetheless privileged the idea more than economic reality. As a result, "the idealism intrinsic in this neo-Kantian thought made the proper consciousness, as embodied in the law, the prerequisite for all economic and social change."[11] In *Die Blendung* Canetti analyzed the prioritization of the idea over and against empirical reality. As his hyperbolic treatment makes clear, he saw in it the symptoms of a pathological public sphere. Rather than engage with the economic and social problems that contribute to a growing disintegration of democracy, Weimar intellectuals perceived a concern with these issues as part of the problem and not as a way of diagnosing the illness.

In his hatred of matter, which he equates with woman as well as with the masses, the intellectual Peter Kien offers a satirical mirror image of the Weimar German identification of reason with ideology. In his quest for autonomy, Kien barricades himself in his library. He goes so far as to refrain from teaching, because doing so would only defile the purity of his intellect. To better facilitate this separation from the impurity of the external world, Kien walls up the windows of his room. The autonomy of the intellectuals must not allow for any contingent influence, not even that of sunlight. The Enlightenment, so it seems, only survives in the radical separation from the outside world, light included. This paradox of enlightenment portends the apocalyptic ending of the novel, in which the autonomous scholar in fact destroys the material basis of his scholarship.[12] Kien feels so threatened by the materiality of both his books and his own body that he sets fire to his library (and to himself). Clearly, Canetti's spoof of Kant functions as a critique of issues that contributed to the collapse of the Weimar republic.

To this extent, intellectuals on the Right and on the Left were united by a common idealist heritage. This tradition gave priority "to the autonomy of rational man over concern with the Marxist definition of objective reality."[13] Canetti not only analyzed the failings of intellectuals. He also saw these failings as mirror images of the Weimar public sphere. Accordingly, every character in *Die Blendung* falls prey to blindness in one form or another. The moot point, however, has to do with the absence of any critical reflection on this social pathology. The one who could critically reflect on this illness (the intellectual Kien) is its symptom. The novel narrates different types of absolutist approaches to empirical reality. Kien's housekeeper Therese (who later becomes his wife) only values sex and money. The porter of the house in which Kien lives can only find pleasure in the sadistic exertion of power as realized in the sexual abuse of his daughter. The obsessive chess champion Fischerle represents the stereotypical representation of "the Jew" just as Therese mirrors the misogynist stereotype of "woman." Canetti does not spare the intellectual from his hyperbolic treatment. With his hatred of the masses Kien mirrors the solitary thinker of German idealism only to turn this isolation itself into the mass-like, that is, into a stereotype. The isolation of the "progressive" mind thus reveals modernity's neglect of the public sphere as the descent into the mindlessness of collectivism. As we have seen, Kien narrows down the concept of education to a divide between matter and spirit. This divide in turn feeds the stereotypical discourse with which other protagonists depict both Jews and women. Misogyny and anti-Semitism often converge.

Canetti shared this concern with the hegemony of idealism in Weimar Germany with his closest intellectual friend during their time of exile in England. As refugees, both thinkers reflected on the historical and philosophical causes of Nazism's rise to power. In closing, I want to draw attention to the importance of the poet and anthropologist Franz Baermann Steiner (1909–1952), whose work helped inspire research on the topic of this study.[14]

Canetti's and Steiner's responses to the Holocaust have contributed to a revised conception of both history and anthropology. Whereas Canetti is well known because he was a Nobel laureate in literature, Steiner has not received the public attention that accords with his contribution to the understanding of modern intellectual history. Whereas many other post-Holocaust Jewish thinkers—including Derrida—have concentrated on a refusal of totality and celebration of otherness, Steiner combined this emphasis with an equal stress on the need for collectively acknowledged limits. Steiner and Canetti both turned their attention to historical anthropology in order to comprehend the Holocaust. The two focused on danger and death, respectively, in their quest to understand the persistent presence of power throughout history. Steiner revised the (in his day) standard theory of history. In contrast to Nobert Elias, Steiner did not depict the movement of civilization in terms of a development that grew out of the West and progressively enriched the developing world. Rather, Steiner conceptualized Occidental history in terms of an ever-increasing demolition of the social structures that set limits to danger and violence. He focused on what he saw as civilization's ambivalence: on one hand, the progress of modern history helps expand the limits of society; on the other, this expansion opens the door to unlimited forms of power and destruction. The limitless violence perpetrated in the Nazi genocide coincides with an absolute identification of power with danger.

Steiner thus analyzed Nazism as the most egregious proof of power's persistence within history. Although it is important to emphasize the historical break of the Holocaust, we also need to keep in mind that the Nazis selected from the past and arranged in a new context the elements that best served their interests and maintained their popularity. Fascism in general and Nazism in particular were scavengers "which attempted to annex all that had appealed to people in the nineteenth- and twentieth-century past: romanticism, liberalism, and socialism, as well as Darwinism and modern technology."[15] In order to analyze these aspects of continuity Steiner wrote a historical anthropology in which he developed a complex sociology of danger.

Steiner's sociology of danger presupposes the acknowledgment of an all-encompassing fact, namely, that value in a postlapsarian world cannot be conceived without its relation to danger. A value thus describes actions that help to alleviate suffering. Steiner made it clear that "suffering as such is not a value."[16] He defined value as "everything that contributes to the alleviation of suffering, everything which gives us strength to overcome suffering, everything which can make suffering cease."[17] As an anthropologist as well as a poet Steiner attempted to come to terms with the dangerous, which causes death and suffering. Apollo, the god of poetry, also practiced medicine. Anthropology, on the other hand, seems to be a value-free science. How can an anthropologist, then, presume to help alleviate suffering? Like his close intellectual friend Canetti, Steiner rejected an understanding of science as "value-free."[18] With Steiner, however, the term *value* has rather ironic connotations. Does value not depend on suffering? If so, a world in which suffering did not exist would therefore be truly value-free. Such a world, however, has not yet come into being. As a result, the human quest for knowledge cannot do without addressing issues related to value.

By analyzing how value depends on suffering, Steiner cast moral philosophy into a rather sober mode of thought. He in fact demolished the German idealist divide between nature and freedom. Rather than conceptualizing value as the overcoming of natural conditions, Steiner argued for protecting humanity's place in nature. This rather humble undertaking was more complex and difficult than it would seem to transcendental philosophers such as Kant and Hegel. Steiner was indeed cognizant of its complexity.

Faced with the limitless destruction of human life during World War II in general and the Nazi genocide in particular, Steiner radically questioned a notion of civilization that would assure us of the identity between historical progression and moral progress. In his aphoristic essay "On the Process of Civilization" (1944) Steiner focused on humanity's domination of nature. By attempting to control natural dangers one actually extends them to the human sphere, where their destructive potential intensifies in the course of "history's progress." The term *civilization* thus describes "the march of danger into the heart of creation."[19] By rendering human society gradually more dangerous until it has reached the point where a single individual is able to exert the destructive power that only specific societies could have unleashed in the past, the progress of civilization propels an increase in suffering. Humanity loses its place in nature. In does so by committing collective suicide. Steiner thus articulated his sense of despair vis-à-vis such blindness to humanity's self-destructive potential:

> Whoever recognizes this [that civilization is the march of danger into the heart of creation] lives in the black night of despair, illuminated only by the star of a dual discipline:
> regarding man, who was created in His image;
> regarding society, whose boundaries are immutably set forth in the covenant.[20]

The star, which illuminates Steiner's night of despair, might well allude to Franz Rosenzweig's *Star of Redemption* (1921). This book responded to the carnage perpetrated on the battlefields of World War I (see chapter 8). Against the background of this carnage, Rosenzweig affirmed both a theology of creation and a Jewish philosophy of law. The teaching of being created in God's image seems to refer to a theology of creation, and the concomitant plea for "boundaries" that "are immutably set forth in the covenant" seems to evoke the covenantal law revealed at Sinai. Significantly, Rosenzweig's book closes with the call "Ins Leben." Life is exactly what Steiner saw as threatened by civilization's march into the heart of creation. Whether he actually had *The Star of Redemption* in mind when he wrote about his "Stern einer Doppellehre" cannot be fully explored here. It should, however, be noted that in Steiner's late poetry (1947–1952) socioreligious concepts such as that of a covenental community seem to be conspicuous by their absence.[21]

How can we account for this apparent tension between Steiner's anthropological project and his late poetry? This tension seems to strike one as particularly odd if one takes into account that Steiner worked on his Taboo lectures between 1950 and 1952. In these lectures he formulated his sociology of danger. There is no such thing as taboo; there are only ways of avoiding danger:

> Danger is narrowed down by taboo. A situation is regarded as dangerous: very well, but the danger may be a socially unformulated threat. Taboo gives notice that danger lies not in the whole situation, but only in certain specified actions concerning it. These actions, these danger spots, are more challenging and deadly than the danger of the situation as a whole, for the whole situation can be rendered free from danger by dealing with or, rather, avoiding the specified danger spots completely.[22]

Here Steiner warned against any attempt to control danger. As he made clear in "On the Process of Civilisation," he saw tendencies toward such control in modern Western societies. According to Steiner, in the modern Western world, danger is to be eliminated by attacking anything that might be conceived of as dangerous. Attempts to control a dangerous situation lack any form of value insofar as the very act of domination extends suffering and death further into the societal sphere rather than helping to alleviate them.

Danger, as "a socially unformulated threat," increases the risk that a specific society turns totalitarian. It does so when a community sets out to attack all possible sources from which the unknown danger seems to originate. Countering such totalitarian behavior, Steiner formulated his sociology of danger. He advocated specific actions by which one avoids rather than attacks manifestations of the dangerous. He thus contrasted the empirical with the conceptual and the context-specific with the categorical. After the Holocaust (his family was killed in the Nazi genocide), he wrote, in "Letter to Mr. Gandhi" (1946), about the precarious situation of European Jews. He explained the achievement of emancipation with reference to both the decline of religion and the rise in nationalism: "When the Europeans after centuries of religious persecution gave freedom to our religion it was not because they had come to respect religions, or our religion, or us—it was simply because religions to them had ceased to be of paramount importance, and nationhood had taken the place of religion."[23] The present study examines the ways in which the modern discourse about reason and nation (the body politic) was framed by a secularized as well as politicized opposition between Jew and Gentile.

What elements, however, constitute the structural differences between the Christian and the Jewish religions? We have seen how the German idealists contrasted the Christian "indetermination" with respect to objects in external reality with the "Jewish" orientation toward the goods of this world.

We have also seen that Kant, Hegel, and Feuerbach labeled such heteronomous orientation "superstitious." In his essay "How to Define Superstition" (1944), Steiner addressed this autonomy-heteronomy opposition. In the Christian context the word *belief,* as opposed to *superstition,* "implies that acceptance of a *structure* which is regarded as a total definition of reality is different from the reality of common experience."[24] The structure of the "total definition of reality" refers to the independence from the goods of this world by means of which one immanently attempts to overcome the limitations of immanence and thus sets out to establish a union with the totality of being. In criticizing this totalizing approach, Steiner of course anticipated Levinas's philosophy of an "otherwise than being."

In a further analytical move, Steiner differentiated opposition between, and a hierarchy of, the autonomous and the heteronomous. An opposition between "the two realities" paved the way to "a hierarchy of the levels of experience." The heteronomous turns out to be superstitious, but with "the declaration that the reality of common sense experience is a delusion." As we have seen, this is precisely the way in which most of the German idealists depicted Judaism (that is, as superstitious, materialistic, or heteronomous). Indeed, Steiner went on to stress that this Christian and post-Christian understanding of *belief* differs from its Jewish sources. He underlined the fact that a "word with this implication does not occur . . . in the Hebrew Bible."[25] To this extent, Steiner associated Jewishness with commonsense reality. In this way his critique of Christian and post-Christian thought shows remarkable similarities with the counternarratives developed by Graetz, Rosenzweig, and Freud. This brief discussion of some aspects of Franz Baermann Steiner's counter-Enlightenment thus illustrates the open-ended character of this study. The list of authors and themes analyzed is by no means comprehensive. Nor is the analysis that has been advanced here.

German Idealism and the Jew first analyzed the blind spots in German idealism. This examination shed light on an unnerving undercurrent in Kant's and Hegel's work on the concepts of freedom and reason. As Adorno has pointed out, even though "Kant inherited the concept of freedom from Greek ethics," he nevertheless "radicalized it to an extraordinary degree."[26] I have offered a sociohistorical explanation of this radicalization. Kant and many of the German idealists who followed him associated the opposite of a free and rational modern state with the posited community of the Jews (both Jewishness and Judaism). Here the Jew embodied the danger of modernity's descent into materialism. As materialists, the Jews represented capitalism or socialism or both at the same time. In this way Judaism and Jewishness embodied the body's inability to transform itself into a free and rational body politic.

The second part of this study examined some German Jewish responses to this hegemonic discourse. At this point, *German Idealism and the Jew* attended to a polyphony of voices that undermined the discourse. I have analyzed German Jewish writing in terms of its reaction to the hegemony of an idealist paradigm in the political and intellectual culture of Germany in the nineteenth and twentieth centuries. In different but related ways, German Jewish writers indeed may have contributed to the diversity of materialist philosophy when they undermined the discriminatory dimension of high-status registers of ideation. In this way, German Jewish thought of the nineteenth and twentieth centuries anticipated a postmodern sensibility concerning issues of narrativity, bodiliness, and timeliness. The responses of German Jews to the unreason in reason might thus prove fruitful for future social theory and practice.

NOTES

Introduction

1. Lionel B. Steiman, *Paths to Genocide: Anti-Semitism in Western History* (Houndsmills, Basingstoke: Macmillan, 1998), p. 240.

2. Theodor W. Adorno, *Kant's Critique of Pure Reason* (1959), ed. Rolf Tiedemann, trans. Rodney Livingstone (Stanford: Stanford University Press, 2001), p. 52.

3. Ibid.

4. Léon Poliakov, *The History of Anti-Semitism*, trans. Miriam Kochan (New York: Vanguard, 1975), 3:180.

5. For a discussion of Kant's influence on highly influential lawyers such as C. W. F. Grattenauer, see ibid., 3:188.

6. Gavin I. Langmuir, *History, Religion, and Anti-Semitism* (Berkeley: University of California Press, 1990), p. 297.

7. Ibid., p. 271.

8. See Langmuir's *Toward a Definition of Anti-Semitism* (Berkeley: University of California Press, 1990), pp. 336–37.

9. Theodor W. Adorno, *Problems of Moral Philosophy*, ed. Thomas Schröder, trans. Rodney Livingstone (Stanford: Stanford University Press, 2000), p. 84.

10. Ibid., p. 129.

11. Dominick LaCapra, "Writing History, Writing Trauma," in LaCapra, *Writing History, Writing Trauma* (Baltimore: Johns Hopkins University Press, 2000), p. 21.

12. See Berel Lang, "Genocide and Kant's Enlightenment," in Lang, *Act and Idea in the Nazi Genocide* (Chicago: University of Chicago Press, 1990), pp. 165–206, and Lang, "The Progress of Evil: The Past and Future of the Holocaust," in Lang, *The Future of the Holocaust: Between History and Memory* (Ithaca: Cornell University Press, 1999), pp. 26–39.

13. Lang, "Genocide and Kant's Enlightenment," p. 195.

14. Ibid.

15. Andrew Colin Gow, *The Red Jews: Antisemitism in an Apocalyptical Age, 1200–1600* (Leiden: Brill, 1995), p. 179.

16. Stefi Jersch-Wenzel, "Population Shifts and Occupational Structure," in Paul Mendes-Flohr et al., *German-Jewish History in Modern Times*, vol. 2, *Emancipation and Acculturation: 1780–1871* (New York: Columbia University Press, 1997), p. 71.

17. Immanuel Kant, *Lectures on Ethics*, ed. Peter Heath and J. B. Schneewind, trans. Peter Heath (Cambridge: Cambridge University Press, 1997), p. 27 (emphasis in original). Unless otherwise indicated, emphasis in quotations is mine throughout.

18. Ibid., p. 442.

19. Johann Gottlieb Fichte, "A State Within a State (1793)," in *The Jew in the*

Modern World: A Documentary History, ed. Paul Mendes-Flohr and Jehuda Reinharz (New York: Oxford University Press, 1995), p. 309.

20. Ibid.

21. Ibid.

22. Ludwig Feuerbach, *Das Wesen des Christentums* (Stuttgart: Reclam, 1984), p. 23. For a discussion of this point see Karl Löwith's "Nachwort" in Feuerbach, *Das Wesen*, pp. 527–34. Feuerbach scholars cannot face the presence of anti-Semitism in work of such a "humanist." Marx W. Wartofsky acknowledges that anti-Semitism can be found in the work of the philosopher but equates this "cultural anti-Semitism" with that of Karl Marx. Wartofsky, *Feuerbach* (Cambridge: Cambridge University Press, 1977), p. 319. V A. Harvey criticizes Wartofsky for having called Feuerbach an anti-Semite. Harvey argues that Feuerbach's remarks, "unlike Marx's, were not directed at a 'race.'" Harvey, *Feuerbach and the Interpretation of Religion* (Cambridge: Cambridge University Press, 1995), p. 85.

23. Feuerbach, *Das Wesen*, p. 79.

24. Ibid., p. 187.

25. Ibid., p. 192.

26. Ibid., p. 196; underscoring indicates Feuerbach's emphasis.

27. Arthur Schopenhauer, *Die Welt als Wille und Vorstellung. Zweiter Teilband* (Zurich: Diogenes, 1977), p. 413.

28. Ibid., p. 438.

29. For a discussion of this point see Alfred Schmidt, *Die Wahrheit im Gewande der Lüge: Schopenhauers Religionsphilosophie* (Munich: Piper, 1986), p. 91.

30. Schopenhauer, *Der handschriftliche Nachlaß (1818–1830)*, ed. Arthur Hübscher (Munich: dtv, 1985), p. 307.

31. Ibid., p. 308.

32. Schopenhauer, *Urwille und Welterlösung: Ausgewählte Schriften* (Wiesbaden: Fourier, 1982), p. 131.

33. See George Mosse, *Toward the Final Solution: A History of European Racism* (New York: Harper Colophon, 1978); Jacob Katz, *From Prejudice to Destruction: Anti-Semitism, 1700–1933* (Cambridge: Harvard University Press, 1980); and Sander L. Gilman, *Jewish Self-Hatred: Anti-Semitism and the Hidden Language of the Jews* (Baltimore: Johns Hopkins University Press, 1986).

34. For a discussion of this point see Sander L. Gilman, *The Jew's Body* (New York: Routledge, 1991), pp. 104–27.

35. Ibid., p. 119.

36. Ibid., p. 179.

37. Karl Marx, "On the Jewish Question," in *The Marx-Engels Reader*, 2d ed., ed. Robert C. Tucker (New York: Norton, 1978), p. 30. Underscoring indicates Marx's emphasis.

38. As Sander L. Gilman has put it, "hidden within Marx's sense of self is the internalization of the German-Christian world's identification of him as a Jew." *Jewish Self-Hatred*, p. 207.

39. Marx, "On the Jewish Question," p. 31.

40. This is indeed the case in the anti-Semitic discourse of "anticapitalism." As Moishe Postone has argued: "This form of 'anticapitalism,' then, is based on a one-sided attack on the abstract. The abstract and concrete are not seen as constituting

an antinomy where the real overcoming of the abstract—of the value dimension—involves the historical overcoming of the antinomy itself as well as of each of its terms." Postone, "Anti-Semitism and National Socialism," in *Germans and Jews Since the Holocaust: The Changing Situation in West Germany*, ed. Anson Rabinbach and Jack Zipes (New York: Holmes & Meier, 1986), p. 311.

41. Gilman, *Jewish Self-Hatred*, p. 197.

42. As Amos Finkenstein has argued: "It seems as if Marx's argument is a caricaturized version of Mendelssohn's. . . . It is not the Jews who have to change in order to be granted emancipation, it is the state which has to change and become its true ugly self. When it does, it will have no choice but to remove the corporative status of Jews—relegate religion 'von der Sphäre des öffentlichen Rechts zur Sphäre des Privatrechts.' Indeed, Marx, like Mendelssohn, also sees the Jews as better fit than any other social segment for the civil state; they are the very incarnation of its true essence, the atomization of society into conflicting economical interest-groups. The civil state is a Jewish state." *Perceptions of Jewish History* (Berkeley: University of California Press, 1993), p. 231.

43. As we will see, Rosenzweig in fact took up Marx's analysis of fetishism.

44. Moishe Postone, *Time, Labor, and Social Domination: A Reinterpretation of Marx's Critical Theory* (Cambridge: Cambridge University Press, 1993), p. 184.

45. See ibid., p. 164.

46. Karl Marx, "Economic and Philosophic Manuscripts of 1844," in *The Marx-Engels Reader*, 2d ed., ed. Robert C. Tucker (New York: Norton, 1978), p. 87.

47. Ibid., p. 94.

48. Ibid., p. 93.

49. Ibid., p. 95.

50. Ibid., pp. 95–96.

51. Marx, "On the Jewish Question," p. 38.

52. Postone, *Time, Labor, and Social Domination*, p. 353.

53. Ibid., p. 383.

54. Seyla Benhabib, *Critique, Norm, and Utopia: A Study of the Foundations of Critical Theory* (New York: Columbia University Press, 1986), p. 36.

55. A critical stance toward studies that make such an equation is thus warranted. See Julius Carlebach, *Marx and the Radical Critique of Judaism* (London: Routledge & Kegan Paul, 1978) and Paul Lawrence Rose, *The German-Jewish Question: Revolutionary Antisemitism in Germany from Kant to Wagner* (Princeton, NJ: Princeton University Press, 1990).

56. Adorno, *Problems of Moral Philosophy*, p. 149.

57. Ibid.

58. Jacques Derrida, *Adieu: To Emmanuel Levinas*, trans. Pascale-Anne Prault and Michel Naas (Stanford: Stanford University Press, 1999), p. 10.

59. Ibid., p. 90.

60. Derrida, *Adieu*, p. 91.

61. "Die politische Kraft einer Demokratie zeigt sich darin, daß sie das Fremde und Ungleiche, die Homogenität Bedrohende zu beseitigen oder fernzuhalten weiß." Carl Schmitt, *Die geistesgeschichtliche Lage des heutigen Parlamentarismus* (Munich: Duncker & Humboldt, 1926), p. 14 .

62. "[D]as Unmenschliche . . . um in unmittelbarer Notwendigkeit das Gute und absolut Menschliche als seinen Gegensatz hervorzurufen." Ibid., p. 74.

63. "[D]as Unmenschliche . . . ähnlich wie nach Hegel (*Phänomenologie* II 257) 'von dem jüdischen Volke gesagt werden kann, daß es gerade darum, weil es unmittelbar vor der Pforte des Heils stehe, das verworfenste sei.'" Ibid., p. 74.

64. Eric L. Santner, *On the Psychotheology of Everyday Life: Reflections on Freud and Rosenzweig* (Chicago: University of Chicago Press, 2001), p. 9.

65. Ibid.

66. Ibid.

67. For a discussion of this point see Paul Mendes-Flohr and Jehuda Reinharz, "Harbingers of Political and Economic Change," in *The Jew in the Modern World: A Documentary History,* ed. Paul Mendes-Flohr and Jehuda Reinharz (New York: Oxford University Press, 1995), pp. 8–9.

68. Gilles Deleuze and Félix Guattari, *A Thousand Plateaus: Capitalism and Schizophrenia,* trans. with a foreword by Brian Massumi (Minneapolis: University of Minnesota Press, 1987), p. 178.

69. Ibid., p. 176.

70. I use quotation marks to distinguish between "Jews"—the fantasized product of anti-Semitic stereotyping—and Jews—members of the Jewish faith. I abandon the redundant quotation marks around "Jewishness" and "Jews" for the rest of this study but of course refer to the fantasized product of discriminatory discourse rather than to real people.

Chapter One

1. Neither Kant nor any of the German philosophers following him disregarded the materiality of natural existence. On the contrary, they took it very seriously, for it is something whose overcoming preconditions the establishment of a transcendental body politic. For a discussion of the devaluation of empirical reality and, related to it, a devaluation of causality see Ernst Topitsch, *Die Voraussetzungen der Transzendentalphilosophie: Kant in weltanschauungsanalytischer Betrachtung* (Hamburg: Hoffmann & Campe, 1975), p. 44.

2. Donald N. Levine, *Visions of the Sociological Tradition* (Chicago: University of Chicago Press, 1995), p. 181.

3. Immanuel Kant, *Kritik der Reinen Vernunft,* ed. W. Weischedel (Wiesbaden: Insel, 1958), 1:293.

4. As Amos Funkenstein has pointed out: "The de-theologization of the foundations of knowledge was doubtless, in his [Kant's] eyes, his contribution to the 'Enlightenment,' that is, to the emancipation of humanity from its 'self-imposed bondage.'" *Theology and the Scientific Imagination from the Middle Ages to the Seventeenth Century* (Princeton, NJ: Princeton University Press, 1986), p. 356.

5. Thus Gordon E. Michaelson Jr. has recently characterized Kant as "a way station between Luther and Marx." *Kant and the Problem of God* (Oxford: Blackwell, 1999), p. 27.

6. "Unser Verstand . . . wird nicht durch die Sinnlichkeit eingeschränkt, sondern schränkt vielmehr dieselbe ein, dadurch, daß er Dinge an sich selbst (nicht als Erscheinungen) Noumena nennt." Kant, *Kritik der Reinen Vernunft,* 1:282–83.

7. Ibid., 1:283.

8. Ibid., 1:181.

9. For a discussion of this progress toward perfection, see Yirmiahu Yovel, *Kant and the Philosophy of History* (Princeton, NJ: Princeton University Press, 1980).

10. Kant, *Kritik der Reinen Vernunft*, 2:702.

11. See ibid., 2:235. Mere reason and imagination seem to coincide in Kant's epistemological critique of metaphysics.

12. Dieter Henrich, "Ethics of Autonomy," trans. Louis Hunt, in Henrich, *The Unity of Reason: Essays on Kant's Philosophy*, ed. and intro. Richard L. Velkkey (Cambridge: Harvard University Press, 1994), p. 93.

13. Giorgio Agamben, *Homo Sacer: Sovereign Power and Bare Life*, trans. Daniel Heller-Roazen (Stanford: Stanford University Press, 1998), p. 51.

14. For a discussion of the Kantian tension between the explanation of the world and its overcoming, see Topitsch, *Die Voraussetzungen der Transzendentalphilosophie*, p. 64.

15. Yirmiyahu Yovel, *Dark Riddle: Hegel, Nietzsche, and the Jews* (University Park: Pennsylvania State University Press, 1998), p. 10.

16. Ibid. (emphasis in original).

17. Robert Pippin, "Dividing and Deriving in Kant's *Rechtslehre*," in *Immanuel Kant: Metaphysische Anfangsgründe der Rechtslehre*, ed. Otfried Höffe (Berlin: Akademie, 1999), p. 63.

18. For a discussion of this point, see ibid., p. 76.

19. See Immanuel Kant, *Schriften zur Ethik und Religionsphilosophie,* ed. Wilhelm Weischdel (Frankfurt am Main: Suhrkamp, 1964), 1:12.

20. Ibid., 1:32.

21. "[E]in Gesetz, wenn es moralisch, d.i. als Grund einer Verbindlichkeit, gelten soll, absolute Notwendigkeit bei sich führen müsse; ... der Grund der Verbindlichkeit hier nicht in der Natur des Menschen, oder den Umständen der Welt, darin er gesetzt ist, gesucht werden müsse, sondern a priori lediglich in Begriffen der reinen Vernunft." Ibid., 1:13.

22. *"[R]äsoniert, so viel ihr wollt, und worüber ihr wollt; nur gehorcht!"* Kant, *Schriften zur Anthroplogie, Geschichtsphilosophie, Politik und Pädagogik,* ed. W. Weischedel (Frankfurt am Main: Insel, 1964), 1:61.

23. Michel Foucault, "What Is Enlightenment?" in *The Foucault Reader*, ed. Paul Rabinow (New York: Pantheon, 1984), p. 36.

24. Kant, *Schriften zur Ethik und Religionsphilosophie*, 2:378.

25. Ibid.

26. Kant, *Schriften zur Anthropologie*, 1:137.

27. Kant, *Kritik der reinen Vernunft*, 2:678.

28. See Susannah Heschel, *Abraham Geiger and the Jewish Jesus* (Chicago: University of Chicago Press, 1998), p. 75.

29. Kant, *Schriften zur Ethik und Religionsphilosophie* 2:400.

30. Ibid.

31. Ibid., 1:25.

32. Ibid., 2:737.

33. Kant, *Religion and Rational Theology*, trans. and ed. Allen W. Wood and George Di Giovanni (Cambridge: Cambridge University Press, 1996), p. 120.

34. Ibid., p. 121; "die Freiheit der Kinder des Himmels und die Knechtschaft eines bloßen Erdensohns." Kant, *Schriften zur Ethik und Religionsphilosophie,* 2:738.

35. Kant, *Religion and Rational Theology*, p. 121; "Das gute Prinzip aber ist nicht bloß zu einer gewissen Zeit, sondern von dem Ursprunge des menschlichen

Geschlechts an unsichtbarerweise vom Himmel in die Menschheit herabgekommen gewesen (wie ein jeder, der auf seine Heiligkeit und zugleich die Unbegreiflichkeit der Verbindung derselben mit der sinnlichen Natur des Menschen in der moralischen Anlage Acht hat, gestehen muß) und hat in ihr rechtlicher Weise *seinen* ersten Wohnsitz. Da es also in einem wirklichen Menschen als einem Beispiel für alle andere erschien, 'so kam er in sein Eigentum, und die Seinen nahmen ihn nicht auf, denen aber, die ihn aufnahmen, hat er Macht gegeben, Gottes Kinder zu heißen, die an seinen Namen glauben,' d.i. durch das Beispiel desselben (in der moralischen Idee) eröffnet er die Pforte der Freiheit für jedermann, die eben so, wie er, allem dem absterben wollen, was sie zum Nachteil der Sittlichkeit an das Erdenleben gefesselt hält." Kant, *Schriften zur Ethik und Religionsphilosophie*, 2:738.

36. Christian Wilhelm von Dohm, "Concerning the Amelioration of the Civil Status of the Jews (1781)," in *The Jew in the Modern World: A Documentary History*, ed. Paul Mendes-Flohr and Jehuda Reinharz (Oxford: Oxford University Press, 1995), p. 29.

37. Ibid., p. 30.

38. For an examination of how widespread the discussion of emancipation was at the end of the eighteenth century see Jonathan M. Hess, "Sugar Island Jews? Jewish Colonialism and the Rhetoric of 'Civic Improvement' in Eighteenth-Century Germany," *Eighteenth-Century Studies* 32.1 (1998): 92–100; Jonathan M. Hess, *Reconstituting the Body Politic: Enlightenment, Public Culture, and the Invention of Aesthetic Autonomy* (Detroit: Wayne State University Press, 1999).

39. Kant, *Schriften zur Ethik und Religionsphilosophie*, 2:734.

40. Kant, *Religion and Rational Theology*, p. 119; "da aber die Gemüter der Untertanen in derselben [i.e., "in der *jüdischen* Theokratie"] für keine andere Triebfedern, als die Güter dieser Welt, gestimmt blieben, und sie also auch nicht anders als durch Belohnung und Strafen in diesem Leben regiert sein wollten, dafür aber auch keiner andern Gesetze fähig waren, als solcher, welche teils lästige Zeremonien und Gebräuche auferlegten, . . . wobei das Innere der moralischen Gesinnung gar nicht in Betrachtung kam: so tat diese Ordnung dem Reiche der Finsternis keinen wesentlichen Abbruch, sondern diente nur dazu, um das unauslöschliche Recht des ersten Eigentümers immer in Andenken zu erhalten." Kant, *Schriften zur Ethik und Religionsphilosophie*, 2:735.

41. Yovel, *Dark Riddle*, p. 7.

42. Baruch Spinoza, *Theological-Political Treatise*, trans. Samuel Shirley, introduction and notes by Seymour Feldman (Indianapolis: Hackett, 1998), p. 39.

43. Ibid.

44. As Steven B. Smith has recently pointed out, "For Spinoza, Judaism served perhaps as a basis for liberalism not because it was a religion of reason, as Moses Mendelssohn believed, but because it was a body of law." *Spinoza, Liberalism, and the Question of Jewish Identity* (New Haven: Yale University Press, 1997), p. xiii.

45. For a discussion of Kant's discriminatory appropriation of Spinoza's writings about Judaism, see Yovel, *Dark Riddle*, pp. 6–20.

46. Kant, *Religion and Rational Theology*, p. 114; "Die Sinnesänderung ist nämlich ein Ausgang vom Bösen, und ein Eintritt in Gute, das Ablegen des alten, und das Anziehen des neuen Menschen, da das Subject der Sünde (mithin auch der Neigungen, sofern sie dazu verleiten) abstirbt, um der Gerechtigkeit zu leben." Kant, *Schriften zur Ethik und Religionsphilosophie*, 2:728.

47. Kant, *Religion and Rational Theology*, p. 276; *Schriften zur Anthropologie, Geschichtsphilosophie, Politik und Pädagogik*, 2:321.

48. Ibid.

49. Kant, *Religion and Rational Theology*, p. 155; "[S]o enthält das Judentum als solches, in seiner Reinigkeit genommen, gar keinen Religionsglauben." Kant, *Schriften zur Ethik und Religionsphilosophie*, 2:791.

50. Kant, *Religion and Rational Theology*, p. 154; Kant, *Schriften zur Ethik und Religionsphilosophie*, 2:790.

51. Kant, *Religion and Rational Theology*, p. 153; Kant, *Schriften zur Ethik und Religionsphilosophie*, 2:788.

52. Kant, *Religion and Rational Theology*, p. 154; "Der *jüdische Glaube* ist, seiner ursprünglichen Einrichtung nach, ein Inbegriff bloß statutarischer Gesetze, auf welchem eine Staatsverfassung gegründet war; denn welche moralische Zusätze entweder damals schon, oder auch in der Folge ihm *angehängt* worden sind, die sind schlechterdings nicht zum Judentum, als solchem gehörig." Kant, *Schriften zur Ethik und Religionsphilosophie*, 2:789.

53. Kant, *Schriften zur Anthropologie*, 1:11.

54. George L. Mosse, *Toward the Final Solution: A History of European Racism* (New York: Harper & Row, 1978), p. 31.

55. Kant, *Religion and Rational Theology*, p. 155; Kant, *Schriften zur Ethik und Religionsphilosophie*, p. 2:791.

56. Kant, *Religion and Rational Theology*, p. 275; "einem *messianischen* Glauben*," Kant, *Schriften zur Anthropologie*, 1:320.

57. Kant, *Religion and Rational Theology*, p. 275; "[W]omit er wahrscheinlicher Weise sagen wollte: Christen, schafft erst das Judentum aus *eurem* eigenen Glauben weg: so werden wir das unsere verlassen." *Schriften zur Anthropologie*, 1: 320. Whereas Mendelssohn wrote that Christianity "is built upon Judaism, and if the latter falls, it must necessarily collapse with it into *one* heap of ruins" (*Jerusalem, or On Religious Power and Judaism*, trans. Allan Arkush, intro. Alexander Altmann [Hanover, NH: University Press of New England/Brandeis University, 1983], p. 87), Kant argued that Christianity only comes into its true essence when it abolishes its Jewish foundations.

58. For a detailed discussion of this point see Michael Mack, "Law, Charity, and Taboo, or Kant's Reversal of Paul's Spirit-Letter Opposition," *Modern Theology* 16 (October 2000): 417–41.

59. Kant, *Schriften zur Ethik und Religionsphilosophie*, 1:288.

60. Ibid., 2:678.

61. Ibid.

62. Ibid.

63. Recent scholarship has shown that Paul did not establish a radical opposition between law and charity and the spiritual and the empirical. See, among other studies, Daniel Boyarin, *A Radical Jew: Paul and the Politics of Identity* (Berkeley: University of California Press, 1994).

64. See Kant, *Schriften zur Ethik und Religionsphilosophie*, 2:318.

65. "[W]ehe dem! Welcher die Schlangenwindungen der Glückseligkeitslehre durchkriecht, um etwas zu aufzufinden, was durch den Vorteil, den es verspricht, ihn von der Strafe, oder auch nur einem Grad derselben entbinde, nach dem pharisäischen Wahlspruch: 'es ist besser, daß ein Mensch sterbe, als daß das ganze Volk,

verderbe'; denn wenn die Gerechtigkeit untergeht, so hat es keinen Wert mehr, daß Menschen auf Erden leben." Ibid., 2:453.

66. Kant, *Schriften zur Ethik und Religionsphilosophie*, 2:735.

67. Boyarin, *Radical Jew*, p. 150.

68. Kant, *Schriften zur Ethik und Religionsphilosophie*, 2:735.

69. Kant, *Schriften zur Anthropologie*, 2:517.

70. Slavoj Zizek, "Class Struggle or Postmodernism? Yes, please!" in *Contingency, Hegemony, Universality: Contemporary Dialogues on the Left*, ed. Judith Butler, E. Laclau, and S. Zizek (London: Verso, 2000), p. 101.

71. See Moishe Postone, *Time, Labor, and Social Domination: A Reinterpretation of Marx's Critical Theory* (New York: Cambridge University Press, 1993), p. 33.

72. Kant, *Schriften zur Anthropologie*, 2:518.

73. Ibid.

74. Kant, *Kritik der Urteilskraft und Schriften zur Naturphilosophie* (Frankfurt am Main: Insel, 1964), 2:365.

75. Recently, Paul Lawrence Rose has emphasized the sociohistorical significance of Kant's anti-Semitic scapegoating, arguing that "what modernized the old Jew-hatred was not the application of biological theories, but the advent of the new vision of revolution and redemption." Rose, *The German-Jewish Question: Revolutionary Antisemitism in Germany from Kant to Wagner* (Princeton: Princeton University Press, 1990), p. 15.

76. Kant, *Schriften zur Anthropologie*, 2:518.

77. Kant, *Schriften zur Metaphysik und Logik*, ed. W. Weischedel (Wiesbaden: Insel, 1958), p. 281 (Quotation from "Was heisst: sich im Denken orientieren?").

78. Kant, *Religion and Rational Theology*, p. 17.

79. Kant, *Schriften zur Ethik und Religionsphilosophie*, 2:735.

80. Rose has rightly drawn attention to the revolutionary rather than the biological aspect of modern anti-Semitism: "What modernized the old Jew-hatred was not the application of biological theories, but the advent of the new vision of revolution and redemption." Rose, *Revolutionary Anti-Semitism*, 15. The only analysis he gives of the revolutionary content of Kant's thought and that of those who took over his transcendental paradigm, however, is to point out its difference from French and British liberalism. My own study, by contrast, analyzes how the transcendental revolution constructs a sense of reason and freedom that might be revolutionary only insofar as it conflates the rational with the transcendence of empirical conditions, for which the Jews and Judaism stand in as scapegoats.

Chapter Two

1. Otto Pöggeler, one of the most renowned Hegel scholars, argues in his "Hegel's Interpretation of Judaism" (*Human Context* 6 [1974]: 523–60) that the mature Hegel overcame the anti-Jewish sentiment of his youth and hence did not discriminate against Jewish students. As will be discussed in this chapter, the mature Hegel of the *Lectures on the Philosophy of Religion* did not abandon a discriminatory description of rabbinic Judaism, although—and here I concur with Pöggeler—the vehemence of his tone changes. Emil Fackenheim characterizes Hegel's view of Judaism as a shortcoming in his system and hence isolates it from the other aspects of his philosophy. Fackenheim, "Hegel and Judaism: A Flaw in the Hegelian Medi-

tation," in *The Legacy of Hegel: Proceedings of the Marquette University Hegel Symposium 1970*, ed. J. J. O'Malley, K. Algozin, H. Kainz, and L. C. Rice (The Hague: Nijhoff, 1973), pp. 161–85. In contrast to Pöggeler and Fackenheim, Paul Lawrence Rose has recently called Hegel a "revolutionary anti-Semite." Rose, however, only discusses the early Hegel, who "characterized Jewish religion as one in which excessive self-love, egoism and the instinct to dominate had driven out true social human love and produced a religion of lovelessness." Rose, *The German-Jewish Question: Revolutionary Antisemitism in Germany from Kant to Wagner* (Princeton, NJ: Princeton University Press, 1990), p. 116. Yirmiyahu Yovel, by contrast, focuses on the mature Hegel of the *Lectures on the Philosophy of Religion* and differentiates between the Hegel who "favored political equality for the Jews" and the idealist philosopher who made Judaism the target of the "same blows which religion *as such* has been dealt throughout the ages by its rationalist opponents." Yovel, *Dark Riddle: Hegel, Nietzsche, and the Jews* (University Park: Pennsylvania State University Press, 1998), p. 82.

2. Robert Pippin, *Hegel's Idealism: The Satisfaction of Self-Consciousness* (Cambridge: Cambridge University Press, 1989), p. 6.

3. Ibid., p. 99 (emphasis in original); see also pp. 181–82.

4. Slavoj Zizek, *The Sublime Object of Ideology* (London: Verso, 1995), p. 205.

5. "Thus Hegel criticizes Judaism as a religion which does not appreciate the dialectical relationship between the visible and the invisible, or else the relationship between finite and infinite. Thus the gap between subject and object is identical with the gap between the finite and the infinite. The ultimate point in Hegel's criticism of Judaism is that it is a non-dialectical religion. This point is the kernel of Hegel's later attempt to interpret Judaism." Nathan Rotenstreich, *The Recurring Pattern: Studies in Anti-Judaism in Modern Thought* (London: Weidenfeld and Nicolson, 1963), p. 58.

6. Interpreting Hegel's elliptic discussion of Judaism in the *Phenomenology of the Spirit*, Yovel offers the following analysis: "The Jewish people reached the gate of salvation but refused to go through it; therefore they will be locked out of the gates of salvation forever. With no evolution and no real hope. In other words, *they will no longer have a history.*" Yovel, *Dark Riddle*, p. 55.

7. Wilhelm Friedrich Hegel, *Wissenschaft der Logik*, ed. Eva Moldenhauer and Karl Markus Michel (Frankfurt am Main: Suhrkamp, 1986), 1:390.

8. Sander L. Gilman, *The Jew's Body* (London: Routledge, 1991), p. 6.

9. Wilhelm Friedrich Hegel, *Enzyklopädie der Philosohischen Wissenschaften*, ed. F. Nicolin and O. Pöggeler (Hamburg: Felix Meiner, 1991), p. 321.

10. "Dieser Unterschied geht in die Parikularitäten hinaus, die man *Lokalgeister* nennen kann, und die sich in der äußerlichen Lebensart, Beschäftigung, körperlicher Bildung und Disposition, aber noch mehr in innerer Tendenz und Befähigung des intelligenten und sittlichen Charakters der Völker zeigen." Ibid., p. 322.

11. As did Kant, in whose writings the notion of freedom derives from Christ's willing death to this world, Hegel used a notion of freedom that grows first out of a religious imagination *(Vorstellung)* and then out of religious thought *(Denken)*. The notion, however, can only be realized thanks to the workings of the modern state. Against this background Hegel stressed that the religion of a people shapes their

customs *(Sittlichkeit)*, their political way of life. Thus the religious must not be separated from the political: "Völker, die nicht wissen, daß der Mensch an und für sich frei sei, diese leben in der Verdumpfung sowohl in Ansehung ihrer Verfassung als ihrer Religion.—Es ist ein Begriff der Freiheit in Religion und Staat. Dieser Eine Begriff ist das Höchste, was der Mensch hat, und er wird vom Menschen realisiert. Das Volk, das einen schlechten Begriff von Gott hat, hat auch einen schlechten Staat, schlechte Regierung, schlechte Gesetze." Wilhelm Friedrich Hegel, *Vorlesungen über die Philosophie der Religion,* ed. Walter Jaeschke (Hamburg: Felix Meiner, 1993), 1:340.

12. Hegel, *Vorlesungen,* 3:265–66.

13. Yovel, *Dark Riddle,* p. 94.

14. For a discussion of this point, see Wilhelm Friedrich Hegel, *Grundlinien der Philosophie des Rechts* (Frankfurt am Main: Suhrkamp, 1976), pp. 16–19.

15. "[T]he abstract, that is, the general and the good, must determine the particular" ("[D]as Abstrakte muß die Bestimmung des Besonderen erhalten"). Ibid., p.252.

16. Wilhelm Friedrich Hegel, *Philosophie des Geistes,* ed. Eva Moldenhauer and Karl Markus Michel (Frankfurt am Main: Suhrkamp, 1973), p. 262. For a discussion of the dependence of Hegel's spirit on sacrifice see Georges Bataille, "Hegel, Death, and Sacrifice," *Yale French Studies* 78 (1990): 9–28.

17. "Aber das Leben, die höchste Darstellung der Idee in der Natur ist nur dies, sich aufzuopfern." Hegel, *Vorlesungen* 3:28.

18. Ibid., 3:251.

19. Leon Kass, *The Hungry Soul: Eating and the Perfection of Our Nature* (New York: Free, 1994), pp. 54, 55.

20. Hegel, *Vorlesungen,* 2:81.

21. Hegel, *Grundlinien.,* p. 107.

22. For a discussion of this point, see ibid., p. 63.

23. For a discussion of this point, see ibid., p. 64.

24. For a discussion of Hegel's patriarchal way of thinking see Heinz Kimmerle, "Die Begründung der Spekulation als eine Form des patriarchalischen Denkens: Ein Beitrag zur Interpretation von Hegels Religionsphilosophie in den Jahren 1801–1807," in *Hegels Logik der Philosophie: Religion und Philosophie in der Theorie des absoluten Geistes,* ed. Dieter Henrich and Rolf-Peter Horstmann (Stuttgart: Klett-Cotta, 1984), pp. 189–210.

25. He makes this clear in the *Phänomenologie des Geistes,* ed. Eva Molderhauer and Karl Markus Michel (Frankfurt am Main: Surhkamp, 1973), p. 536.

26. Ibid., p. 526.

27. Ibid., p. 527.

28. For a discussion of this point see ibid., p. 538.

29. Ibid., p. 540.

30. Ibid., p. 91.

31. Ibid., p. 335.

32. "Im *Zustande der Not* [war] aber . . . ist es die Souveränität [of the state] in deren einfachen Begriff der dort in seinen Besonderheiten bestehende Organismus zusammengeht und welcher die Rettung des Staates mit der Aufopferung dieses sonst berechtigten anvertraut ist, wo jener Idealismus zu seiner eigentümlichen Wirklichkeit kommt." Hegel, *Grundlinien.,* p. 444. Mark C. Taylor has described

this point as follows: "The speculative form of the teleological argument does not reveal the divine as an alien other who directs the world from without. To the contrary, God is the immanent structural principle that sustains and directs the universe." Taylor, *Nots* (Chicago: University of Chicago Press, 1993), p. 16.

33. Hegel, *Grundlinien*, p. 491.

34. Seyla Benhabib, "On Hegel, Women and Irony," in Benhabib, *Situating the Self: Gender, Community, and Postmodernism in Contemporary Ethics* (New York: Routledge, 1992), p. 246.

35. Ibid., p. 247.

36. Hegel, *Vorlesungen*, 3:xiii. As Wolfgang Pannenberg has pointed out in an important essay, from a Christian perspective the finite is not a passing moment but originates from a creator and thus carries spiritual value. In this way the trinitarian dogma incorporates another notion of spirit than that developed by Hegel. According to Christian doctrine, spirit is not absolute; rather, it proceeds from the father, who is not himself the spirit. For a discussion of this point see Pannenberg, "Der Geist und sein Anderes," in *Hegels Logik der Philosophie: Religion und Philosophie in der Theorie des absoluten Geistes,* ed. Dieter Henrich and Rolf-Peter Horstmann (Stuttgart: Klett-Cotta, 1984), pp. 151–59.

37. This is Yovel's argument, based on, as mentioned at the beginning of this chapter, the description of the Jews as the most reprobate people because they are closest to salvation as found in the *Phenomenology.* As a consequence of this reading, Yovel argues that Hegel was "Christocentric, but not, on that account, necessarily an anti-Semite" (Yovel, *Dark Riddle*, p. 98). I would argue instead that he is anti-Judaic, in the sense that he discriminates against rabbinic Judaism, and anti-Semitic, in the sense that he helps develop the anti-Semitic conflation of a Jewish way of life and materialism. Hegel based his fantasy about Jewishness on religious "sources," but in doing so, he did not attempt to serve a specific religious creed (i.e., that of Christianity). That Hegel did not discriminate against Jews in contemporary German society has to do with his attempt *not* be Christocentric, not to favor one particular religion and one particular culture, because this would undermine the "modern" principle of generality and indifference to difference.

38. For a discussion of this point see Hegel, *Vorlesungen,* 3:xxxi.

39. Hegel, *Phenomenology of Spirit,* trans. A. V. Miller (Oxford: Oxford University Press, 1977), p. 206.

40. Hegel, *Vorlesungen,* 2:15.

41. Ibid.

42. Hegel, *Phänomenologie,* p. 257.

43. Ibid.

44. Yovel, *Dark Riddle,* p. 55, quoting Hegel, *Phenomenology of Spirit,* p. 206.

45. Hegel, *Phenomenology of Spirit,* p. 206.

46. For Hegel's interpretation of this theme, see his *Vorlesungen,* 2:348–49. This point will be discussed in the following section.

47. Ibid., 2:352.

48. Kass, *Hungry Soul,* p. 220.

49. Ibid., p. 221.

50. Hegel, *Grundlinien.,* p. 511.

51. Hegel, *Wissenschaft der Logik,* 1:20.

52. Hegel, *Vorlesungen,* 2:140.

53. Hegel discusses this point in ibid., 2:178.

54. Ibid., 2:256.

55. "Die Bestimmung der Dinge ist dann eben diese, daß sie Geschöpfe sind, daß sie in die Kategorien getreten sind des Äußerlichen, Nichtselbständigen, oder die Natur der natürlichen Dinge wird hier prosaisch; sie ist entgöttert, sie sind Unselbständigkeiten in ihnen selbst; alle Selbständigkeit ist in den Einen konzentriert." Hegel, *Vorlesungen,* 2:329.

56. Gillian Rose, *Hegel Contra Sociology* (London: Athlone, 1981), pp. 80–81.

57. Hegel, *Vorlesugen,* 2:348.

58. Immanuel Kant, *Schriften zur Ethik und Religionsphilosophie,* ed. Wilhelm Weischdel (Frankfurt am Main: Suhrkamp, 1964), 2:735. For a discussion of Kant's usage of the word *Sklavensinn* and its relation to Paul's view of Judaism, see Michael Mack, "Kant's Reversal of St. Paul's Spirit-Letter Opposition," *Modern Theology* 16 (October 2000): 417–41.

59. Hegel, *Vorlesungen,* 2:345.

60. Ibid., 2:346–47.

61. Ibid., 2:352.

62. Yovel, *Dark Riddle,* p. 74. As Yovel has argued, the metaphysical connotations of Hegel's "sublime" are deceptive, for "the fear which characterizes Judaism is not primarily metaphysical dread but a material concern. The Jew is afraid for his life and his property; he prefers life over values and thereby becomes a slavish servant of God and his proxies" (p. 81).

63. Hegel, *Vorlesungen,* 2:364.

64. Ibid., 2:355.

65. Ibid., 2:364.

66. For Hegel's discussion of this point see ibid., 1:59.

67. Ibid., 2:529.

68. Ibid., 2:534.

69. Sander L. Gilman, *Creating Beauty to Cure the Soul: Race and Psychology in the Shaping of Aesthetic Surgery* (Durham: Duke University Press, 1999), p. 41. Gilman has drawn attention to Karl Rosengarten (1805–1879), "Hegel's best-known student," who "justified his undertaking an aesthetics of the ugly by stating in his introduction that the study of the ugly is to the examination of beauty what the study of pathology is to illness" (p. 40).

70. Hegel, *Vorlesungen,* 3:364.

71. Ibid., 3:408.

72. Ibid., 2:231.

Chapter Three

1. Stating that Wagner's attempted popularization of Kant's, Hegel's, Feuerbach's, and Schopenhauer's moral philosophy has not been discussed previously is not to say that his debt to German Enlightenment thought has been overlooked. In *The German-Jewish Question: Revolutionary Antisemitism in Germany from Kant to Wagner* (Princeton: Princeton University Press, 1990), Paul Lawrence Rose has in fact claimed that German revolutionary thought differed from its French and British counterparts and that Wagner followed this tradition in his anti-Semitic works.

What, however, are the implications of this difference? Rose does not address this issue.

2. Anette Hein's *"Es ist viel Hitler in Wagner"*: *Antisemitismus und Deutschtumsideologie in den Bayreuther Blättern* (Tübingen: Niemeyer, 1997) has documented the impact of Wagner's aesthetics and politics on middle-class professionals (above all, teachers) in Germany at the end of the nineteenth and the beginning of the twentieth century. For a discussion of this issue see also Saul Friedländer, "Hitler and Wagner," in *Richard Wagner im Dritten Reich,* ed. Saul Friedländer and Jörn Rüsen (Munich: Beck, 2000).

3. Richard Wagner, *Gesammelte Schriften,* ed. Julius Kapp (Leipzig: Hesse & Becker, 1920), 14:11.

4. Ibid.

5. Ibid., 14:24.

6. Ibid.

7. Barry Millington has argued that "what is idiosyncratic about Wagner's anti-semitism . . . is the way he lifted it into the realm of theology." Millington, *Wagner* (Princeton: Princeton University Press, 1992), p. 106. As we have seen, this is also "idiosyncratic" with regard to anti-Semitism in German transcendental thought.

8. Wagner, *Gesammelte Schriften,* 14:25.

9. Ibid.

10. Nietzsche has called Wagner "Hegel's heir." Friedrich Nieztsche, *Sämtliche Werke: Kritische Studienausgabe,* ed. Giorgio Colli and Mazzino Montinari (Berlin: de Gruyter, 1967–77), 6:36. Theodor Adorno has given a more detailed discussion of the relations between Hegel and Wagner, referring specifically to their shared notion of totality. See Adorno, "Musikalische Aphorismen," in *Gesammelte Schriften,* ed. Rolf Tiedemann and Klaus Schultz (Frankfurt am Main: Suhrkamp, 1984), 18:23. For a discussion of Hegel's influence on Wagner see Siegfried Mauser, "Wagner und Hegel—Zum Nachwirken des Deutschen Idealismus im 'Ring des Nibelungen,'" *Schriften der Hochschule für Musik* 4 (1983): 45–59; John Deathridge and Carl Dahlhaus, *The New Grove Wagner* (London: Macmillan, 1984); Sandra Corse, *Wagner and the New Consciousness: Language and Love in the Ring* (London: Associated University Presses, 1990); and Petra-Hildegard Wilberg, *Richard Wagners Mythische Welt: Versuche wider den Historismus* (Freiburg im Breisgau: Rombach, 1996), p. 124.

11. William Friedrich Hegel, *Phänomenologie des Geistes,* ed. Eva Moldenhauer and Karl Markus Michel (Frankfurt am Main: Surhkamp, 1973), p. 335.

12. Wagner, *Gesammelte Schriften,* 14:25.

13. Ibid. Slavoj Zizek, "'There Is No Sexual Relationship': Wagner As a Lacanian," *New German Critique* 69 (fall 1996): 7–35, quotation on 14.

14. For a discussion of this point see Maurice Olender, *The Language of Paradise: Race, Religion, and Philology in the Nineteenth Century,* trans. Arthur Goldhammer (Cambridge: Harvard University Press, 1992).

15. See, e.g., Werner Sombart, *The Jews and Modern Capitalism,* trans. M. Epstein (Glencoe, IL: Free, 1951).

16. Wagner, *Gesammelte Schriften,* 14:33.

17. Ibid.

18. Ibid., 14:76.

19. Ibid., 14:82.

20. Ibid., 14:101.

21. For a discussion of Wagner's monarchism from his revolutionary period to his later, more conservative affiliations, see Wilberg, *Richard Wagners Mythische Welt,* p. 175.

22. For a traditional theory of the king's two bodies see Ernst H. Kantorowicz, *The King's Two Bodies: A Study in Medieval Political Theory* (Princeton: Princeton University Press, 1957).

23. Wagner, *Gesammelte Schriften,* 14:111.

24. Ibid.

25. Ibid.

26. Ibid., 14:102.

27. Richard Wagner, *Stories and Essays,* ed. Charles Osborne (La Salle, IL: Open Court, 1991), pp. 27–28.

28. Wagner, *Gesammelte Schriften,* 13:13.

29. Ibid.

30. Ibid., 13:48.

31. For a discussion of the "Aryan Christ" in Fichte see Rose, *Revolutionary Anti-Semitism,* p. 122. For a discussion of the "Aryan Christ" in Schopenhauer see Alfred Schmidt, *Die Wahrheit im gewande der Lüge: Schopenhauer's Religiosphilosophie* (Munich: Piper, 1986), p. 148.

32. Wagner, *Gesammelte Schriften,* 14:150.

33. For a discussion of this point, see Sander L. Gilman, *Freud, Race, and Gender* (Princeton: Princeton University Press, 1993), pp. 150–51.

34. Wagner, *Gesammelte Schriften,* 14:151.

35. Wagner, *Stories and Essays,* p. 38.

36. Ibid., p. 39.

37. Wagner, *Gesammelte Schriften,* 14:190.

38. Ibid., 14:175.

39. Ibid.

40. See Cosima Wagner, *Die Tagebücher, 1869–1877,* ed. Martin Gregor-Dellin and Dietrich Mack (Munich: Piper, 1976), 1:241.

41. Fritz K. Ringer, *The Decline of the German Mandarins: The German Academic Community, 1890–1933* (Cambridge: Harvard University Press, 1969), pp. 38–39.

42. Wagner, *Stories and Essays,* p. 24.

43. Ibid., p. 25.

44. For a discussion of the conflation of the Jews and exploiters, see Theodor Adorno, "Versuch über Wagner," in *Gesammelte Schriften,* ed. Gretel Adorno and Rolf Tiedemann (Frankfurt am Main: Suhrkamp, 1971), 13:23–25.

45. Wagner, *Stories and Essays,* p. 52.

46. Wagner, *Gesammelte Schriften,* 14:135.

47. Ibid., 14:141.

48. Richard Wagner, *Gesammelte Dichtungen und Schriften,* ed. Dieter Borchmeyer (Frankfurt am Main: Insel, 1983), 4:290.

49. Wagner, *Gesammelte Schriften,* 14:186.

50. Ibid., 14:189.

51. In this context see David J. Levin, *Richard Wagner, Fritz Lang, and the Ni-*

belungen: The Dramaturgy of Disavowal (Princeton: Princeton University Press, 1998); Marc A. Weiner, *Richard Wagner and the Anti-Semitic Imagination* (Lincoln: University of Nebraska Press, 1995); and Leon Stein, *The Racial Thinking of Richard Wagner* (New York: Philosophical Library, 1950). Jacob Katz's *The Dark Side of Genius: Richard Wagner's Anti-Semitism* (Hanover: University Press of New England, 1986) seems to separate Wagner's operas from his theoretical writings.

52. Richard Wagner, *Das Rheingold,* ed. Wilhelm Zentner (Stuttgart: Reclam, 1996), pp. 30, 28.

53. For a discussion of the relationship between Alberich and Wotan see Carolyn Abbate, *Unsung Voices: Opera and Musical Narrative in the Nineteenth Century* (Princeton: Princeton University Press, 1991), p. 172. For a discussion of parallels between Wotan and Kundry see Ernest Newman, *The Life of Richard Wagner* (New York: Knopf, 1946), 4:603.

54. For a discussion of this point see Udo Bermbach, "Politik und Anti-Politik im Kunst-Mythos," in *Richard Wagners "Ring des Nibelungen": Ansichten des Mythos,* ed. Udo Bermbach and Dieter Borchmeyer (Stuttgart: Metzler, 1995).

55. Wagner, *Das Rheingold,* p. 35.

56. Ibid., 57.

57. Wagner, *Die Walküre,* ed. Egon Voss (Stuttgart: Reclam, 1997), p. 53.

58. Wagner, *Das Rheingold,* p. 43.

59. For a discussion of this point see Levin's *Richard Wagner,* pp. 5–95.

60. Wagner, *Das Rheingold,* p. 65.

61. Wagner, *Götterdämmerung,* ed. Egon Voss (Stuttgart: Reclam, 1997), p. 27.

62. Ibid., p. 51.

63. Ibid., p. 88.

64. Ibid., p. 89.

65. Wagner, *Siegfried,* ed. Egon Voss (Stuttgart: Reclam, 1998), p. 123.

66. For a discussion of the binary opposition between Siegfried's fearlessness and the Nibelungen's fearfulness see Newman, *Life of Richard Wagner,* 2:337.

Chapter Four

1. Moses Mendelssohn, "Morgenstunden oder Vorlesungen über das Dasein Gottes: Vorbericht," in *Schriften über Religion und Aufklärung,* ed. Martina Thom (Darmstadt: Wissenschaftliche Buchgesellschaft, 1989), p. 469.

2. It also seems to have informed Kant's and Hegel's understanding of Jewishness.

3. As Paul Mendes-Flohr has pointed out: "But Humboldt was an exception. Most cultured Germans expected Mendelssohn and his fellow Jews to shed their Judaism and primordial identity, if not forthwith, certainly incrementally and unfalteringly. This demand was aggravated by the pervasive assumption that Judaism was incompatible with liberal culture and sensibility." *German Jews: A Dual Identity* (New Haven: Yale University Press, 1999), p. 14.

4. Moses Mendelssohn, "Schreiben an Herrn Diakonus Lavater zu Zürich," in *Schriften über Religion und Aufklärung,* ed. Martina Thom (Darmstadt: Wissenschaftliche Buchgesellschaft, 1989), p. 312. For a discussion of the Lavater affair see Alexander Altmann, *Moses Mendelssohn: A Biographical Study* (University City: University of Alabama Press, 1973), pp. 194–263.

5. Amos Funkenstein, *Perceptions of Jewish History* (Berkeley: University of California Press, 1993), p. 229.

6. Mendes-Flohr, *German Jews,* pp. 3–4.

7. See Paul Guyer, *Kant on Freedom, Law, and Happiness* (Cambridge: Cambridge University Press, 2000).

8. See Julius Guttmann, "Mendelssohn's *Jerusalem* and Spinoza's *Theological-Political Treatise,*" in *Studies in Jewish Thought: An Anthology of German-Jewish Scholarship,* ed. Alfred Jospe (Detroit: Wayne Sate University Press, 1981).

9. Moses Mendelssohn, *Jerusalem, or On Religious Power and Judaism,* trans. Allan Arkush with an introduction and commentary by Alexander Altmann (Hanover, NH: University Press of New England, 1983), p. 97. "Die Stimme, die sich an jenem großen Tag auf Sinai hören ließ, rief nicht: 'Ich bin der Ewige, dein Gott! Das notwendige, selbstständige Wesen, das allmächtig ist und allwissend, das den Menschen in einem zukünftigen Leben vergilt nach ihrem Tun.' Dieses ist die allgemeine *Menschenreligion,* nicht Judentum; und allgemeine Menschenreligion, ohne welche die Menschen weder tugendhaft sind noch glückselig werden können, sollte hier nicht geoffenbart werden." Mendelssohn, *Schriften über Religion und Aufklärung,* p. 415.

10. Ibid.

11. Whereas Allan Arkush's *Moses Mendelssohn and the Enlightenment* (Albany: SUNY Press, 1994) calls into doubt whether Mendelssohn's usage of the word *revelation* should be taken at face value, David Sorkin affirms the importance of revelation in Mendelssohn's oeuvre as follows: "Arkush contends that for Mendelssohn 'revelation was, in effect, of secondary importance,' yet totally ignores Mendelssohn's pronouncements on the nature of revelation in his commentary on the book of Exodus." "The Mendelssohn Myth and Its Method," *New German Critique* 77 (spring–summer 1999): 25.

12. Mendelssohn, *Jerusalem,* p. 127. "Die Gesetze wurden *geoffenbart,* d.i. von Gott durch *Worte* und *Schrift* bekanntgemacht." Mendelssohn, *Schriften über Religion und Aufklärung,* p. 446.

13. Mendelssohn, *Jerusalem,* pp. 127–28. "Jedoch ist nur das Wesentlichste davon den Buchstaben anvertraut worden; und auch diese niedergeschriebenen Gesetze sind ohne die ungeschriebenen, mündlich überlieferten und durch mündlichen, lebendigen Unterricht fortzupflanzenden Erläuterungen, Einschränkungen und näheren Bestimmungen größtenteils unverständlich oder mußten es mit der Zeit werden." Mendelssohn, *Schriften über Religion und Aufklärung,* p. 446.

14. Mendelssohn, *Jerusalem,* pp. 102–3. "Lehrbegriffe und Gesetze, Gesinnungen und Handlungen. Jene waren nicht an Worte und Schriftzeichen gebunden, die für alle Menschen und Zeiten, unter allen Revolutionen der Sprachen, Sitten, Lebensart und Verhältnissen immer dieselben bleiben, uns immer die dieselbe steife Formen darbieten sollen, in welche wir unsere Begriffe nicht einzwängen können, ohne sie zu verstümmeln. Sie wurden dem lebendigen, geistigen Unterrichte anvertraut, der mit allen Veränderungen der Zeiten und Umstände gleichen Schritt halten und nach dem Bedürfnisse, nach der Fähigkeit und Fassungskraft des Lehrlings abgeändert und gemodelt werden kann. . . . Das Zeremonialgesetz selbst ist eine lebendige, Geist und Herz erweckende Art von Schrift, die bedeutungsvoll ist und ohne Unterlass zu Betrachtung erweckt und zum mündlichen Unterrichte Anlaß und Gelegenheit gibt." Mendelssohn, *Schriften über Religion und Aufklärung,* 420–21.

15. David Sorkin, *Moses Mendelssohn and the Religious Enlightenment* (Berkeley: University of California Press), p. 13.

16. Mendelssohn, *Jerusalem*, p. 100. "Dem Glauben wird nicht befohlen; denn er nimmt keine andere Befehle an, als die den Weg der Überzeugung zu ihm kommen." Mendelssohn, *Schriften über Religion und Aufklärung*, p. 418.

17. Mendelssohn, *Jerusalem*, p. 132. "[I]n der echten Politik eine Gottheit erblicken, wo gemeine Augen einen Stein sehen." Mendelssohn, *Schriften über Religion und Aufklärung*, p. 450.

18. Mendelssohn, *Jerusalem*, p. 132. "Schon zu den Zeiten des Propheten Samuel gewann das Gebäude einen Riß, der sich immer weiter auftat, bis die Teile völlig zerfielen. Die Nation verlangte einen sichtbaren, fleischlichen König zum Regenten. Es sei nun, daß die Priesterschaft, wie von den Söhnen des Hohenpriesters in der Schrift erzählt wird, schon angefangen, ihr Ansehen beim Volke zu mißbrauchen, oder daß der Glanz einer benachbarten Hofhaltung die Augen geblendet; genug; sie forderten *einen König, wie alle andere Völker haben.* Der Prophet, den dieses *kränkte,* stellte ihnen vor, was ein menschlicher König sei, der seine eigenen Bedürfnisse hat und sie nach Wohlgefallen erweitern kann, und wie schwer ein Schwacher Sterblicher zu befriedigen sei, dem man das Recht einer Gottheit einräumet. . . . Staat und Religion [waren] nicht mehr ebendasselbe, und Kollision der Pflichten war schon nicht mehr unmöglich." *Schriften zur Religion und Aufklärung,* pp. 450–51.

19. Emmanuel Levinas, "Preface to the Translation of *Jerusalem,*" in *In the Time of Nations,* trans. Michael B. Smith (Bloomington: Indiana University Press, 1994), p. 144.

20. Mendelssohn, *Jerusalem*, p. 113. "[D]aß das Bedürfnis der Schriftzeichen die erste Veranlaßun zur Abgötterei gewesen." Mendelssohn, *Schriften über Religion und Aufklärung,* p. 432.

21. Mendelssohn, *Jerusalem,* p. 100. "Gebot und Verbot, Belohnung und Strafen sind nur für Handlungen, für Tun und Lassen, die in des Menschen Willkür stehen und durch Begriffe vom Guten und Bösen, also auch von Hoffnung und Furcht, gelenkt werden. Glaube und Zweifel, Beifall und Widerspruch hingegen richten sich nicht nach unserem Begehrungsvermögen, nicht nach Wunsch und Verlangen, nicht nach Fürchten und Hoffen, sondern nach unserer Erkenntnis von Wahrheit und Unwahrheit." Mendelssohn, *Schriften über Religion und Aufklärung,* p. 418.

22. Mendelssohn, *Jerusalem,* p. 93. "Jene ewigen Weisheiten hingegen, insoweit sie zum Heile und zur Glückseligkeit der Menschen nützlich sind, lehrt Gott auf eine der Gottheit gemäßere Weise: nicht durch Laut und Schriftzeichen, die hier und da, diesem und jenem verständlich sind, sondern durch die Schöpfung selbst und ihre innerliche Verhältnisse, die allen Menschen leserlich und verständlich sind." Mendelssoh, *Schriften über Religion und Aufklärung,* p. 411.

23. Mendelssohn, *Jerusalem,* p. 107. "[D]ie Dinge selbst." Mendelssohn, *Schriften über Religion und Aufklärung,* p. 426.

24. Mendelssohn, *Jerusalem,* p. 119. "Die zur Glückseligkeit der Nation sowohl als der einzelnen Glieder derselben nützlichen Wahrheiten sollten von allem Bildlichen äußerst entfernt sein." Mendelssohn, *Schriften über Religion und Aufklärung,* p. 437.

25. See Mendelssohn, *Jerusalem,* pp. 110–13.

26. Mendelssohn, *Jerusalem,* p. 118. "Bilder und Bilderschrift führen zu Aberglauben und Götzendienst, und unsere alphabetische Schreiberei macht den Menschen macht den Menschen zu spekulativ. Sie legt die symbolische Erkenntnis der Dinge und ihrer Verhältinisse gar zu offen auf der Oberfläche aus, überhebt uns der Mühe des Eindringens und Forschens und macht zwischen Lehr und Leben eine gar zu weite Trennung. Diesen Mängeln abzuhelfen, gab der Gesetzgeber dieser Nation das *Zeremonialgesetz.* Mit dem alltäglichen Tun und Lassen der Menschen sollten religiöse und sittliche Erkenntnisse verbunden sein. Das Gesetz trieb sie zwar nicht zum Nachdenken an, schrieb ihnen bloß Handlungen, bloß Tun und Lassen vor." Mendelssohn, *Schriften über Religion und Aufklärung,* p. 437.

27. Sorkin, *Mendelssohn and the Religious Enlightenment,* p. 153. Similarly, Amos Funkenstein characterizes Mendelssohn's difference from mainstream German Jewish thought in the nineteenth century as follows: "He was not altogether free from the apologetic tendencies that were to become dominant later. Perhaps we ought to say, he has not yet reached the point where assimilation or at least accommodation even of religious tenets seemed a necessary price for emancipation into the state, because the state he conceived of was not yet the national state of the early nineteenth century, itself a surrogate for religious fervor. And, for the same reason, he could not yet see the gap between political and social integration." *Perceptions of Jewish History,* p. 229.

28. Stefi Jersch-Wenzel, "Legal Status and Emancipation," in *German-Jewish History in Modern Times,* vol. 2, *Emancipation and Acculturation: 1780–1871,* ed. Michael A. Meyer et al. (New York: Columbia University Press, 1997), p. 33.

29. Michael A. Meyer, "Jewish Communities in Transition," in *German-Jewish History in Modern Times,* vol. 2, *Emancipation and Acculturation: 1780–1871,* ed. Michael A. Meyer et al. (New York: Columbia University Press, 1997), p. 117.

30. Jersch-Wenzl, "Legal Status and Emancipation," p. 41.

31. Samson Raphael Hirsch, "Religion Allied to Progress (1854)," in *The Jew in the Modern World: A Documentary History,* ed. Paul Mendes-Flohr and Jehuda Reinharz (Oxford: Oxford University Press, 1995), p. 199.

32. Here it is worthwhile recalling that, like Geiger, Hirsch received a university education (University of Bonn).

33. Hirsch, "Religion Allied to Progress (1854)," p. 201.

34. David Sorkin, *The Transformation of German Jewry, 1780–1840* (Oxford: Oxford University Press, 1987), p. 170.

35. Funkenstein, *Perceptions of Jewish History,* p. 36. Funkenstein is not the first to have coined the notion "counterhistory." Compare David Biale, *Gershom Scholem: Kabbala and Counterhistory* (Cambridge: Harvard University Press, 1979).

36. Abraham Geiger, *Abraham Geiger and Liberal Judaism: The Challenge of the Nineteenth Century,* comp. Max Wiener, trans. Ernst J. Schlochauer (Philadelphia: Jewish Publication Society of America, 1962), p. 209.

37. Susannah Heschel, *Abraham Geiger and the Jewish Jesus* (Chicago: University of Chicago Press, 1998), p. 3.

38. Ibid.

39. Ibid., p. 153.

40. Geiger, *Abraham Geiger and Liberal Judaism,* p. 183.

41. Ibid.

42. "Es ist in der That auffallend, welche innige Wahlverwandtschaft zwischen den beiden Völkern der Sittlichkeit, den Juden und Germanen, herrscht." Heinrich Heine, *Historisch-kritische Gesamtausgabe der Werke*, vol. 10, *Shakespeares Mädchen und Frauen*, ed. Manfred Windfuhr (Hamburg: Hoffmann & Campe, 1993), p. 125.

43. "[. . .] daß man das ehemalige Palestina für ein orientalisches Deutschland ansehen könnte, wie man das heutige Deutschland für die Heimath des heiligen Wortes, für den Mutterboden des Prophetentums, für die Burg der reinen Geistheit halten sollte." Ibid., p. 125.

44. Ibid.

45. Immanuel Wolf, "On the Concept of a Science of Judaism (1822)," in *The Jew in the Modern World: A Documentary History*, ed. Paul Mendes-Flohr and Jehuda Reinharz (Oxford: Oxford University Press, 1995), p. 220.

46. Quoted from S. S. Prawer, *Heine's Jewish Comedy: A Study of His Portrait of Jews and Judaism* (Oxford: Oxford University Press, 1983), p. 238.

47. Ibid. "Diese können, bey politischen Fragen, so republikanisch als möglich denken, ja sich sogar sanskülotisch im Kothe wälzen; kommen aber religiöse Begriffe ins Speil, dann bleiben sie unterthänige Kammerknechte ihres Jehova, des alten Fetischs, der doch von ihrer ganzen Sippschaft nichts mehr wissen will und sich zu einem Gott-reinen Geist umtaufen lassen." Heinrich Heine, "Aus den Memoiren des Herrn von Schnabelewopski," in *Historisch-kritische Gesamtausgabe der Werke*, vol. 5, *Almansor, William Ratcliffe*, ed. M. Windfuhr (Hamburg: Hoffmann & Campe, 1994), p. 180.

48. Heinrich Heine, *Historisch-kritische Gesamtausgabe*, vol. 11, *Ludwig Börne: Eine Denkschrift und kleinere politische Schriften*, ed. M. Windfuhr (Hamburg: Hofmann & Campe, 1978), p. 18.

49. "Ich sage nazarenisch, um mich weder des Ausdrucks 'jüdisch' noch 'christlich' zu bedienen, obgleich beide Ausdrücke für mich synonym sind und von mir nicht gebraucht werden, um einen Glauben, sondern ein Naturell zu bezeichnen. [A]lle Menschen sind entweder Juden oder Hellenen, Menschen mit ascetischen, bildfeindlichen, vergeistigungssüchtigen Trieben, oder Menschen von lebensheiterem, entfaltungsstolzem und realistischem Wesen." Ibid., 11:18–19.

50. Ibid., 11:31–32.

51. See Sander Gilman, *Jewish Self-Hatred: Anti-Semitism and the Hidden Language of the Jews* (Baltimore: Johns Hopkins University Press, 1986), pp. 167–88.

52. Prawer, *Heine's Jewish Comedy*, p. 688.

53. Roger F. Cook, *By the Rivers of Babylon: Heinrich Heine's Late Songs and Reflections* (Detroit: Wayne State University Press, 1998), p. 31. For an overview of secondary literature on Heine, see Jeffrey L. Sammons, "The Exhaustion of Current Heine Studies: Some Observations, Partly Speculative," in *The Jewish Reception of Heinrich Heine*, ed. Mark H. Gelber. Conditio Judaica, vol. 1 (Tübingen: Niemeyer, 1992), pp. 5–19.

54. Heinrich Heine, *The Complete Poems of Henrich Heine: A Modern English Version by Hal Draper* (Boston: Suhrkamps/Insel, 1982), p. 654.

55. Heine, *Historisch-kritische Gesamtausgabe der Werke*, vol. 3, pt. 1, *Romanzero Gedichte, 1853 und 1854: Lyrischer Nachlass*, ed. M. Windfuhr (Hamburg: Hoffmann & Campe, 1992), p. 128.

56. Cook, *By the Rivers of Babylon*, p. 99.

Chapter Five

1. Heinrich von Treitschke, "A Word About Our Jewry (1880)," in *The Jew in the Modern World: A Documentary History,* ed. Paul Mendes-Flohr and Jehuda Reinharz (Oxford: Oxford University Press, 1995), p. 344.

2. Ibid.

3. Moishe Postone, "Anti-Semitism and National Socialism," in *Germans and Jews Since the Holocaust: The Changing Situation in West Germany,* ed. Anson Rabinbach and Jack Zipes (New York: Holmes & Meier, 1986), p. 311.

4. Treitschke, "A Word," p. 344.

5. Ismar Schorsch, "Ideology and History in the Age of Emancipation," in Heinrich Graetz, *The Structure of Jewish History and Other Essays,* trans., ed., and intro. Ismar Schorsch (New York: Jewish Theological Seminary of America, 1975), p. 45.

6. Heinrich Graetz, *History of the Jews,* vol. 5, *From the Chmielncki Persecution of the Jews in Poland (1648 C.E.) to the Present Time (1870 C.E.),* trans. Bella Löwy (Philadelphia: Jewish Publication Society of America, 1895), p. 365.

7. Ibid., p. 707.

8. Ibid.

9. Ibid.

10. Ibid., p. 712.

11. Ibid.

12. Ibid., pp. 711–12.

13. Ibid., p. 712.

14. Heinrich Graetz, "The Stucture of Jewish History," in *The Structure of Jewish History and Other Essays,* trans., ed. and intro. Ismar Schorsch (New York: Jewish Theological Seminary of America, 1975), p. 70.

15. Ibid., pp.70–71.

16. Michael A. Meyer, "Jewish Identity in the Decades After 1848," *German-Jewish History in Modern Times,* vol. 2, *Emancipation and Acculturation: 1780–1871* (New York: Columbia University Press, 1997), p. 336.

17. Gilles Deleuze and Felix Guattari, *Anti-Oedipus: Capitalism and Schizophrenia,* trans. Robert Hurley, Mark Seem, and Helen R. Lane (Minneapolis: University of Minnesota Press, 1983), p. 105.

18. See Theodor Herzl, *The Jewish State,* intro. Louis Lipsky, trans. Sylvia d'Avigdor (Mineola, NY: American Zionist Emergency Council, 1988), p. 76.

19. See Sander L. Gilman, *Jewish Self-Hatred: Anti-Semitism and the Hidden Language of the Jews* (Baltimore: Johns Hopkins University Press, 1986), pp. 290–93.

20. Herzl, *Jewish State,* p. 82.

21. For a discussion of the establishment of a similar immanent idea of the sensuous as formulated by Georg Simmel in his critique of Kant's legal theory see Michael Mack, "Law, Charity, and Taboo, or Kant's Reversal of St. Paul's Spirit-Letter Opposition and Its Theological Implications," *Modern Theology* 16 (2001): 417–41.

22. Eric Voeglin, *Collected Works,* vol. 2, *Race and State,* trans Ruth Hein, ed. with an introduction by Klaus Vondung (Baton Rouge: Louisiana State University Press, 1997), p. 190.

23. Ibid., p. 191.

24. For a discussion of Chamberlain's obsession with biblical and talmudic law see ibid., p. 201.

25. Houston Stewart Chamberlain, "The Foundation of the Nineteenth Century (1899)," in *The Jew in the Modern World: A Documentary History*, ed. Paul Mendes-Flohr and Jehuda Reinharz (Oxford: Oxford University Press, 1995), p. 359.

26. Ibid.

27. Ibid.

28. Chandak Sengoopta, *Otto Weininger: Sex, Science, and Self in Imperial Vienna* (Chicago: University of Chicago Press, 2000), p. 10.

29. See ibid., p. 17.

30. Otto Weininger, *Sex and Character*, trans. not named (London: Heinemann, 1906), p. 292. "Die Frau will nicht als Subjekt behandelt werden, sie will stets und in alle Wege—das ist eben ihr Frau-Sein—lediglich passiv bleiben, einen Willen auf sich gerichtet fühlen." Weininger, *Geschlecht und Charakter: Eine Prinzipielle Untersuchung* (Vienna: Braumüller, 1903), p. 391.

31. Weininger, *Sex and Character*, pp. 292–93. "Die Materie, das absolut Unindividualisierte, das, was jede Form annehmen kann, selbst aber keine bestimmten und dauernden Eigenschaften hat, ist das, was so wenig Essenz besitzt, wie der bloßen Empfindung, . . . zukommt." Weininger, *Geschlecht und Charakter*, p. 392.

32. "We cannot do better than begin with Immanuel Kant, Otto Weininger's intellectual ideal and the prototypical German thinker of the Enlightenment, who believed that women and men had different 'characters' and that this difference was ordained by a higher power. Women, according to Kant, acted on inclination and needed to be governed by men, who acted according to reason. Morally women could not be their own masters and, therefore, could not be full and active citizens." Sengoopta, *Otto Weininger*, p. 29.

33. Weininger, *Sex and Character*, p. 306. "[D]as Judentum . . . durchdränkt von . . . Weiblichkeit." Weininger, *Geschlecht und Charakter*, p. 409.

34. Weininger, *Sex and Character*, p. 309. "Die Juden leben sonach nicht als freie, selbstherrliche, zwischen Tugend und Laster wählende Individualitäten wie die Arier." Weininger, *Geschlecht und Charakter*, p. 415.

35. Weininger, *Sex and Character*, p. 329. "Weiber und Juden kuppeln, ihr Ziel ist es: den Menschen schuldig werden zu lassen." Weininger, *Geschlecht und Charakter*, p. 441.

36. Sengoopta, *Otto Weininger*, p. 59. Sengoopta is quoting his translation from Weininger's *Geschlecht und Character: Eine prinzipielle Untersuchung* (1903; reprint, Munich: Matthes & Seitz, 1980), p. 332.

37. Weininger, *Sex and Character*, p. 313. "[F]ür die gehorsame Befolgung eines mächtigen fremden Willens das Wohlergehen auf Erden in Aussicht stellt und die Eroberung der Welt verheißt." Weininger, *Geschlecht und Charakter*, p. 420.

38. Weininger, *Sex and Character*, p. 313. "Das Verhältnis zum Jehovah, dem abstrakten Götzen, vor dem er die Angst des Sklaven hat, dessen Namen er nicht einmal auszusprechen wagt, charakterisiert den Juden." Weininger, *Geschlecht und Charakter*, p. 420.

39. Weininger, *Sex and Character*, p. 303; "eine Geistesrichtung," Weininger, *Geschlecht und Charakter*, p. 406.

40. As Allan Janik and Stephen Toulmin have put it, "when he realized the im-

possibility both of assimilation and of continuing to live as a Jew in non-Jewish society, he chose the only reasonable solution to his dilemma; believing as he did that the Jewish character was by nature the lowest, most depraved type of character—the lowest form of 'womanhood'—and that all character was eternal and immutable, he had no alternative." *Wittgenstein's Vienna* (New York: Simon & Schuster, 1973), p. 71.

41. For a discussion of Weininger's sense of Jewish immutability, see Sander L. Gilman, "Otto Weininger and Sigmund Freud: Race and Gender in the Shaping of Psychoanalysis," in *Love* + Marriage = Death and Other Essays on Representing Difference, Stanford Studies in Jewish History and Culture (Stanford: Stanford University Press, 1998), pp. 113–33.

42. Nancy A. Horrowitz and Barbara Hyams, "A Critical Introduction to the History of Weininger Reception," in *Jews and Gender: Responses to Otto Weininger,* ed. Horrowitz and Hyams (Philadelphia: Temple University Press, 1995), p. 10.

43. See Carl Schmitt, *Die geistesgeschichtliche Lage des heutigen Parlamentarismus,* 2d ed. (Munich: Duncker & Humbolt, 1926), p. 74.

44. See ibid., pp. 20–23.

Chapter Six

1. Franz Rosenzweig, "Einleitung in die Akademieausgabe der Jüdischen Schriften Hermann Cohens" (1923), in Rosenzweig, *Kleinere Schriften,* ed. Edith Rosenzweig (Berlin: Schocken, 1937), p. 339.

2. Ibid.

3. For Rosenzweig's discussion of this point see his *Stern der Erlösung* (Frankfurt am Main: Suhrkamp, 1990), p. 24.

4. Moses Mendelssohn, *Schriften über Religion und Aufklärung,* ed. Martina Thom (Darmstadt: Wissenschaftliche Buchgesellschaft, 1989), p. 312.

5. Steven M. Lowenstein, Paul Mendes-Flohr, Peter Pulzer, and Monika Richarz, introduction to Mendes-Flohr et al., *German-Jewish History in Modern Times,* vol. 3, *Integration in Dispute: 1871–1918* (New York: Columbia University Press, 1997), p. 1. As the authors make clear, "The principle of legal equality was enshrined in a law passed by the Reichstag of the North German Confederation on July 3, 1869, which in a single paragraph declared, 'All remaining restrictions in civil and political rights based on differences of religion are hereby abolished.' It was not new. The Basic Rights of the German People, adopted by the Frankfurt parliament in 1848, had included a similar declaration in almost identical wording. . . . [T]he practical implementation of civic equality remained a matter of dispute" (p. 1).

6. Ibid.

7. As Ismar Schorsch has pointed out, Cohen himself perceived of Judaism as closely joined to Protestantism in the 1880s: "Whereas in 1880 he [Cohen] had dwelt exclusively on the fundamental unity of Judaism and Protestantism, taking an equivocal stand on the issue of Jewish survival, during the last decades of the Empire, he emerged as the most profound spokesman for the right of German Jewry to retain its religious identity." See Schorsch, *Jewish Reactions to Anti-Semitism, 1870–1914* (New York: Columbia University Press, 1972), p. 140.

8. Ibid., p. 1.

9. Deutsch-Israelitischer Gemeindebund (1869–1881), Verein Zur Abwehr des Antisemitismus (1891–1914), Centralverein deutscher Staatsbürger jüdischen Glaubens (1893–1914).

10. Schorsch, *Jewish Reactions,* p. 75.

11. This very duality within Cohen's notion of reason and religion bespeaks a correlation between his pattern of thought and the particular constellation of German Jewish identity that Paul Mendes-Flohr has recently called a "dual identity." See Mendes-Flohr, *German Jews: A Dual Identity* (New Haven: Yale University Press, 1999).

12. Cohen's neo-Kantianism has of course also shaped his understanding of Judaism. Thus he marks "the ritualism of our religion" off from "its eternal essence." Cohen, "Affinities Between the Philosophy of Kant and Judaism," in Cohen, *Reason and Hope: Selections from the Jewish Writings of Hermann Cohen,* trans Eva Jospe (New York: Norton, 1971), p. 89.

13. Hugo Bergman's *Faith and Reason: An Introduction to Modern Jewish Thought,* trans. and ed. Alfred Jospe (Washington, D.C.: B'Nai B'Rith Hillel Foundation, 1961), is one of the few studies that draws attention to Cohen's critical relation to Kantian thought. Bergman examines the difference in philosophical outlook between Cohen's Marburg and Berlin periods. However, Bergmann confines this movement from the Kantian independence of reason (autonomy) to an acknowledgment of human dependence on outside influences to a concern with bridging the gap between faith and reason: "In Cohen's early period we can find no place for faith: now faith encompasses reason as part of itself" (p. 54). Developing Bergman's reading in his essay "Hermann Cohen," Nathan Rotenstreich argues that whereas Kant conceives of morality as a self-sufficient immanent entity, Cohen connects ethics to the relationship between man and God. Rotenstreich, *Essays in Jewish Philosophy in the Modern Era,* intro. Paul Mendes-Flohr, ed. Reiner Munk (Amsterdam: Gieben, 1996). In a similar manner, Julius Gutman's *Philosophy of Judaism: The History of Jewish Philosophy from Biblical Times to Franz Rosenzweig,* intro. R. J. Zwi Werblowsky, trans. David W. Silverman (New York: Holt, Rinehart and Winston, 1964), focuses on the interdependence of the ethical and the religious in Cohen's thought. Thus, Bergman's, Rotenstreich's, and Gutman's discussions concentrate on religion without attending to the difference between Cohen's and Kant's understanding of the rational. Rather than a dual notion of rationality in Cohen's work, one type of reason—the Mendelssohnian—turns out to be Cohen's notion of religion, whereas the other—the Kantian—is defined as neo-Kantian rationality. Authors of more recent studies seem not to allow for a notion of heteronomy in Cohen's understanding of religion. Robert Gibbs's *Correlation in Rosenzweig and Levinas* (Princeton, NJ: Princeton University Press, 1992), concedes that "Cohen goes further *in the systematic writings* than idealists have ever gone before" (p. 185). Leora Batnitzky's *Idolatry and Representation: The Philosophy of Franz Rosenzweig Reconsidered* (Princeton, NJ: Princeton University Press, 2000) associates Cohen's critique of idolatry with Maimonides' philosophy over and against Mendelssohn's emphasis on worship, while neglecting a Cohenian concern with an interpenetration of teaching and moral action that follows the trajectory of Mendelssohn's Enlightenment thought.

14. See Leo Strauss, "Introductory Essay to Hermann Cohen, *Religion of Reason Out of the Sources of Judaism,*" in *Jewish Philosophy and the Crisis of Moder-*

nity: Essays and Lectures in Modern Jewish Thought, ed. and intro. Kenneth Hart Green (Albany: SUNY Press, 1997).

15. Cohen might be referring to Kant's critique of Mendelssohn's antievolutionist view of history. See Immanuel Kant, "Über den Gemeinspruch: Das mag in der Theorie richtig sein, Taugt aber nicht für die Praxis," *Schriften zur Anthropologie, Geschichtsphilosophie, Politik und Pädagogik,* ed. W. Weischedel (Frankfurt am Main: Insel, 1964), 1:165–72.

16. Immanuel Kant, *Religion and Rational Theology,* trans and ed. Allen W. Wood (Cambridge: Cambridge University Press, 1996), p. 155.

17. Hermann Cohen, *Religion of Reason Out of the Sources of Judaism,* trans. and intro. Simon Kaplan, with an introductory essay by Leo Strauss (New York: Ungar, 1972), p. 357. For the German original see Cohen, *Die Religion der Vernunft aus den Quellen des Judentums* (Leipzig: Fock, 1919), p. 421.

18. Cohen, *Religion of Reason,* p. 357. "Schon Kant hatte daher unrecht, wenn er Mendelssohns Auffassung einen 'Mangel an Menschlichkeit' vorwarf. Diese Ansicht ist nur möglich, wenn man es für selbstverständlich und unbezweifelbar hält, daß die jüdischen Gesetze schlechterdings nur als ein hartes Joch gefühlt werden können." Cohen, *Die Religion der Vernunft,* p. 422.

19. Cohen, *Religion of Reason,* pp. 368–69. "Nicht die Isolierung ist der einzige Zweck des Gesetzes, sondern die Idealisierung alles irdischen Tuns mit dem Göttlichen. Der Gottesdienst beschränkt sich nicht auf die Synagoge: das Gesetz erfüllt und durchdringt das ganze Leben mit ihm. . . . Man kennt den Juden in seinem Äußeren, aber nicht hinreichend in der Fortwirkung des Gesetzes in seinem Innenleben und in dessen hereditären Grundlagen." Cohen, *Die Religion der Vernunft,* pp. 434–35.

20. Cohen, *Religion of Reason,* p. 370. "Denn das ist der Sinn des Gesetzes: die Verbindung zu stiften und aufrechtzuhalten zwischen der Erkenntnis und der Handlung, und daher auch zwischen der Erkenntnis als Religion, und der Handlung, als der sittlichen Tat." Cohen, *Die Religion der Vernunft,* p. 437.

21. Michael Zank, *The Idea of Atonement in the Philosophy of Hermann Cohen,* Brown Judaic Studies, no. 234 (Providence, RI: Brown University Press, 2000), p. 34.

22. See ibid., pp. 55–56.

23. Ibid., p. 294.

24. "Der Aufschwung des Willens darf des Schwungs nicht verlustig gehen, den der Affekt und er allein zu erteilen vermag." Hermann Cohen, *Gesammelte Werke,* vol. 7, *Ethik des reinen Willens,* intro, Steven S. Schwarzschild (Hildesheim: Olms, 1981), p. 199.

25. See Cohen, *Die Religion der Vernunft,* p. 7.

26. Rotenstreich, *Essays in Jewish Philosophy in the Modern Era,* pp. 113–14.

27. See Kant, *Schriften zur Ethik und Religionsphilosophie,* ed. Wilhelm Weischdel (Frankfurt am Main: Suhrkamp, 1964), 2:734; Kant, *Religion and Rational Theology,* p. 118.

28. Gordon E. Michaelson, *Kant and the Problem of God* (Oxford: Blackwell, 1999), p. 104.

29. Cohen, *Religion of Reason,* p. 169. See Cohen, *Die Religion der Vernunft,* p. 197. For a discussion of Cohen's critique of the Christian paradigm that permeates Kant's moral philosophy see Zank, *Idea of Atonement,* pp. 261–62.

30. Cohen, *Religion of Reason*, p. 456. "[E]in Fehler des Pessimismus und der gemeinen Ansicht von dem radikal Bösen im Menschen, welche Kant allerdings ebenso richtig wie tiefsinnig idealisiert hat." Cohen, *Die Religion der Vernunft*, p. 538.

31. Cohen, *Religion of Reason*, p. 223. "Gott Macht unschuldig." Cohen, *Die Religion der Vernunft*, p. 262.

32. Kant, *Religion and Rational Theology*, p. 77. "[D]aß die aus dem natürlichen Hange entspringende Fähigkeit oder Unfähigkeit der Willkür, das moralische Gesetz in seine Maxime aufzunehmen, oder nicht, das *gute oder das böse Herz* genannt werden kann." Kant, *Schriften zurEthik und Religionsphilosophie*, p. 676.

33. Cohen, *Religion of Reason*, p. 182. "Auf die Gedanken der Genesis also kann sich der Gedanke nicht berufen, der unsere Frage nach dem Ursprung des Bösen durch die Anlage des menschlich Herzens, des menschlichen Willens zum Bösen erledigen wollte." Cohen, *Die Religion der Vernunft*, p. 214.

34. Cohen, *Religion of Reason*, p. 461. "Es ist bedeutsam für das jüdische Sprachbewußtsein, daß das hebräische Wort Olam für Welt zugleich die Ewigkeit bedeutet: 'Auch die Welt hat er in sein Herz gegeben' (Koh. 3, 11). Diese Welt ist auch die Ewigkeit, so daß man auch die Ewigkeit, als in das Herz des Menschen von Gott gegeben, übersetzen kann." Cohen, *Die Religion der Vernunft*, p. 544.

35. Cohen, *Religion of Reason*, p. 193. "*[D]ie Schuld darf nicht zum Anstoß*, nicht zum Hindernis der Befreiung von ihr werden." Cohen, *Die Religion der Vernunft*, p. 227.

36. Zank, *Idea of Atonement*, p. 35.

37. Cohen, *Religion of Reason*, p. 223. "Die Schuld darf nicht 'zum Anstoß' sein. Die Schuld stabiliert keineswegs einen bösen Charakter des Menschen, sondern sie ist vielmehr nur der Durchgang zu seiner Vollendung, zu seinem höheren Aufstieg für die Wiedergewinnung der Unschuld." Cohen, *Die Religion der Vernunft*, p. 262.

Chapter Seven

1. Fritz K. Ringer, *The Decline of the German Mandarins: The German Academic Community, 1890–1933* (Cambridge: Harvard University Press, 1969), p. 139.

2. Franz Rosenzweig, *The Star of Redemption*, trans. William W. Hallo (Notre Dame, IN: Notre Dame University Press, 1985), p. 3; Franz Rosenzweig, *Der Stern der Erlösung* (Frankfurt am Main: Suhrkamp, 1990), p. 3.

3. Rosenzweig, *Star of Redemption*, p. 3.

4. Ibid., p. 6. "Zum Schweigen bracht wurde die Stimme, welche in einer Offenbarung die jenseits des Denkens entspringende Quelle göttlichen Wissens zu besitzen behauptete. Die philosophische Arbeit von Jahrhunderten ist dieser Auseinandersetzung des Wissens mit dem Glauben gewidmet; sie kommt zum Ziel in dem gleichen Augenblick, wo das Wissen vom All in sich selber zum Abschluß kommt." Rosenzweig, *Der Stern der Erlösung*, p. 6.

5. Rosenzweig, *Star of Redemption*, p. 6; Rosenzweig, *Der Stern der Erösung*, p. 7.

6. Rosenzweig, *Star of Redemption*, p. 7; Rosenzweig, *Der Stern der Erlösung*, p. 7.

7. This serious mistranslation of the German adverb *gerade* has led to some

misunderstanding of Rosenzweig's relation to Kant. Rosenzweig, *Star of Redemption,* p. 10. "[U]nd gerade bei Kant hat durch die Formulierung des Sittengesetzes als der allgemeingültigen Tat wieder der Begriff des All über das Eins des Menschen den Sieg davongetragen." Rosenzweig, *Der Stern der Erlösung,* p. 11.

8. Rosenzweig, *Star of Redemption,* p. 10. "Kant selbst steht bei Hegel's Weltgeschichte Pate, nicht bloß in seinen staats- und geschichtsphilosophischen Ansätzen, sondern schon in den ethischen Grundbegriffen." Rosenzweig, *Der Stern der Erlösung,* p. 11.

9. Rosenzweig, *Star of Redemption,* p. 14. "Das Gesetz ist dem Menschen, nicht der Mensch dem Gesetz gegeben." Rosenzweig, *Der Stern der Erlösung,* p. 15.

10. Richard A. Cohen, *Elevations: The Height of the Good in Rosenzweig and Levinas* (Chicago: University of Chicago Press, 1994), p. 96.

11. Rosenzweig, *Star of Redemption,* p. 214. "[U]nd die Forderung der Autonomie fordert, daß der Mensch nur schlechthin, nur überhaupt will." Rosenzweig, *Der Stern der Erlösung,* p. 239.

12. Rosenzweig, *Star of Redemption,* p. 214. "[M]an kann nicht 'etwas' wollen und trotzdem nur 'überhaupt' wollen." Rosenzweig, *Der Stern der Erlösung,* p. 239.

13. Paul Mendes-Flohr, "Rosenzweig and Kant: Two Views of Ritual and Religion," in *Divided Passions: Jewish Intellectuals and the Experience of Modernity* (Detroit: Wayne State University Press, 1991), p. 295.

14. Rosenzweig, *Star of Redemption,* p. 217. "Indem aber die Welttat im Islam Ausübung des Gerhorsams ist, wird nun sein Menschenbegriff ganz deutlich. . . . Und wieder findet diese auf dem Grunde einer freien, mühsam immer neu gewonnenen Selbstverleugnung schlicht gehorsame Frömmigkeit merkwürdigerweise ihre genaue Entstprechung in in der Weltfrömigkeit des freien sich Einfügens in das allgemeine Gesetz, wie sie die neuere Zeit etwa in der Ethik Kants und seiner Nachfolger sowie überhaupt im allgemeinen Bewußtsein." Rosenzweig, *Der Stern der Erlösung,* pp. 242–43.

15. Rosenzweig, *Star of Redemption,* p. 188. "Es war der ungeheure Irrtum des Idealismus, daß er meinte, in seiner 'Erzeugung' des All sei wirklich des All sei wirklich das All ganz erhalten." Rosenzweig, *Der Stern der Erlösung,* p. 209.

16. Rosenzweig, *Star of Redemption,* p. 141. "Aber der Idealismus liebt diesen Hinweis [daß A=B eingeschloßen ware zwischen ein zeugendendes A=A und ein gebärendes B=B] auf ein ihm zugrunde liegendes dunkles Chaos des Besonderen nicht und sucht schnell davon wegzukommen." Rosenzweig, *Der Stern der Erlösung,* p. 157.

17. For a discussion of Rosenzweig's reading of Schelling see Else Rahel-Freund, *Franz Rosenzweig's Philosophy of Existence: An Analysis of* The Star of Redemption, trans. Stephen L. Weinstein and Robert Israel, ed. Paul Mendes-Flohr (Dordrecht: Kluwer, 1979); and Ernest Rubinstein, *An Episode of Jewish Romanticism: Franz Rosenzweig's* The Star of Redemption (Albany: SUNY Press, 1999).

18. *Franz Rosenzweig: His Life and Thought,* comp. Nahum N. Glatzer (Cambridge, MA: Hackett, 1998), p. 96.

19. F. W. J. von Schelling, *The Abyss of Freedom: Ages of the World: An Essay by Slavoj Zizek and the Complete Text of Schelling's* Die Weltalter *(second draft, 1813),* trans. Judith Norman (Ann Arbor: University of Michigan Press, 2000), p. 150.

20. Rosenzweig, *Star of Redemption,* p. 188. "Der Idealismus hatte sich uns

erwiesen als eine Konkurrenz nicht mit der Theologie überhaupt, sondern nur mit der Theologie der Schöpfung. Von der Schöpfung hatten wir den Weg zur Offenbarung gesucht." Rosenzweig, *Der Stern der Erlösung*, p. 209.

21. Rosenzweig, *Star of Redemption*, p. 103. "Auch Offenbarung, auch Erlösung sind eben in gewisser, noch nicht auseinanderzusetzender Weise Schöpfung." Rosenzweig, *Der Stern der Erlösung*, p. 114.

22. Cohen, *Elevations*, p. 95.

23. Rosenzweig, *Star of Redemption*, p. 7. "[D]en Blick . . . in jedes Jenseits verschlossen." Rosenzweig, *Der Stern der Erlösung*, p. 8.

24. Rosenzweig, *Star of Redemption*, p. 14. "So ist die Welt dem eigentlich Logischen, der Einheit, gegenüber ein Jenseits." Rosenzweig, *Der Stern der Erlösung*, p. 15.

25. Rosenzweig, *Star of Redemption*, p. 4. "[D]aß die Philosophie das Einzelne aus der Welt schaffen muß, diese Abschaffung des Etwas ist auch der Grund, weshalb sie idealistisch sein muß." Rosenzweig, *Der Stern der Erlösung*, p. 4.

26. Emmanuel Levinas, *Totality and Infinity: An Essay on Exteriority*, trans. Alphonso Lingis (Pittsburgh: Duquesne University Press, 1969), p. 43.

27. Ibid., p. 28.

28. "Such is the definition of freedom: to maintain oneself against the other, despite every relation with the other to ensure the autarchy of the an I." Ibid., p. 46.

29. Ibid., p. 88.

30. For a discussion of how in Levinas "autonomy is itself a mark of irresponsibility, of moral failing," see Robert Gibbs, *Correlations in Rosenzweig and Levinas* (Princeton, NJ: Princeton University Press, 1992), p. 222.

31. Emmanuel Levinas, *Difficult Freedom: Essays on Judaism*, trans. Seàn Hand (Baltimore: Johns Hopkins University Press, 1990), p. 293.

32. Levinas, *Totality and Infinity*, p. 40.

33. Eric L. Santner, *On the Psychology of Everyday Life: Reflections on Freud and Rosenzweig* (Chicago: University of Chicago Press, 2001), p. 66.

Chapter Eight

1. Franz Rosenzweig, *Philosophical and Theological Writings*, trans and ed. Paul W. Frank and Michael L. Morgan (Indianapolis: Hackett, 2000), p. 17. "Statt—in der Ewigkeit des philosophischen Gedankens oder in der Zeitlichkeit des geschichtlichen Prozesses—das Menschliche unter der Gewalt des Göttlichen zu zeigen, versucht man, umgekehrt das Göttliche als die Selbstprojektion des Menschlichen an den Himmel des Mythos zu verstehen. Das Volk ist hier die menschliche Wirklichkeit, die sich schon als solche einem positivistisch gewisssenhaften Geschlecht zum Glaubensinhalt empfiehlt." Franz Rosenzweig, "Atheistische Theologie (1914)," in *Kleinere Schriften* (Berlin: Schocken, 1937), pp. 283–84.

2. "Von ihm [Wagner] führt der Weg einerseits über Feuerbach zu Hegel, andrerseits über die Jungdeutschen z.T. auch zu Hegel." Rosenzweig, *Briefe*, ed. Edith Rosenzweig and Ernst Simon (Berlin: Schocken, 1935), p. 43.

3. "[D]as Imperium schlechthin, wenn auch selbst nur in 'kultureller' Beziehung." Rosenzweig, *Briefe*, p. 44.

4. Ibid. See Paul Mendes-Flohr, "Rosenzweig and the Crisis of Historicism," in *Divided Passions: Jewish Intellectuals and the Experience of Modernity* (Detroit: Wayne State University Press, 1991).

5. Rosenzweig, *Philosophical and Theological Writings,* p. 18; "rational-istische[n] Vergötterung des Volks," Rosenzweig, "Atheistische Theologie," p. 284.

6. Rosenzweig, *Philosophical and Theological Writings,* p. 18. "Statt der Menschwerdung behauptete man so das Menschsein Gottes, statt seines Nieder-steigens zum Berge der Gesetzgebung die Autonomie des Sittengesetzes." Rosen-zweig, "Atheistische Theologie," p. 285.

7. Karl Marx, "Theses on Feuerbach," in *The Marx-Engels Reader,* 2d ed., ed. Robert C. Tucker (New York: Norton, 1978), p. 143.

8. Ibid., p. 145.

9. Rosenzweig, *Philosophical and Theological Writings,* pp. 16–17. "Nicht ohne Berührung mit jenem älteren Volkstumsbegriff des deutschen Idealismus, aber doch wesentlich neu, bildete sich eine Vorstellung von Volk, die ihm den Rang seiner Daseinsberichtigung einräumte. Wer es vermag, durch die pseudonaturalistischen Umhüllungen des Rassebegriffs, denen dieser seine breite Popularität verdankt, hin-durchzuschauen, der erkennt hier das Bestreben, den Volksbegriff so umzubilden, daß das Volk unabhängig von sachlichen Leistungen einfach aus seinem Dasein das Recht dazusein schöpft." Rosenzweig, "Atheistische Theologie," p. 283.

10. Rosnzweig, *Philosophical and Theological Writings,* p. 100. "Kann der andre, wenn er so ist, wie ich ihn hier abmale, denn noch—leben?" Rosenzweig, "Apologetisches Denken: Bemerkungen zu Brod und Baeck," *Kleinere Schriften,* p. 35.

11. Rosenzweig, *Philosophical and Theological Writings,* p. 101. "Nicht lebensfähig wären diese humor- und seelenlosen Gesetzesmaschinen, die sich der Christ so gern unter den 'Pharisäern' vorstellt." Rosenzweig, "Apologetisches Denken," p. 35.

12. "[A]pologetisches Denken bleibt abhängig von der Veranlassung, vom Gegner. Und in diesem Sinn bleibt jüdisches Denken apologetisches Denken." Rosenzweig, "Apologetisches Denken," p. 33. See Paul Mendes-Flohr, "Men-delssohn and Rosenzweig," in *Der Philosoph Franz Rosenzweig (1886–1929): Internationaler Kongreß—Kassel 1986,* vol. 1, *Die Herausforderung jüdischen Ler-nens,* ed. Wolfdietrich Schmied-Kowarzik (Freiburg: Alber, 1988), pp. 213–23.

13. Rosenzweig, "Neues Lernen: Entwurf der Rede zur Eröffnung des Freien Jüdischen Lehrhauses (1920)," *Kleinere Schriften,* p. 97.

14. Leora Batnitzky sets the records straight by showing that Rosenzweig did not, as has often been claimed by Christian theologians, theorize the relation be-tween Judaism and Christianity in terms of mutual affirmation. Instead, he de-scribed this dialogue in terms of mutual judgment. In this way "Judaism's prideful particularity saves Christianity from its own totalitarian tendency to believe that it has reached its goal." Batnitzky, *Idolatry and Representation: Franz Rosenzweig Reconsidered* (Princeton: Princeton University Press, 2000), p. 158.

15. For a discussion of Mendelssohn's influence on Rosenzweig, see Bat-nitzky's *Idolatry and Representation.* See also Michael Mack's review of *Idolatry and Representation* (*Journal of Religion* 81 [April 2001]: 312).

16. There are only a few references to Marx in Rosenzweig's work. However, as a letter of 19 August 1917 illustrates, he was familiar with the complexities of Marxist thought. In this letter he appreciates Marx's defense of the rights of the in-dividual over and against the interference of the state. See Rosenzweig, *Briefe,* p. 260.

17. Batnitzky, *Idolatry and Representation*, p. 74.

18. Franz Rosenzweig, *The Star of Redemption*, trans. William W. Hallo (Notre Dame, IN: Notre Dame University Press, 1985), p. 299. "Wir allein vertrauten dem Blut und ließen das Land; also sparten wir den kostbaren Lebenssaft, der uns Gewähr der eigenen Ewigkeit bot, und lösten allein unter allen Völkern der Erde unser Lebdendiges aus jeder Gemeinschaft der Toten." Rosenzweig, *Der Stern der Erlösung* (Frankfurt am Main: Suhrkamp, 1990), p. 332.

19. It has so far remained unexamined.

20. For Rosenzweig's analysis of this point see his *Hegel und der Staat* (Berlin: Oldenbourg, 1920), 2:243.

21. "Und dieses Schicksals ein Teil ist der Staat! Das ist der Augenblick, wo jede Staatsansicht, die den Einzelnen vor dem Ganzen sähe, ein Unding geworden ist." Ibid., 2:88.

22. Ibid.

23. For Rosenzweig's discussion of God's freedom as saying no to nothingness, see *Der Stern der Erlösung*, p. 32.

24. Franz Rosenzweig, "Franz Rosenzweig's *The New Thinking*," trans and ed. Alan Udoff and Barbara E. Galli (Syracuse: Syracuse University Press, 1999), p. 57. "Meine 'Freiheit,' und zwar nicht meine Freiheit wie sie die Philosophen umlügen, indem sie ihr das rote Blut der Willkür abzapfen und es in das Gefäß der 'Sinnlichkeit,' des 'Triebs,' der 'Motive' laufen lassen und nur den blutlosen Rückstand des Gehorsams gegen das Gesetz der Freiheit kennen wollen." Rosenzweig, "'Urzelle' des Stern der Erlösung: Brief an Rudlolf Ehrenberg vom 18. XI. 1917," *Kleinere Schriften*, pp. 357–72, p. 366.

25. See Micha Brumlik, *"Deutscher Geist und Judenhass": Das Verhältnis des philosophischen Idealismus zum Judentum* (Munich: Luchterhand, 2000).

26. Mendes-Flohr, "Mendelssohn and Rosenzweig," 1:221.

27. Rosenzweig, *Star of Redemption*, p. 331. "Ja der Jude ist eigentlich der einzige Mensch in der christlichen Welt, der den Krieg nicht ernst nehmen kann, und so ist er der einzige echte 'Pazifist.' So aber scheidet er sich, gerade weil er die vollkommene Gemeinschaft in seinem geistlichen Jahr erlebt, ab von der weltlichen Zeitrechnung." Rosenzweig, *Der Stern der Erlösung*, p. 368.

28. Rosenzweig, *Star of Redemption*, p. 332. "Im Gottesvolk ist das Ewige schon da, mitten in der Zeit. In den Völkern der Welt ist reine Zeitlichkeit. Aber der Staat ist der notwendig immer zu erneuernde Versuch, den Völkern in der Zeit Ewigkeit zu geben." Rosenzweig, *Der Stern der Erlösung*, p. 369.

29. Rosenzweig, *Der Stern der Erlösung*, p. 369.

30. "Im Gesetz ist eben alles Diesseitige, was darin ergriffen wird, alles geschaffene Dasein, schon unmittelbar zum Inhalt der künftigen Welt belebt und beseelt." Rosenzweig, *Der Stern der Erlösung*, p. 451.

31. "Indem der Jude, weil er sein Fleisch und Blut unter dem Joch des Gesetzes heiligte, ständig in der Wirklichkeit des Himmelreichs lebt, lernt der Christ, daß es ihm selber nicht erlaubt ist, die Erlösung, gegen die sich sein stets unheiliges Fleisch und Blut zur Wehr setzt, im Gefühl vorwegzunehmen." Rosenzweig, *Der Stern der Erlösung*, p. 460.

32. Rosenzweig, *Star of Redemption*, p. 216. "Die Gebote Gottes, soweit zur 'zweiten Tafel' gehören, welche die Liebe des Nächsten spezifiert, stehen durchweg in der Form des 'Du sollst nicht.' Nur als Verbote, nur in der Absteckung von Gren-

zen dessen, was keineswegs mit der Liebe zum Nächsten vereinbar ist, können sie Gesetzeskleid anziehen." Rosenzweig, *Der Stern der Erlösung*, p. 241.

Chapter Nine

1. The most recent is Eric L. Santner's *On the Psychotheology of Everyday Life: Reflections on Freud and Rosenzweig* (Chicago: University of Chicago Press, 2001).

2. Regina M. Schwartz, "Freud's God," in *Post-Secular Philosophy: Between Philosophy and Theology*, ed. Philip Blond (New York: Routledge, 1998), p. 292.

3. Peter Gay, *Freud: A Life for Our Time* (London: Macmillan, 1989), p. 524.

4. "This entanglement of autobiography with science has bedeviled psycho-analysis from its beginnings." Ibid., p. 89. "Das Skandalon dieses 1899 erschienenen Werkes bestand darin, daß Freud eine Theorie entwarf, bei der er sich auf ein Material äußerster Subjektivität berief, auf ein Material, das für andere Wissenschaftler direkt weder zugänglich noch nachprüfbar war (bekanntlich ist man immer allein in seinen Träumen). Die Hypothesen, die Freud aufstellte, konnten nur an der Evidenz der eigenen Träume kontrolliert werden. Wer sich auf Freuds Traumdeutung einließ, war somit gezwungen, seine eigene Subjektivität in den Forschungsprozeß einzubeziehen." Mario Erdheim, "Psychoanalyse als moderne Form der Weisheit," in *Weisheit: Archäologie der literarischen Kommunikation*, ed. Aleida Assmann (Munich: Fink, 1991), 3:225–26.

5. "[S]o ist damit die Herrschaft einer inneren psychischen Realität über die Realität der Außenwelt erreicht." Sigmund Freud, *Kulturtheoretische Schriften* (Frankfurt: Fischer, 1986), p. 525. (This is identical with the *Studienausgabe*, vol. 9, ed. Alexander Mitscherlich, Anglika Richards, and James Strachey).

6. "[D]er Weg zur Psychose eröffnet." Freud, *Kulturtheoretische Schriften*, p. 525.

7. "Aufgabe der Kur sei, die Amnesien aufzuheben. Wenn alle Erinnerungslücken ausgefüllt, alle rätselhaften Effekte des psychischen Lebens aufgeklärt sind, ist der Fortbestand, ja eine Neubildung des Leidens unmöglich gemacht." Sigmund Freud, *Studienausgabe: Ergänzungsband: Schriften zur Behandlungstechnik*, ed. Alexander Mitscherlich, Anglika Richards, and James Strachey (Frankfurt: Fischer, 1975), p. 105.

8. Paul Ricoeur, *Freud and Philosophy: An Essay on Interpretation*, trans. Denis Savage (New Haven: Yale University Press, 1970), p. 83.

9. Thus Ricoeur calls Freud's notion of the libido "the first concept that can be said to be both energetic and nonanatomical." Ibid., p. 84.

10. See Erna Lesky, *The Vienna Medical School of the 19th Century*, trans. L. Williams and I. S. Levij (Baltimore: Johns Hopkins University Press, 1976), p. 280.

11. "Unser Unbewußtes ist nicht ganz dasselbe wie das der Philosophen, und überdies wollen die meisten Philosophen vom 'unbewußten Psychischen' nichts wissen Freud." Freud, *Sudienausgabe: Ergänzungsband*, p. 118.

12. According to the assumption of Christian innocence, the Savior has already come, and we are supposed to be redeemed and purified through his sacrificial death.

13. "[D]ies Strafbedürfnis ist der schlimmste Feind unserer therapeutischen Bemühung." Freud, *Studienausgabe*, 1:541. See the *Studienausgabe: Ergänzungsband*, p. 245.

14. As Richard Wollheim has put it, "the 'unconscious sense of guilt,' which Freud could now discern in the resistance to therapy as well as in the standard form of criminality, could be traced to two historic features of the super-ego; first, that it is the heir to an external authority, and, secondly, that it is an internalized version of that authority." Wollheim, *Freud* (Glasgow: Fontana, 1982), p. 198.

15. See Sander L. Gilman, *The Jew's Body* (New York: Routledge, 1991).

16. Sigmund Freud, *Psychoanalysis and Faith: The Letters of Sigmund Freud and Oskar Pfister*, ed. Heinrich Meng and Ernst L. Freud, trans. Eric Mosbacher (New York: Basic, 1963), p. 76.

17. "Aber es wurde nicht die Mordtat erinnert." Freud, *Kulturtheoretische Schriften*, p. 534.

18. "[D]iese Phantasie als Erlösungsbotschaft (*Evangelium*)." Ibid. Freud, *Kulturtheoretische Schriften*, p. 534.

19. "Der Kastrationskomplex ist die tiefste unbewußte Wurzel des Antisemitismus, denn schon in der Kinderstube hört der Knabe, daß dem Juden etwas am Penis . . . abgeschnitten werde." Freud, *Studienausgabe*, 7:36 n. 2.

20. "[E]r meint, ein Stück des Penis." Ibid.

21. "[U]nd dies gibt ihm das Recht, den Juden zu verachten." Ibid.

22. "Auch die Überhebung über das Weib hat keine stärkere unbewußte Wurzel. Weininger, jener hochbegabte und sexuell gestörte junge Philosoph, . . . hat . . . den Juden und das Weib mit der gleichen Feindschaft bedacht und mit den nämlichen Schmähungen überhäuft." Ibid.

23. Gay, *Freud*, pp. 237–38.

24. Freud, *Psychoanalysis and Faith*, p. 63.

25. "Aber die innere Entwicklung der neuen Religion kam bald zum Stillstand, vielleicht weil es an der Vertiefung fehlte, die im jüdischen Falle der Mord am Religionsstifter verursacht hatte." Freud, *Kulturtheoretische Schriften*, p. 540.

26. "Die anscheinend rationalistischen Religionen des Ostens." Ibid.

27. "[S]ind ihrem Kern nach Ahnenkult, machen also auch halt bei einer frühen Stufe der Rekonstruktion des Vergangenen." Ibid.

28. The most striking example of this kind of reading may well be Jean-Joseph Goux, *Oedipus, Philosopher*, trans. Catherine Porter (Stanford: Stanford University Press, 1993). On this point see also Estelle Roith, *The Riddle of Freud: Jewish Influences on His Theory of Female Sexuality* (London: Tavistock, 1987); and Samuel Slipp, *The Freudian Mystique: Freud, Women, and Feminism* (New York: New York University Press, 1993).

29. As Jonathan Lear has argued, "Freud-bashing retraces Oedipus' steps, partaking of a manic, Enlightenment defense which does not even acknowledge the problem which psychoanalysis sets out to address." Lear, *Open Minded: Working Out the Logic of the Soul* (Cambridge: Harvard University Press, 1999), p. 54.

30. Translating Freud's *Ich* as "ego" can be misleading: the term *ego* seems to be related to the notion of egoism. Freud's *Ich* does not encompass such semantic associations. However, I refer to the common translation of "ego" for *Ich* in order not to confuse the reader.

31. "[P]sychologische Forschung . . . , welche dem Ich nachweisen will, daß es nicht einmal Herr ist im eigenen Hause, sondern auf kärgliche Nachrichten angewiesen bleibt von dem, was unbewußt in seinem Seelenleben vorgeht." Freud, *Studienausgabe*, 1:284.

32. As Donald N. Levine has argued, "Kant's radical distinction between the worlds of nature and freedom and his insistence that the good is to be attained through a process in which nature is somehow transcended gave expression to thoughtways so deeply embedded in German culture that his ideas were embraced and reworked by hundreds of German philosophers and poets." Levine, *Visions of the Sociological Tradition* (Chicago: University of Chicago Press, 1995), p. 184.

33. The editors of the *Studienausgabe* point out that Freud's term *philosopher* here refers to Kant: *Studienausgabe,* 1:511, n. 2.

34. Ibid., 1:511.

35. That is to say, the *I* cannot organize them in a perception of the external world in which she or he can feel at home.

36. Jean Laplanche discusses this point as follows: "The ego, consequently, if it is the instrument of reality, does not *bring* a privileged access to the real, but by its simple presence, will permit external reality alone to function, whereas it disqualifies the pseudoreality of internal origin. Which is to say that its function is essentially inhibitive: to prevent hallucination, to cut off that 'excess of reality' coming from internal excitation in order to allow the indication of reality for external perception (which had always existed without any need for an ego) to operate henceforth alone, without the rivalry of hallucinatory reactivation functioning thereafter as a valid *criterion.*" Laplanche, *Life and Death in Psychoanalysis,* trans. Jeffrey Mehlman (Baltimore: Johns Hopkins University Press, 1976), p. 62.

37. "Als Vergangenheit erkannt, entwertet und ihrer Energiebesetzung enttraubt können sie erst werden, wenn sie durch die analytische Arbeit bewußt geworden sind." Freud, *Studienausgabe,* 1:511.

38. "[U]nd darauf beruht nicht zum kleinsten Teil die therapeutische Wirkung der analytischen Behandlung." Ibid.

39. Ibid., 1:284.

40. Jean-Joseph Goux's *Symbolic Economies After Marx and Freud,* trans. Jennifer Curtis Gage (Ithaca: Cornell University Press, 1990) has given an intriguing reading of psychoanalysis as a critique of philosophical *immaterialism.* I have also found encouragement for such analysis in Eric L. Santner's *Psychotheology of Everyday Life* and in Jonathan Lear's *Love and Its Place in Nature* (New Haven: Yale University Press, 1990).

41. There have been many attempts at reading Freud as a Kantian—from R. D. Chessik's *Freud Teaches Psychotherapy* (Cambridge, MA: Hackett, 1980), Stanely Cavell's "Psychoanalysis and Cinema: The Melodrama of the Unknown Woman," in *The Trial(s) of Psychoanalysis,* ed. F. Meltzer (Chicago: University of Chicago Press, 1988), and Jakob Hessing's *Der Fluch des Propheten: Drei Abhandlungen zu Sigmund Freud* (Frankfurt: Suhrkamp, 1993) to David Levingstone Smith's *Freud's Philosophy of the Unconscious* (Dordrecht: Kluwer, 1999)—and there have been some attempts, such as Philip Rieff's *Freud: The Mind of the Moralist* (Chicago: University of Chicago Press, 1959)—to read Freud as radically anti-Kantian. Rather than being Kantian or anti-Kantian, I would argue, he revised a Kantian Enlightenment project.

42. For a discussion of this point see Michael Mack, "Between Kant and Kafka: Walter Benjamin's Notion of Law," *Neophilologus* 85 (2001): 257–72.

43. Immanuel Kant, *Schriften zur Ethik und Religionsphilosophie,* ed. Wilhelm Weischedel (Wiesbaden: Insel, 1956), 2:735.

44. Ibid., 2:738.

45. "[D]as Wesen des sinnvollen und lebensfrohen Judentums." Freud, *Briefe 1873–1939,* ed. Ernst Freud and Lucie Freud (Frankfurt am Main: Fischer, 1960), p. 32.

46. Judith van Herik, *Freud on Femininity and Faith* (Berkeley: University of California Press, 1982), p. 192. See also Joy Geller, "A Paleontolotgical View of Freud's Study of Religion: Unearthing the *Leitfossil* Circumcision," *Modern Judaism* 13 (April 1993): 49–70. Recently, Howard Eilberg-Schwartz has argued that for Freud "the prohibition on images was analogous to the discovery of paternity. Both, he suggests, were triumphs of the spirit over sensuality. The prohibition on images forced the people to conceptualize rather than image God." Eilberg-Schwartz, *God's Phallus and Other Problems for Men and Monotheism* (Boston: Beacon, 1994), p. 56.

47. Van Herik, *Freud on Femininity,* p. 72.

48. Eric L. Santner, *My Own Private Germany: Daniel Paul Schreber's Secret History of Modernity* (Princeton: Princeton University Press, 1995), 109. Recently Daniel Boyarin has shown that Weininger's *Sex and Character* influenced Freud more "than he was prepared to admit." Boyarin, *Unheroic Conduct: The Rise of Heterosexuality and the Invention of the Jewish Man* (Berkeley: University of California Press, 1997), p. 218.

49. Boyarin, *Unheroic Conduct,* 242. See Marthe Robert, *From Oedipus to Moses: Freud's Jewish Identity,* trans. Ralph Mannheim (New York: Anchor, 1976).

50. Quoted in Boyarin, *Unheroic Conduct,* p. 226.

51. Ibid.

52. This might be one reason why he frequently ridiculed philosophy and philosophers.

53. In his *Anthropology from a Pragmatic Point of View* he labeled the Jews "a nation of cheaters" and attributed the cause of cheating to rabbinic Judaism. Kant, *Schriften zur Anthropologie, Geschichtsphilosophie, Politik und Pädagogik,* ed. W. Weischedel (Wiesbaden: Insel, 1956), 2:518.

54. Boyarin, *Unheroic Conduct,* p. 251.

55. In this context it should be noted that Freud differentiated his work on the death drive from that of the Kantian philosopher Schopenhauer as follows: "Moreover, what we are saying is not even true to Schopenhauer. We are not saying that death is the only goal of life: we are not overlooking that there is life next to death." *(Und weiter, was wir sagen, ist nicht einmal richtiger Schopenhauer. Wir behaupten nicht, der Tod sei das einzige Ziel des Lebens; wir übersehen nicht neben dem Tod das Leben.)* Freud, *Studienausgabe,* 1:540.

56. "[D]aß das Tabu eigentlich noch in unserer Mitte fortbesteht; obwohl negativ gefaßt und auf andere Inhalte gerichtet, ist es seiner psychologischen Natur nach doch nichts anderes als der 'kategorische Imperativ' Kants, der zwangsartig wirken will und jede bewußte Motivierung ablehnt." Freud, *Kulturtheoretische Schriften,* 292.

57. For a discussion of a Jewish intellectual who—as a social anthropologist— compares "primitive" taboo with Jewish law, see Michael Mack, *Anthropology as Memory: Elias Canetti's and Franz Baermann Steiner's Responses to the Shoah* (Tübingen: Niemeyer, 2001), pp. 81–203.

58. Kant, *Schriften zur Anthropologie,* 2:518.

59. This bourgeois property and ownership distinction in a paradoxical manner enforces Kantian autonomy by restraining one's desire for material gain. See Brian Tierney, "Kant on Property: The Problem of Permissive Law," *Journal of the History of Ideas* 62 (2001): 301–12; Michael Mack, "Law, Charity, and Taboo, or Kant's Reversal of St. Paul's Spirit-Letter Opposition and Its Theological Implication" *Modern Theology* 16 (October 2000): 417–41.

60. "Denn wenn andere Triebfedern nötig sind, die Willkür zur gesetzmäßigen Handlung zu bestimmen, als das Gesetz selbst (z.B. Ehrbegierde, Selbstliebe, überhaupt, ja gutherziger Instinkt, dergleichen das Mitleiden ist): so ist es bloß zufällig, daß diese mit dem Gesetz übereinstimmen: denn sie könnten eben sowohl zur Übertretung antreiben." Kant, *Schriften zur Ethik und Religionsphilosophie*, 2:678.

61. "Die Tabuverbote entbehren jeder Begründung; sie sind unbekannter Herkunft; für uns unverständlich erscheinen sie jenen selbstverständlich, die unter ihrer Herrschaft stehen." Freud, *Kulturtheoretische Schriften*, p. 311.

62. "Der Ursprung der obersten Gewalt ist für das Volk, das unter derselben steht, in praktischer Absicht unerforschlich: d.i. der Untertan soll nicht über diesen Ursprung, als ein noch in Ansehung des ihr schuldigen Gehorsams zu bezweifelndes Recht (ius controversum), werktätig vernünfteln." Kant, *Schriften zur Ethik und Religionsphilosophie*, 2:437.

63. Ibid.

64. Lear, *Open Minded*, p. 114.

65. Without analyzing the complex issue of Freud's response to Kant's idealism, Jonathan Lear has discussed this point as follows: "Rather than see irrationality as *coming from the outside* as from an Unconscious Mind which disrupts Conscious Mind, one should see irrational disruptions as themselves an inherent expression of mind. In a nutshell: mind has a tendency to disrupt its own rational functioning." Ibid., p. 84.

66. "[J]ede bewußte Motivierung ablehnt." Freud, *Kulturtheoretische Schriften*, p. 292.

67. Eric L. Santner, "Freud's Moses and the Ethics of Nomotropic Desire," *October* 88 (spring 1999): 3–41, p. 23.

68. "[V]on außen (von einer Autorität) aufgedrängt und gegen die stärksten Gelüste der Menschen gerichtet." Freud, *Kulturtheoretische Schriften*, p. 326.

69. "[D]ie Menschen, die dem Tabu gehorchen, haben eine ambivalente Einstellung gegen das vom Tabu Betroffene. Die dem Tabu zugeschriebene Zauberkraft führt sich auf die Fähigkeit zurück, die Menschen in Versuchung zu führen . . . weil sich das verbotene Gelüste im Unterbewußten auf anderes verschiebt." Freud, *Kulturtheoretische Schriften* , p. 326.

70. "[U]nterwirft sich das Ich dem kategorischen Imperativ seines Über-Ichs." Freud, *Studienausgabe*, 3:315.

71. "Das Über-Ich wird den Charakter des Vaters bewahren, und je stärker der Ödipuskomplex war, je beschleunigter (unter dem Einfluß von Autorität, Religionslehre, Unterricht, Lektüre), seine Verdrängung erolgte, desto strenger wird später das Über-Ich als Gewissen, vielleicht als unbewußtes Schuldgefühl über das Ich herrschen.—Woher es die Kraft zu dieser Herrschaft bezieht, den zwangsartigen Charakter, der sich als kategorsicher Imperativ äußert, darüber werde ich später eine Vermutung vorbringen." Ibid., 3:302.

72. "Während das Ich wesentlich Repräsentant der Außenwelt, der Realität

ist, tritt ihm das Über-Ich als Anwalt der Innenwelt, des Es, gegenüber. Konflikte zwischen Ich und Ideal werden, darauf sind wir nun vorbereitet, in letzter Linie den Gegensatz von Real und Psychisch, Außenwelt und Innenwelt, wiederspiegeln." Ibid., 3:303.

73. "[D]aß die Neurose den Verzicht auf das reale Objekt involviert, auch daß die dem realen Objekt entzogene Libido auf ein phantasiertes Objekt und von da aus auf ein verdrängtes zurückgeht (Introversion)." Ibid., 3:155.

74. "Bei jedem Ansteigen der Trieberregung muß der schützende Wall um die Ersatzvorstellung um ein Stück weiter hinausverlegt werden. Die ganze Konstruktion, die in analoger Weise bei den anderen Neurosen hergestellt wird, trägt den Namen einer *Phobie*. Der Ausdruck der Flucht vor bewußter Besetzung der Ersatzvorstellung sind die Vermeidungen, Verzichte und Verbote." Ibid., 3:142–43.

75. Lear, *Love and Its Place in Nature*, p. 145.

76. Ibid., pp. 145–46.

77. For a discussion of this transcendental bent in Freud, see Françoise Meltzer, "Introduction: Partitive Plays, Pipe Dreams," in *The Trial(s) of Psychoanalysis*, ed. Meltzer (Chicago: University of Chicago Press, 1988), pp. 1–7.

78. "Der kategorische Imperativ ist so der direkte Erbe des Oedipuskomplexes." Freud, *Studienausgabe*, 3:351.

79. "Dies Über-ich ist nämlich ebensosehr der Vertreter des Es wie der Außenwelt." Ibid., 3:350.

80. "Der Kantsche Satz, daß Zeit und Raum notwendige Formen unseres Denkens sind, kann heute infolge gewisser psychoanalytischer Erkenntnisse einer Diskussion unterzogen werden." Ibid., 3:238.

81. "[I]nnere Erregungen . . . als ob sie nicht von innen, sondern von außen her einwirkten." Ibid., 3:239.

82. "Dies ist die Herkunft der *Projektion,* der eine so große Rolle bei der Verursachung pathologischer Prozesse vorbehalten ist." Ibid.

83. Lear, *Love and Its Place in Nature*, p. 153.

84. Pharaoh Akhenaten first inaugurated monotheism. After his demise it suffered a subterranean existence of latency, until "Moses the Egyptian" rediscovered it.

85. Jan Assmann, *Moses the Egyptian: The Memory of Egypt in Western Monotheism* (Cambridge: Harvard University Press, 1997), p. 167.

86. For a discussion of such "deconstructive memory" and its opposition to a "memory of conversion" see ibid., pp. 7–8.

87. For a detailed discussion of Assmann's Moses book about Moses see Santner, "Freud's Moses," pp. 6–14.

88. "[D]ie Vorstellung eines universellen Gottes." Freud, *Kulturtheoretische Schriften*, p. 472.

89. "Maat, die Göttin der Wahrheit, Ordnung, Gerechtigkeit." Ibid.

90. "[D]aß der Fortschritt ein Bündnis mit der Barbarei geschlossen hat." Ibid., p. 503.

91. Harold Bloom, *The Strong Light of the Canonical: Kafka, Freud, and Scholem as Revisionists of Jewish Culture and Thought* (New York: City College Papers, 1987), p. 46.

92. Ibid.

93. See Freud's *Kulturtheoretische Schriften*, pp. 507, 575.

94. "[D]er Befreier und Gesetzgeber des jüdischen Volkes." Ibid., p. 468.

95. "[Z]wang sie in den Dienst einer neuen Religion." Ibid., p. 469.
96. "Jähzornig und Aufwallungen von Leidenschaften unterworfen." Freud, *Studienausgabe,* 10: 217.
97. "Er gedachte seiner Mission und verzichtete für sie auf die Befriedigung seines Affekts." Ibid., 10:214.
98. "Jahve . . . ein Vulkangott . . . Er ist ein unheimlicher, blutgieriger Dämon, der bei Nacht umgeht und das Tageslicht scheut." Freud, *Kulturtheoretische Schriften,* p. 484.
99. "[H]errisch, jähzornig, ja gewalttätig . . . der sanftmütigste und geduldigste aller Menschen." Ibid., p. 490.
100. "[V]ielleicht gehören sie dem anderen, dem Midianiter, an." Ibid.
101. "Moses wie Ikhnaton fanden dasselbe Schicksal, das aller aufgeklärten Despoten wartet." Ibid., p. 496.
102. "Aber während die zahmen Ägypter damit warteten, bis das Schicksal die geheiligte Person des Pharaoh beseitigt hatte, nahmen die wilden Semiten das Schicksal in ihre Hand und räumten den Tyrannen aus dem Wege." Ibid., pp. 496–97.
103. Gilman, *Freud, Race, and Gender* (Princeton: Princeton University Press, 1993), p. 193.
104. Ibid., p. 192.
105. Kant, *Schriften zur Ethik und Religionsphilosophie,* 2:735.
106. Ibid., 2:737.
107. For Freud's discussion of this point, see his *Kulturtheoretische Schriften,* p. 513.
108. Kant speaks of the Jews' "slave-like mind-set" as regards their heteronomous relation to both the positivity of religion and the positivity of the material world. Kant, *Schriften zur Ethik und Religionsphilosophie,* 2:735.
109. Freud compared Moses as enlightened despot to the "person of the Pharaoh, regarded as holy" *(die geheiligte Person des Pharaoh).* Freud, *Kulturtheoretische Schriften,* p. 496.
110. "[O]hne rationelle Begründung," Ibid., 566.
111. "Um miteinander in Frieden leben zu können, verzichteten die siegreichen Brüder auf die Frauen, derentwegen sie den Vater erschlagen haben." Ibid., p. 576.
112. "[D]as jüdische Volk in seiner gesitteten *Epoche.*" Immanuel Kant, *Kritik der Urteilskraft und Schriften zur Naturphilosophie* (Wiesbaden: Insel, 1956), 2:365.
113. "[D]as moralische Gesetz aber ist an sich selbst in uns hinreichend und ursprünglich bestimmend, so daß es nicht einmal erlaubt ist, uns nach einem Bestimmungsgrunde außer demselben umzusehen." Ibid., 2:366.
114. Freud, *Kulturtheoretische Schriften,* p. 572.
115. "[D]aß das Ich die Triebbefriedigung mit Rücksicht auf äußere Hindernisse unterläßt, nämlich dann, wenn es einsieht, daß die betreffende Aktion eine ernste Gefahr für das Ich hervorrufen würde." Ibid., p. 562.
116. Ibid.
117. "[S]o ist damit die Herrschaft einer inneren psychischen Realität über die Realität der Außenwelt erreicht, der Weg zur Psychose eröffenet." Ibid., p. 525.
118. Ibid.
119. "[E]in Staat im Staat." Ibid. For a discussion of Freud's etiology of anti-Semitism see Gilman, *Freud, Race, and Gender,* 196. Anti-Semites such as Wilhelm

Marr accused the Jews of seeking to build a state within a state. For discussion of this topic, see Paul Lawrence Rose, *The German-Jewish Question: Revolutionary Antisemitism in Germany from Kant to Wagner* (Princeton: Princeton University Press, 1990), p. 282.

120. Freud, *Kulturtheoretische Schriften*, p. 552.

121. "Es ist nicht selbstverständlich und nicht ohne weiteres einzusehen, warum ein Fortschritt in der Geistigkeit, eine Zurücksetzung der Sinnlichkeit, das Selbstbewußtsein einer Person wie eines Volkes erhöhen sollte." Ibid., p. 561.

122. "Gehorsam gegen das Realitätsprinzip, ist auf keinen Fall lustvoll." Ibid., p. 562.

123. Ibid., p. 580.

124. Theodor Adorno, *Problems of Moral Philosophy,* ed. Thomas Schröder, trans. Rodney Livingstone (Stanford: Stanford University Press, 2000), p. 70.

Chapter Ten

1. John McCole, *Walter Benjamin and the Antinomies of Tradition* (Ithaca: Cornell University Press, 1993), p. 56.

2. Walter Benjamin, "Experience and Poverty," trans. Rodney Livingstone, in *Selected Writings,* vol. 2, *1927–1934,* ed. Michael W. Jennings et al. (Cambridge: Belknap Press of Harvard University Press, 1999), p. 731. "[D]ie Erfahrung ist im Kurse gefallen und das in einer Generation, die 1914–1918 eine der ungeheuersten Erfahrungen der Weltgeschichte gemacht hat." Walter Benjamin, *Gesammelte Schriften,* ed. Rolf Tiedemann and Hermann Schweppenhäuser (Frankfurt am Main: Suhrkamp, 1980), 2:214.

3. Walter Benjamin, "On the Coming Philosophy," trans. Mark Ritter, in *Selected Writings,* vol. 1, *1913–1926,* ed. Marcus Bullock and Michael W. Jennings (Cambridge: Belknap Press of Harvard University Press, 1996), pp. 105–6.

4. Ibid., 1:101. "[Daß Kants Werk] gleichsam auf den Nullpunkt, auf das Minimum von Bedeutung reduzierten Erfahrung vorgenommen wurde." Benjamin, *Gesammelte Schriften,* 2:159.

5. Benjamin, "On the Coming Philosophy," *Selected Writings,* 1:101. "Ja man darf sagen daß eben die Größe seines Versuches, der ihm eigene Radikalismus eine solche Erfahrung zur Vorraussetzung hatte, deren Eigenwert sich der Null näherte und die eine (wir dürfen sagen: trarige) Bedeutung durch ihre Gewißheit hätte erlangen können." Benjamin, *Gesammelte Schriften,* 2:159.

6. Walter Benjamin, "Program for Literary Criticism," in *Selected Writings,* 2:292.

7. Walter Benjamin, *The Origin of the German Baroque Tragic Drama,* trans. John Osborne (London: NLB, 1977), p. 92. "[R]estlose Säkularisierung des Historischen im Schöpfungszustand." Benjamin, *Gesammelte Schriften,* 1:271.

8. Benjamin, *Origin of the German Baroque Tragic Drama,* pp. 216–17. "[D]er menschliche Körper durfte keine Ausnahme von dem Gebot machen, das das Organische zerschlagen hieß, um in seinen Scherben die wahre, die fixierte und schrifgemäße Bedeutung aufzulesen." Benjamin, *Gesammelte Schriften,* 1:391.

9. Walter Benjamin, "Mickey Mouse," *Selected Writings,* 2:545. "Also nicht 'Mechanisierung,' nicht das 'Formale,' nicht ein 'Mißverständnis' hier für den ungeheuren Erfolg dieser Filme die Basis, sondern daß das Publikum sein eigenes Leben in ihnen wiedererkennt." Benjamin, *Gesammelte Schriften,* 4:145.

10. Benjamin, "Mickey Mouse," 2:545. "Eigentumsverhältnisse im Mickey-Mouse-Film: hier erscheint zum ersten Mal, daß einem der eigene Arm, ja der eigene Körper gestohlen werden kann." Benjamin, *Gesammelte Schriften*, 4:144.

11. Walter Benjamin, "Goethe's Elective Affinities," *Selected Writings*, 1:308.

12. Benjamin, "Mickey Mouse," 2:545. "Diese Filme desavourieren, radikaler als je der Fall war, alle Erfahrung. Es lohnt sich in einer solchen Welt nicht, Erfahrungen zu machen." Benjamin, *Gesammelte Schriften*, 4:144.

13. Walter Benjamin, "Capitalism as Religion," trans. Rodney Livingstone, *Selected Writings*, 1:289. "Darin liegt das historisch Unerhörte des Kapitalismus, daß Religion nicht mehr Reform des Seins sondern dessen absolute Zertrümmerung ist. Die Ausweitung der Verzweiflung zum religiösen Weltzustand aus dem die Heilung zu erwarten sei. Gottes Transzendenz ist gefallen. Aber er ist nicht tot, er ist ins Menschenschicksal einbezogen." Benjamin, *Gesammelte Schriften*, 4:101.

14. For a discussion of Benjamin's "Identifikation mit dem Angreifer," see Walter Glogauer, "Widerspruch, Paradoxie oder 'Rettung' Zum Begriff der Wahrheit in Walter Benjamin's *Ursprung des Deutschen Trauerspiels*," *Neophilologus* 69 (1985): 115–25, p. 119.

15. Immanuel Kant, *Schriften zur Ethik und Religionsphilosophie* (Wiesbaden: Insel, 1956), 2:735.

16. "Die Moral, so fern sie auf dem Begriff des Menschen, als eines freien, eben darum aber auch sich selbst durch seine Vernunft an unbedingte Gesetze bindenden Wesens, gegründet ist, bedarf weder einer Idee eines anderen Wesens über ihm, um seine Pflicht zu erkennen noch einer anderen Triebfeder als des Gesetzes selbst, um sie zu beobachten." Ibid., 2:649.

17. Benjamin, "Capitalism as Religion," 1:290. "Kapitalismus und Recht. Heidnischer Charakter des Rechts. . . . Methodisch wäre zunächst zu untersuchen, welche Verbindungen mit dem Mythos je im Laufe der Geschichte das Geld eingegangen ist, bis es aus dem Christentum soviel mythische Elemente an sich ziehen konnte, um den eigenen Mythos zu konstituieren." Benjamin, *Gesammelte Schriften*, 6:102.

18. Benjamin, "Capitalism as Religion," 1:290. "Das Christentum zur Reformationszeit hat nicht das Aufkommen des Kapitalismus begünstigt, sondern es hat sich in den Kapitalismus umgewandelt." Benjamin, *Gesammelte Schriften*, 6:102.

19. Walter Benjamin, "Soviel Heidnische Religionen," trans. Michael Mack. "Soviel heidnische Religionen, soviel natürliche Schuldbegriffe. Schuldig ist stets irgendwie das Leben, die Strafe an ihm der Tod. Eine Form der natürlichen Schuld ist die Sexualität. . . . Eine andere die des Geldes. . . . Jüdisch: nicht das Leben, sondern allein der handelnde Mensch kann schuldig werden." Benjamin, *Gesammelte Schriften*, 6:56.

20. Walter Benjamin, "World and Time," in *Selected Writings*, 1:226. "[S]ie [die mosaischen Gesetze] bestimmen Art und Zone *unmittelbarer* göttlicher Einwirkung. Und ganz unmittelbar da wo diese Zone sich ihre Grenze setzt, wo sie zurücktritt, grenzt das Gebiet der Politik, des Profanen, der im religiösen Sinne gesetzlosen Leiblichkeit an." Benjamin, *Gesammelte Schriften*, 6:99.

21. Benjamin, "On Kantian Ethics," trans. Michael Mack. "[D]ie Lehre von 'vernünftigen Wesen' . . . die Anzahl der ethischen Subjekte von der der menschlichen Leiber." Benjamin, *Gesammelte Schriften*, 6:55.

22. Benjamin, "On Kantian Ethics," trans. Michael Mack. "Der Begriff 'Nei-

gung,' den Kant für einen ethisch indifferenten oder wider-ethischen hält, ist durch einen Bedeutungswandel zu einem der höchsten Begriffe der Moral zu machen, in der er vieleicht berufen ist, an die Stelle zu treten, welche die 'Liebe' inne hatte." Benjamin, *Gesammelte Schriften*, 6:55.

23. Walter Benjamin, "Critique of Violence," *Selected Writings*, 1:248. "Rechtsetzung ist Machtsetzung und insofern ein Akt von unmittelbarer Manifestation der Gewalt." Benjamin, *Gesammelte Schriften*, 2:198.

24. Benjamin, "Critique of Violence," *Selected Writings*, 1:249. "Denn unter dem Gesichtspunkt der Gewalt, welche das Recht allein garantieren kann, gibt es keine Gleichheit, sondern bestenfalls gleich große Gewalten. . . . Gesetze und umschriebene Grenzen bleiben, wenigstens in Urzeiten, ungeschriebene Gesetze. Der Mensch kann sie ahnungslos überschreiten und so der Sühne verfallen. Denn jeder Eingriff des Rechts, den die Verletzung des ungeschriebenen und unbekannten Gesetzes heraufbeschwört, heißt zum Unterschied von der Strafe die Sühneibid." Benjamin, *Gesammelte Schriften*, 2:198–99.

25. Walter Benjamin, "The Little Hunchback," *Selected Writings*, 2:808. "Das Zeitalter, in dem Kafka lebt, bedeutet ihm keinen Fortschritt über die Uranfänge. Seine Romane spielen in einer Sumpfwelt. Die Kreatur erscheint bei ihm auf der Stufe, die Bachofen als die hetärische bezeichnet." Benjamin, *Gesammelte Schriften*, 2:428.

26. Walter Benjamin, "Potemkin," *Selected Writings*, 2:797. "Gesetze und umschriebene Normen bleiben in der Vorwelt ungeschrieben Gesetze." Benjamin, *Gesammelte Schriften*, 2:412.

27. Benjamin, "Potemkin," *Selected Writings*, 2:797. "Hier steht zwar das geschriebene Recht in Gesetzbüchern, jedoch geheim, und auf sie gestützt, übt die Vorwelt ihre Herrschaft nur schrankenloser." Benjamin, *Gesammelte Schriften*, 2:412.

28. For a discussion of the accuracy of Benjamin's discussion of the keeping secret of law by the ruling classes, see Michael Mack, "Law and Zionism: Franz Kafka and Franz Baermann Steiner," *Litteraria Pragensia* 10.19 (2000): 37–50.

29. Walter Benjamin, "A Childhood Portrait," *Selected Writings*, 2:805.

30. Walter Benjamin, "Sancho Panza," 2:815. "Das Recht, das nicht mehr praktiziert und nur studiert wird, ist die Pforte der Gerechtigkeit. Die Pforte der Gerechtigkeit ist das Studium. Und doch wagt Kafka nicht, an dieses Studium die Verheißungen zu knüpfen, welche die Überlieferung an das der Thora geschlossen hat. Seine Gehilfen sind Gemeindediener, denen das Bethaus, seine Studenten Schüler, denen die Schrift abhanden kam." Benjamin, *Gesammelte Schriften*, 2: 437.

31. Benjamin, "The LittleHunchback," *Selected Writings*, 2:810. "Was die Korruption im Recht ist, das ist in ihrem Denken die Angst. Sie verpfuscht den Vorgang und ist doch das einzig Hoffnungsvolle in ihm." Benjamin, *Gesammelte Schriften*, 2:431.

32. Benjamin, "Critique of Violence," *Selected Writings*, 1:201. "Falsch und niedrig ist der Satz, daß Dasein höher als gerechtes Dasein stehe, wenn Dasein nichts als bloßes Leben bedeuten soll. . . . Eine gewaltige Wahrheit aber enthält er, wenn Dasein (oder besser Leben) . . . den unverrückbaren Aggregatzustand von 'Mensch' bedeutet. Wenn der Satz sagen will, das Nichtsein des Menschen sei etwas Furchtbareres als das (unbedingt: bloße) Nochnichtsein des gerechten Menschen. . . . Der

Mensch fällt eben um keinen Preis zusammen mit dem bloßen Leben des Menschen, so wenig mit dem bloßen Leben in ihm wie mit irgendwelchen andern seiner Zustände und Eigenschaften, ja nicht einmal mit der Einzigartigkeit seiner leiblichen Person." Benjamin, *Gesammelte Schriften,* 2:201.

33. Benjamin, "Capitalism as Religion," *Selected Writings,* 1:288. "[D]er Kapitalismus [ist] eine reine Kultreligion ... er kennt keine spezielle Dogmatik, keine Theologie." Benjamin, *Gesammelte Schriften,* 6:100.

34. Immanuel Kant, *Religion and Rational Theology,* trans. A. W. Wood and G. Di Giovanni (Cambridge: Cambridge University Press, 1996), p. 128.

35. Benjamin, "On the Coming Philosophy," *Selected Writings,* 1:108. "Auf Grund des Kantischen Systems einen Erkenntnisbegriff zu schaffen, dem der Begriff einer Erfahrung korrespondiert, von der die Erkenntnis Lehre ist. Eine solche Philosophie wäre entweder in ihrem allgemeinen Teile selbst als Theologie zu bezeichnen oder wäre dieser, sofern sie etwa historisch philosophische Elemente einschließt, übergeordnet." Benjamin, *Gesammelte Schriften,* 2:168. *Lehre* is the word that the translator of "Capitalism as Religion" translates as "doctrine."

36. Benjamin, "On the Coming Philosophy," *Selected Writings,* 1:108. "[V]ernichtend zu nennen ... in Rücksicht auf Güter, Recht, Leben u. dgl., niemals absolut in Rücksicht auf die Seele des Lebendigen." Benjamin, *Gesammelte Schriften,* 2:200.

37. Benjamin, "Critique of Violence," *Selected Writings,* 1:252. "Von neuem stehen der reinen göttlichen Gewalt alle ewigen Formen frei, die der Mythos mit dem Recht bastardierte. Sie vermag im wahren Kriege genauso erscheinen wie im Gottesgericht der Menge am Verbrecher. Verwerflich aber ist alle mythische Gewarlt, die rechtsetzende, welche die schlatende genannt werden darf. Verwerflich auch die rechtserhaltende, die verwaltende, die ihr dient." Benjamin, *Gesammelte Schriften,* 2:203.

38. Benjamin, "World and Time," *Selected Writings,* 1:227. "Das Soziale ist in seinem jetzigen Stande Manifestation gespenstischer und dämonischer Mächte, allerdings in ihrer höchsten Spannung zu Gott, ihrem aus sich selbst Herausstreben. Göttliches manifestiert sich in ihnen nur in der revolutionären Gewalt. .... In dieser Welt is höher: göttliche Gewalt als göttliche Gewaltlosigkeit. In der kommenden göttliche Gewaltlosigkeit höher als göttliche Gewalt." Benjamin, *Gesammelte Schriften,* 6:99.

39. Benjamin, "Bert Brecht," *Selected Writings,* 2:369. "Wenn Marx sich ... das Problem gestellt hat, die Revolution aus ihrem schlechtweg anderen, dem Kapitalismus, hervorgehen zu lassen." Benjamin, *Gesammelte Schriften,* 2:665.

40. Benjamin, "The Little Hunchback," *Selected Writings,* 2:811. "Dies Männlein ist der Insasse des entstellten Lebens; es wird verschwinden, wenn der Messias kommt, von dem ein großer Rabbi gesagt hat, daß er nicht mit Gewalt die Welt verändern wolle, sondern nur um ein Geringes sie zurechtstellen werde." Benjamin, *Gesammelte Schriften,* 2:432.

Conclusion

1. Albert S. Lindemann, *Anti-Semitism Before the Holocaust* (London: Longman, 2000), p. 59.

2. Paul Mendes-Flohr, *German Jews: A Dual Identity* (New Haven: Yale University Press, 1999), p. 9.

3. Norman Cohen, *Warrant for Genocide: The Myth of the Jewish World-Conspiracy and the Protocols of the Elders of Zion* (London: Eyre & Spottiswoode, 1967), p. 137.

4. Fritz K. Ringer, *The Decline of the German Mandarins: The German Academic Community, 1890–1933* (Cambridge: Harvard University Press, 1969), p. 139.

5. Cohen, *Warrant for Genocide*, p. 172.

6. Daniel Goldhagen, *Hitler's Willing Executioners: Ordinary Germans and the Holocaust* (London: Abacus, 1996), p. 28.

7. Michael Mack, *Anthropology as Memory: Elias Canetti's and Franz Baermann Steiner's Reponses to the Shoah* (Tübingen: Niemeyer, 2001), p. 111.

8. See Friedrich Kluge, *Etymologisches Wörterbuch der deutschen Sprache* (Berlin: de Gruyter, 1982), p. 92.

9. Jakob Grimm and Wilhelm Grimm, *Deutsches Wörterbuch* (Leipzig: S. Hirzel, 1860), 2:106.

10. George Mosse, introduction to *Germans and Jews: The Right, the Left, and the Search for a "Third Force" in Pre-Nazi Germany* (Detroit: Wayne State University Press, 1987), p. 7.

11. George Mosse, "Left-Wing Intellectuals in the Weimar Republic," in *Germans and Jews,* p. 177.

12. Clearly Kien desires the Kantian refinement of a kind of thought that has become disembodied. The end of *Auto-da-Fé* illustrates the irony of this ideal. As Jean-François Lyotard has pointed out, "Thought without a body is the prerequisite for thinking of the death of all bodies, solar or terrestrial, and of the death of thoughts that are inseparable from those bodies." Lyotard, "Can Thought Go on Without a Body?" in Lyotard, *The Inhuman: Reflections on Time,* trans. Geoffrey Bennington and Rachel Bowlby (Cambridge, UK: Polity, 1991), p. 14.

13. George Mosse, "The Heritage of Socialist Humanism," in Mosse, *Masses and Man: Nationalist and Fascist Perceptions of Reality* (New York: Fertig, 1980), p. 154.

14. For a detailed analysis of Steiner's work see Mack, *Anthropology as Memory.*

15. George Mosse, "Toward a General Theory of Fascism," in Mosse, *Masses and Man,* p. 178.

16. Franz Baermann Steiner, "Letter to Georg Rapp," in *Selected Writings,* vol. 2, *Orientpolitik, Value, and Civilisation,* ed Jeremy Adler and Richard Fardon with a memoir by M. N. Sriniva (Oxford: Berghahn, 1999), p. 116.

17. Ibid.

18. For a discussion of Canetti's and Steiner's critiques of positivism see Mack, *Anthropology as Memory,* pp. 149–157.

19. Franz Baermann Steiner, "On the Process of Civilisation," trans. Jeremy Adler and Michael Mack, in *Selected Writings,* vol. 2, *Orientpolitik, Value, and Civilisation,* ed Jeremy Adler and Richard Fardon with a memoir by M. N. Sriniva (Oxford: Berghahn, 1999), p. 128.

20. Ibid.

21. See Mack, *Anthropology as Memory.*

22. Franz Baermann Steiner, *Selected Writings,* vol. 1, *Taboo, Truth, and Religion,* ed. Jeremy Adler and Richard Fardon, with a memoir by Mary Douglas (Oxford: Berghahn, 1999), p. 213.

23. Franz Baermann Steiner, "Letter to Mr. Gandhi," in *Selected Writings,* vol. 2, *Orientpolitik, Value, and Civilisation,* ed Jeremy Adler and Richard Fardon with a memoir by M. N. Sriniva (Oxford: Berghahn, 1999), p. 131.

24. Franz Baermann Steiner, "How to Define Superstition," in *Selected Writings,* vol. 1, *Taboo, Truth, and Religion,* ed. Jeremy Adler and Richard Fardon, with a memoir by Mary Douglas (Oxford: Berghahn, 1999), p. 225.

25. Ibid.

26. Theodor Adorno, *Problems of Moral Philosophy,* ed. Thomas Schröder, trans. Rodney Livingstone (Stanford: Stanford University Press, 2000), p. 146.

INDEX